Following
the
Narrow Path

Devotions From the
World of Horses

by Vicki Watson

TABLE OF CONTENTS

INTRODUCTION

Many believe that becoming a Christian will make your life easy, but Jesus said the path that leads to eternal life is narrow, difficult, and hard to find. In this devotional, I share some of my experiences in finding and staying on that narrow path. I hope my stories will encourage you on your journey.

The truths of the Bible can be understood intellectually, but those truths are more fully absorbed through life experiences that shed additional light on them and drive them deeper into our hearts. We can know theoretically what it means to forgive someone, however a deeper understanding of that word is gained when we must forgive someone who has wronged us.

God leads us through various life experiences to embed His truths deep within us. The truth doesn't change, but the lessons He sends to imprint those truths on us will be specific to each believer. Spiritual truths have been confirmed to me through the horses God has blessed me with. I share some of those experiences and insights in this devotional.

I'm not a Hebrew and Greek scholar, but I've always been fascinated with words, their origins, and meanings. I didn't become a Christian until my late twenties. At that time, I begged the pastor of the church I attended to have a Bible study. He refused. Unfortunately, I've had some bad church experiences over the years.

But God worked even that out for good. He steered me to a church with a Kay Arthur Precepts study on James. What a perfect start to my study of the Bible! Not only did I learn a lot about the book of James, I learned how to study the Bible for myself. Among other things, Kay Arthur explained how to find the words in the original languages and look up their meaning. I still love it when I uncover a gem when looking up a word from the Bible.

Many of the devotions address our behavior and attitudes. Our study of the Bible should produce wisdom we apply in our lives not just head knowledge.

I'm confident my position on that aligns with scripture. We don't perform good deeds to earn our way into heaven. But after we are saved through faith in Christ, we will have a desire to serve God out of love for Him. That will inevitably result in fruit being produced. A lack of fruit should be a cause for concern.

> For it is by grace you have been saved through faith, and this not from yourselves; it is the gift of God, not by works, so that no one can boast. For we are God's workmanship, created in Christ Jesus to do good works, which God prepared in advance as our way of life.
>
> *Ephesians 2:8-10*

I believe the Bible is God's inerrant word, which I interpret literally unless it's clearly intended to be symbolic.

> The Law of the LORD is perfect, reviving the soul;
> the testimony of the LORD is trustworthy, making wise the simple.
> The precepts of the LORD are right, bringing joy to the heart;
> the commandments of the LORD are radiant, giving light to the eyes.
> The fear of the LORD is pure, enduring forever;
> the judgments of the LORD are true, being altogether righteous.
> They are more precious than gold, than much pure gold;
> they are sweeter than honey, than honey from the comb.
> By them indeed Your servant is warned; in keeping them is great reward.
>
> *Psalm 19:7-11*

Horses are a favorite "proof" for evolutionists. I believe the opposite. Horses seem to be one of God's favorite animals. For anyone with an open mind, the complexity of their design points to an intelligent designer.

I mention several racehorses in this book. That doesn't mean I endorse horse racing. There are many evils connected with the sport, but horses love to run. The fact that people turn that into something bad doesn't take away from the horses' amazing athletic abilities.

The primary translation used for the quoted scriptures is the Berean Study Bible. It's a newer translation (2016), comparable to the ESV. The translation is a product of the Bible Hub (biblehub.com). Although it is copyrighted (to maintain its accuracy), the publisher's intent is to allow a more free distribution of God's word.

I hope this book helps you to see God working through the animals, people, and everyday events in your own life.

Many of the photos are ones I've taken. Check out the notes at the end of the book for comments about each of my photos.

Special thanks to:

Pat Marvenko Smith, revelationillustrated.com, for permission to use her Four Horsemen and Christ on a White Horse artwork.

And Nadina Ironia, ironia-art.com, for permission to use her Secretariat painting.

(Sassy and I performing in a drill team, 4ᵗʰ from the left)

1

WHY THIS OBSESSION WITH HORSES?

I don't know where the longing came from or when it started. I can't remember a time when I didn't want a horse.

The librarian in our small town must have understood horse-crazy girls. Perhaps she had been one herself. All the horse books were stored on a shelf right at my eye level. In those days, a library was a silent place. The quiet contributed to my awe of this building full of books. Those horse books pulled me like a magnet to their shelf. I carefully selected a book and took it to the large desk at the back of the library. The prim and proper librarian removed the card from the pocket in the book, stamped it with the due date, and handed it to me. I neatly printed my name, smiled shyly, and handed the card back to her.

Back home, I devoured each book, dreaming of the day I would have my own horse. One afternoon, I saw the teenage neighbor ride into our backyard on her horse. She must have noticed me staring at her. "Would you like a ride?"

Too shy to speak to her, I nodded. She helped me up behind the saddle. I wrapped my arms around her waist, and we were off. To a scrawny, eight-year-old girl, the palomino seemed like the tallest and most beautiful horse in the world. I inhaled the aroma of horsehair and leather, listened to the squeak of the saddle and the thud of the horse's hooves on the hard ground.

After a brief lap around the yard, she helped me down, and I ran my hands over the palomino's soft coat. The neighbor never returned, but that one ride was enough for me to be hooked. My longing for a horse grew so intense it seemed my whole body ached. I thought about horses constantly, read about them, and drew pictures of them.

One night, I dreamed someone gave me a plastic, inflatable horse. As I blew into the toy, it began to take shape. When fully inflated, the toy horse came to life. Finally, I had a horse of my very own! I was so excited—until I woke up.

I cried when I realized the horse, that had been so alive in my dream, didn't really exist.

I was very quiet and shy even with my parents. They were aware of my longing although I'm sure they didn't understand it.

Later that year, I spotted my father walking down the road, leading a small, silver dapple pony. Cricket came with a beautiful saddle—black leather with a red, stitched seat.

It turned out to be one of those fortunately-unfortunately stories. Fortunately, I now had a real, live pony. But unfortunately, the pony wasn't trained. Cricket bucked me off or ran away with me every time I tried to ride her. I wasn't hurt, and Cricket's behavior didn't diminish my love for horses.

The following year, we moved to a small farm where my dad began to raise pigs. A neighbor, Mr. Steffens, had several well-trained horses and ponies. His own children were young, so I became the Steffens' "adopted" farm-hand daughter, helping with work around their place. In exchange, he taught me how to ride.

Mr. Steffens traded a stocky, bay pony, Dolly, to us in exchange for Cricket and one of my dad's pigs. Now, I had a pony of my own I could actually ride! Dolly was twelve hands tall. She was also trained to pull a cart.

Mr. Steffens offered to take Dolly and me to local horse shows, but I didn't have any show clothes. In exchange for painting their chicken coop, the Steffens took me to a nearby tack shop and bought me an outfit to show in.

In those days, you didn't need the fancy, expensive outfits worn in horse shows today. I remember being delighted with a red-checked western shirt, black jeans, and a black cowboy hat. For several years, I had a great time traveling with the Steffens family to shows.

Dolly had a wonderfully smooth jog, but she was too lazy to canter much. I didn't win many ribbons, but enough to keep me happy. It didn't matter that Dolly wasn't a great show horse. She was mine, and I loved her.

Those are some of my best childhood memories. The Steffens family played a big role in my life. They were Christians, and looking back from an adult perspective, I see how they put their faith into action by reaching out to a shy, lonely, horse-crazy girl.

From the perspective of many years, I know my intense childhood longing for a horse, even when fulfilled, would never ultimately satisfy. Horses were the wrong object of my longing. God saw fit to grant the desires of that insecure little girl, and I hope I have used my horses in a way that is honoring to Him.

> As the deer pants for streams of water, so my soul longs after You, O God. My soul thirsts for God, the living God.
>
> *Psalm 42:1,2*

For a while in my early adult life, I was horseless. During those years, I never lost my love for horses. I subscribed to a magazine called *The Perfect Horse*, a publication by Christian trainer, John Lyons. Lyons occasionally inserted Christian principles into the magazine that related to his experience with horses. My faith was new at the time, and I appreciated his spiritual insights. But it was another trainer, Lew Sterrett, who really opened my eyes to the similarity of a horse's relationship to his master and our relationship to God. It's not a perfect comparison by any means, but real-life examples can make spiritual concepts more understandable and memorable.

By then, I had three daughters. I wanted them to have the opportunity to enjoy horses as I had. My girls and I attended a horse exposition, Equine Affaire, in Columbus. They held a special church service in the coliseum on Easter Sunday.

Lew Sterrett entered the ring, riding one horse and leading another—a pretty roan mare named Jessie. He was given the mare because no one else had been able to tame her. Whenever anyone tried to ride her, Jessie would rear up so high she sometimes fell over backward. This is one of the most dangerous behaviors for a horse. Sterrett demonstrated the rearing as he tried to get on the mare.

He explained how Jessie's rebelliousness was like people rebelling against God. If Jessie had submitted to training, she would have been useful to her master and well cared for. But she didn't have much of a future in her current state—as a dangerous, unrideable horse.

It's the same with us. When we refuse to submit to God, we miss out on what He wants to accomplish in our lives.

Some might raise their eyebrows at attending a horse expo on Easter Sunday, but it's been twenty-five years since that presentation with Jessie, and Sterrett's message is still fresh in my mind. Later that year, my girls and I attended one of Sterrett's *Sermon on the Mount* presentations. He covered training principles in more detail and explained how they related to Christian discipleship. I absorbed a lot, but most of his talk went over my daughters' heads.

By the following year, we were back in the horse business. The *Parable of the Pink Jacket* explains how that came about.

I believe the interests and material possessions God gives us are intended to be used to reach out to others. With the examples of Lyons and Sterrett in the back of my mind, I decided to use our horses to start the Christian Cowgirl Club. My daughters and I held summer day camps where we helped girls learn to care for and ride horses. We also had crafts, music, snacks, and a lesson that conveyed a spiritual message through the horses.

Lew Sterrett's insights were too high level, so I brought the lessons down several notches for the girls. The more I thought about the parallels between my own experiences with horses and my relationship to God, the more examples I came up with on my own.

God helped me out by sending a lot of animals our way who had unique, quirky personalities.

2

THE SECRET OF CONTENTMENT

When I received Cricket, my silver-dapple Shetland pony, I thought I was in heaven—that is until the first time I rode her.

I climbed onto that beautiful saddle, and Cricket promptly bucked me off. She took off running across several neighbors' yards into a vacant field. That's the way all my riding sessions on Cricket went.

I wasn't the only one surprised with a pony that day. Cricket was half of a matched pair that were sold at an auction. The other half was a gelding named Jumper. My dad and a friend pooled their money to buy the two ponies. The neighbor girls who received Jumper were friends of mine.

Mary and Jane weren't crazy about horses as I was, so they were also surprised when their father brought a pony home. As it turned out, Jumper was better trained than Cricket—or maybe he simply had a more easygoing disposition. I watched in amazement as my friends rode their pony around the field behind their house.

That's the first time I recall being envious. It wasn't that I wanted to take Jumper from my friends; I just couldn't understand why they had gotten the better pony. I was the one that loved horses, and I was stuck with a pony I couldn't ride. In some ways, it was worse than having no pony at all.

> I know what it is to be in need, and I know what it is to have plenty. I have learned the secret of being content in any and every situation, whether well fed or hungry, whether living in plenty or in want.
>
> *Philippians 4:12 NKJV*

It was many years ago that I received that pony. I wish I could say I've mastered the art of being content, but unfortunately, at times, I still struggle with it. The problem creeps up here and there in various forms—wishing for a better horse, a better barn (with an indoor arena), a more beautiful saddle, a nice truck, or a higher income.

When I stop and think about it, I realize those are all wants rather than needs. I don't actually need any of those things. God has already blessed me beyond anything I deserve.

> Every good and perfect gift is from above, coming down from the Father of the heavenly lights,
>
> *James 1:17*

Just as we feel disappointed when someone doesn't seem to appreciate a gift we've carefully selected for them, it must hurt God when I don't appreciate the gifts He's given to me.

The year after my dad bought Cricket, our family moved to a small farm. Dad traded Cricket—and a pig—to a neighbor for a pony named Dolly. I learned to ride at their stable, and my disappointment with Cricket was soon forgotten. My lifelong horse and pony adventure had begun!

3
PARABLE OF THE PINK JACKET

The first year my daughters and I attended the horse exposition, Equine Affaire, my youngest daughter, Julie, was four years old. The expo ran for four days in mid-April, from Thursday through Sunday. When we prepared to leave home for the first day of the event, I grabbed a cute, pink jacket for Julie to wear.

As we wandered around that day, taking in the horse exhibits and demonstrations, the weather grew unusually warm. At some point, I noticed Julie no longer had her jacket. We'd been in at least five different barns on the sprawling fairgrounds. None of us had any idea where she had lost it. I was certain we would never see that jacket again.

We enjoyed the exhibits and clinics each day, but that Sunday was Easter, and a special church service had been organized by Christian horse trainer, John Lyons. During the service, one man explained that he'd first gotten involved with horses when a young woman, soon to be heading off to college, drove past his farm. It looked like a perfect place for a horse to live, so she stopped to ask if he would like to have her expensive show horse.

At that time, I was horseless and feeling a bit sorry for myself. No one had ever given me a horse.

Later in the service, one of the leaders asked everyone to stand who had witnessed a miracle. A surprising number of people stood. Again I wondered why I'd never had that experience.

After we left the church service, it was almost time for Equine Affaire to end. Everyone began closing down their exhibits. My girls wanted to go back to a particular barn one last time before leaving the expo. We walked around, gazing at the beautiful horses, then headed for the door to leave for home.

As we walked in front of one of the last booths, a woman held something up in the air, asking the lady next to her if she knew whether there was a "Lost and Found."

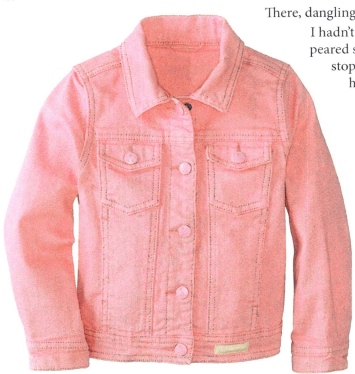

There, dangling right in front of me, was Julie's pink jacket!

I hadn't given the jacket a thought since it had disappeared several days earlier, and I didn't remember stopping at that booth the day the jacket was lost. I have no idea how it ended up there.

The timing was eerily perfect. My daughters had picked that barn to visit one last time. We just happened to walk past the booth at the precise moment the woman held up the jacket. (I had just met Sissy Burggraf of Lost Acres Horse Rescue and Rehabilitation that year, but we have been friends since that day.)

I realized we had just experienced our own small-scale miracle. God was trying to get something through my thick head.

In the next weeks, some exciting things happened. We located a pony, Ebony, that was "child-safe," and my husband agreed to buy her for our daughters. Then, we got a call from my mom. Someone she worked with had an extra horse they weren't using. The woman wanted to lease her to us for the summer—for $1.00!

This all happened so soon after the recovery of Julie's jacket, I began to think of it as the *Parable of the Pink Jacket*.

The pink jacket object lesson reminded me that God is in control. I needed to stop complaining and worrying. God is more than capable of providing for me.

It was amazing that those horses suddenly appeared for us, but I realized I needed to be content with what I had—whether it was two horses or no horses! God had already blessed me tremendously. It was sinful to complain about anything I didn't have.

Now to Him who is able to do immeasurably more than all we ask or imagine, according to His power that is at work within us, to Him be the glory in the church and in Christ Jesus throughout all generations, forever and ever. Amen.

Ephesians 3:20-21

4

THE BEST GIFT

Gary Chapman, author of the book, *The 5 Love Languages*, describes different categories for how we express and receive love. They're listed, in no particular order, to the right.

- Words of affirmation
- Quality time
- Physical touch
- Acts of service
- Receiving gifts

It's possible for the ways you receive love to differ from the ways you best express it. Gifts aren't at the top of my list for receiving love, but gift giving is my second-best way to express love—after quality time.

My favorite experience of gift giving was buying a horse for my oldest daughter's birthday. Buying a horse is always an interesting experience. I've found that you should trust no one when going horse shopping.

This was in the days before the internet, so I was scanning newspapers and our local *County Classifieds*. I came across an ad for a palomino mare, unregistered but mostly Quarter Horse, about an hour from where we lived. After arranging for some Grandma time for the girls, I set off to check out the horse.

When I arrived, a young woman greeted me and led me to the barn. She opened the stall door, and the mare moseyed out. Maggie stood calmly in the aisle, unhaltered, as the woman groomed her. She had apparently had a long fixation on the palomino's tail. Due to this careful attention, Maggie's tail was sparkling white.

Maggie didn't possess perfect conformation. Her neck and shoulders were too narrow in comparison to her large hindquarters, a somewhat pear-shaped horse. It was the mare's calm temperament that impressed me.

I asked a variety of questions. The owner's answers shifted based on what she thought I wanted in a horse. At one point, she told me how fast Maggie was, that she had once outrun her husband's contesting horse. After experiencing the reality of Maggie for many years, that statement still brings a smile. The mare wasn't fond of running—ever. If she outran a contesting horse, the woman's husband should have gotten a new one!

Despite the owner's attempt to portray Maggie as a racehorse (the opposite of what I wanted), I decided to buy the mare. The horse's behavior seemed to be more honest than the woman's words. I arranged to pick her up the following week.

This was all top secret, of course. My girls knew nothing about it. I worried that my mom, not known for her ability to keep a secret, would let something slip, but she managed to keep quiet this time.

The day I went to pick up our new horse, a friend rode along with me. Once again, I sent the girls to my mom's. We made it back home and got Maggie situated. I placed a big "Happy Birthday" poster covered with bows and ribbons on her stall door.

After we finished, I called Mom to let her know it was time for the big reveal. When they arrived, my friend said she wanted to see our pony, Ebony. The girls led the way to the barn, eager to show off their pony. As we entered, a palomino head turned toward us over a stall door. I couldn't stop grinning as it slowly registered on my girls, and especially my oldest, what this was all about.

Maggie was not only the calmest horse we ever owned, but the calmest one I've EVER seen. Nothing bothered her. She would travel along any trail or down a city street in the middle of a noisy parade without batting an eye. Maggie rarely even looked to the side. Head low, facing straight ahead, the mare just kept going wherever you pointed her. Years after buying her, the previous owner called me, wanting to buy her back. By then, she had a little boy and wanted Maggie for his horse, but we had no intention of parting with her.

Coincidentally, our pony Ebony's previous owner later tried to buy her back, also. A good horse is truly hard to find. I've had a variety of horses over the years, but Maggie and Ebony were by far the best. Many happy memories are connected to those two. Both were with us until the end, and I still miss them.

That was the most fun I had giving a gift. But, of course, God is the greatest gift giver of all.

> For God so loved the world that He gave His one and only Son, that everyone who believes in Him shall not perish but have eternal life.
>
> *John 3:16*

Jesus said this to Nicodemus, explaining what was required for one to be born again. This one verse summarizes all God went through to make our salvation possible. Not only is John 3:16 the best known and most quoted verse from the Bible, it consists of multiple "greatests."

> **For God**—the greatest Giver
> **so loved**—the greatest love
> **the world**—the greatest number of recipients
> **that He gave**—the greatest act
> **His one and only Son**—the greatest Gift
> **that everyone who believes in Him**—the greatest opportunity
> **shall not perish**—the greatest promise
> **but**—the greatest difference
> **have eternal life**—the greatest reward

I hope you have experienced this incredible gift from God!

> Every good and perfect gift is from above, coming down from the Father of the heavenly lights, with whom there is no change or shifting shadow.
>
> *James 1:17*

5
SACRIFICE—JET'S STORY

An idea came to me years ago for a story about a young girl's pony who died while protecting her newborn foal from an attack by a coydog (coyote-dog hybrid).

I'd never had a secret desire to write a book, and I was reluctant to write this story, unsure whether I could make it believable. On the other hand, I didn't want to make it too believable, either. People would hate me for "killing" a kid's pony—even if it was only a fictional one. A close friend told me absolutely not to write it—it would be too sad.

But the idea would not leave me alone. It bounced around in my head to the point that it was driving me crazy. I considered what my friend had said about it being too sad.

Why wasn't it too sad for Christian parents to tell their children about Jesus' horrible death on the cross? Was a pony more important than Jesus?

The following excerpt from *Rosie and Scamper* picks up midway through the book, after the grandmother discovered Rosie's pony, Jet, had died. Grandma rescued the foal, Scamper, and spent the night in the barn caring for him. Early the next morning, the granddaughter, Rosie, and her mother, Kristy, arrive at the stable to

help care for the horses. When Rosie learns of her pony's death, she asks the hard question, "Why?" The grandmother attempts to explain how the actions of Jet, in dying to save her foal, are like Christ giving His life for us.

"Mom! Mom!" Rosie shrieked. "Jet had her foal! Come and see!" She ran toward her mother, then turned and went back to the foal's stall.

"Grandma, where's Jet? Why isn't she with her baby?" Rosie opened the stall door. She placed one arm around Scamper's neck and stroked his forehead with the other. The foal found one of her fingers and sucked, thinking he had found his breakfast. Rosie laughed with delight. "He's trying to eat my finger!"

Grandma walked over and wearily sat down on the tack box, tears streaming down her cheeks. She took a deep breath and slowly let it out. "Rosie, would you come here for a minute?"

"Aw, but I want to play with the baby." Rosie reluctantly stepped out of the stall, gently pushing the foal back enough so she could close the door. She looked in the stall to the left of Scamper's. "Where is Jet?"

Grandma patted the tack box, motioning for Rosie to sit beside her. Kristy sat on the other end. As Grandma explained the events of the night before, all three held each other and cried.

Finally, Rosie was able to speak. "Why, Grandma? Why did my pony have to die? It's not fair."

Grandma brushed away more tears. Would they never end?

She had cried so much the night before, she couldn't believe she had any tears left. "Rosie, I won't pretend to understand why this happened. But I know God can use the painful things in our lives for good."

Grandma closed her eyes briefly and silently prayed for words that would help Rosie understand. "The Bible says that God knows when a sparrow falls to the ground. God created Jet, and He loved her as much, or more, than you and I did. You know the verse John 3:16, right?"

Rosie nodded slowly. Jemimah jumped into her lap, and she absently stroked the cat's head.

"When it says 'God gave His only Son,' it's talking about when Jesus came and lived as a man on earth."

Rosie's tears slowed, but Grandma sensed she had no idea what this had to do with Jet.

"Jesus died on the cross to pay the penalty for our sins. He gave His life for ours, so we could have eternal life. Why would He do that for us?"

Rosie shrugged.

"That's what the 'For God so loved the world' part of the verse is about. Jesus came because of God's amazing love for us."

Grandma continued. "The animal that attacked Jet was what some people call a coydog, part coyote and part dog, probably starving after the hard winter. Being part dog, they are less fearful than coyotes. Since the foal was weak and helpless, it probably went after him first. When Jet tried to protect her foal, it attacked her. Do you see now? Jet loved her baby so much; she gave her life so he could live."

"It's not exactly the same, of course," Grandma added. "But what Jet did for her foal helps me understand what Jesus did for me—for all of us."

Grandma watched Rosie turn this over in her mind.

"I kind of understand, but it doesn't make me feel any better."

"I know. It will hurt for a long time." Grandma nodded sadly. "Jet made many children happy by teaching them how to ride. Maybe someday the story of her death can do something even better if it helps them understand what Christ did for us on the cross."

"I don't think I could tell anyone about it," Rosie said slowly.

"It will take time." They sat together quietly for several minutes, then Grandma broke the silence by blowing her nose on a damp wad of tissues retrieved from her coat pocket. "I named him Scamper. He needs to be fed every two hours for the next few days. Will you help me take care of him?"

Rosie shrugged. "I guess so."

"You can stay here with Grandma for a few days," Kristy offered. "I mean—if you feel up to it."

Grandma stood up, feeling her age for the first time in her life. Her back ached as she returned to the tack room for Scamper's bottle. After cleaning it and mixing a fresh batch of milk, she held it out to her granddaughter.

Rosie sniffed and raised her hand to take the bottle. "What do I do with it?"

"He knows what to do," Grandma said.

Rosie nudged Jemimah off her lap and shuffled toward the stall. Grandma slid the door open. Scamper butted the bottle and eagerly began to drink.

"Tip it up so the milk comes out more easily," Grandma said.

Rosie smiled briefly through her tears as the hungry little colt energetically attacked the bottle she held with both hands.

Over the next few months, Rosie and Grandma spent many hours at the barn caring for Scamper. Each day, the time between his feedings was gradually extended. As he grew stronger, they taught him to drink his milk from a bucket instead of the bottle. He also began to nibble at small bits of hay and grain.

Jet was buried in the back pasture beside her mother, Ebony. Rosie and Grandma remembered with sadness and joy the pony they had loved so dearly.

No other pony/horse (or human) dies in the series. Was I right to put something so sad in that first book? I debated back and forth on it years ago and obviously decided to do it—for several reasons.

Children experience the death of dearly loved pets. I still remember the death of a cat from when I was very young. It's a sadness everyone who loves animals goes through, sometimes repeatedly. The story shows that it's normal and acceptable to cry and grieve for them.

Love and sadness seem intertwined. If we love, we'll most likely experience loss and the resulting sadness, whether it's the death of an animal or a person.

C. S. Lewis experienced this when his wife died from cancer. "The pain I feel now is the happiness I had before. That's the deal."

Children who grow up in Christian families hear about the crucifixion of Christ from a young age. It's easy to lose the emotional impact of the suffering He went through for us, simply because we've heard it so often. By having Jet die, I wanted the emotional response to be strong and real, something young people could relate to. The comparison between a pony dying to protect her foal and Jesus' death on the cross is imperfect, but I think it's close enough to give children a deeper appreciation for Christ's sacrifice for us.

Death, disease, and other types of evil happen because of our sin and the curse on this world. I don't believe God is pleased with any of that, but He can use bad experiences in the lives of believers to bring about good.

> And we know that God works all things together for the good of those who love Him, who are called according to His purpose.
>
> *Romans 8:28*

Rosie doesn't see this happen immediately. It's not a magic formula—and it doesn't erase the sadness of our traumatic experiences. But later in the book, Jet's story is one of the seeds planted in the life of another character, Carrie, that helps her come to Christ.

> Greater love has no one than this, that he lay down his life for his friends.
>
> *John 15:13*

6

KINGDOM OF DARKNESS

Sometimes God reveals things to me in His word, and I see a confirmation or parallel in the world of horses. Other times, I see things when working with horses that remind me of a verse or scriptural principle.

One day, I was captivated by the thought expressed in Colossians 1:13. Here it is in several versions.

> For he has rescued us from the dominion of darkness and brought us into the kingdom of the Son he loves, NIV
>
> For he has rescued us from the kingdom of darkness and transferred us into the Kingdom of his dear Son, NLT
>
> Who hath delivered us from the power of darkness, and hath translated us into the kingdom of his dear Son: KJV
>
> He has delivered us from the power of darkness and conveyed us into the kingdom of the Son of His love, NKJV
>
> He rescued us from the power of darkness and brought us safe into the kingdom of his dear Son, GNT
>
> He has rescued [rhyomai] us from the dominion of darkness and brought us into [methistēmi] the kingdom of His beloved Son, BSB
>
> **rhyomai**—to draw to one's self, to rescue, to deliver. This is the same word used in Matthew 6:13. And lead us not into temptation, but deliver [rhyomai] us from the evil one.
>
> **methistēmi**—to transpose, transfer, translate, remove from one place to another; of a change of situation or place

Before we are saved, we live in a kingdom of darkness. God can rescue us from that darkness, but many choose to remain there. If we allow Him to, He will scoop us up out of the dark and deposit us into the kingdom of light, ruled by His beloved Son, Jesus.

> Men love darkness rather than light because their deeds are evil.
>
> *John 3:19*

Have you ever suddenly left a dark place and faced bright sunlight? It's a drastic change. Your eyes want to close, and you blink until they become accustomed to the light. But it's a wonderful change. Light is superior to gloomy darkness.

As I considered this transference from a kingdom of darkness to a kingdom of light, I thought of the ponies who worked underground in coal mines.

The first recorded use of horses or ponies in mines in Britain was in 1750. The Mining Act of 1842 limited the use of children as workers in the mines. This resulted in ponies taking over many of the jobs the young miners had previously performed.

Because the mine tunnels were low and narrow, small ponies, averaging twelve hands or less, were best suited for the work. Shetland was the most common breed. Geldings were used almost exclusively because they had fewer behavioral issues than mares and stallions. The British Coal Mines Act of 1911 required ponies to be at least four years old before they could work in the mines. By 1913, there were 70,000 pit ponies working in the UK.

The pony's training began when he arrived at the colliery (coal mine). But no amount of training could prepare the animals for what they would experience in the mines.

When his brief harness training was complete, the day came for the pony to begin work. In a deep-shaft mine, that meant a trip to the bottom. Small ponies traveled down in a cage-like elevator similar to the one used to transport the miners. Larger ponies and horses were lowered down the shaft in a sling.

> The horses which draw the wagons on the underground railways are sometimes sent down into the mine fastened to a rope, but generally in the English collieries on a properly constructed platform and cage, either in nets or baskets. When the former mode is adopted the horses do not make the slightest movement, being paralysed with fear and to all appearances dead, but when they reach the bottom of the pit they gradually recover their senses.
>
> *Bright, p. 33*

As he began his work underground, the pony pulled empty tubs behind an experienced animal. The narrowest passages left at most a foot, sometimes only inches, on either side of the coal cars. The driver often had to stoop to avoid banging his head on the roof. If the inexperienced pony became frightened, he couldn't run away—there was no place to go. I feel claustrophobic just thinking about that.

In deep mines, the ponies didn't return to the surface after each shift, but were housed in an underground stable which might contain up to a hundred animals. The stable was located at a distance from the main tunnels to provide a quiet area for the ponies to rest. Since they had to constantly keep their heads low when traveling through the tunnels, the stable roofs were required to be high enough for the ponies to raise their heads when stalled. To reduce the risk of fire, very little wood was used in the stable. Walls were typically rock or brick. Most stables were white to help spread the dim lighting.

The pit ponies are special to me because my pony, Toby, is the size of many of those who worked the mines. If he'd been born in a different time and place, Toby might have been dangled, petrified, from a sling that lowered him to the bottom of a mine shaft where he would have spent his lifetime pulling heavy coal carts through dark tunnels.

Some of the pit ponies spent their entire working lives underground while other mines gave the ponies a two-week holiday each year. Those who experienced the luxury of that vacation were released into a pasture near the mine where they were able to briefly enjoy the life of a normal horse.

The ponies' transition from the depth of the mine to a pasture reminds me of Colossians 1:13.

Imagine the sheer delight of those hard-working ponies when they were raised from the drab darkness of the mine into the sunshine and beautiful colors of the world above. Green grass!

I can picture them, once their eyes adjusted to the light, being undecided whether they should gallop about, roll on the soft ground, or of course—graze on the beautiful grass. I've watched Toby do the last two almost simultaneously. He sometimes lies down to roll and snatches a few bites of grass while he's down.

As Christians rescued by God, we never have to return to that old kingdom of darkness. The poor ponies did. After their brief vacation, they were once again lowered down the shaft to resume their work in the mine.

Although the work was hard, pit ponies weren't often mistreated. The miners' income depended on getting as much coal out as possible. It was common for the drivers to form a strong bond with their equine partners. They bragged of the intelligence, strength, or heroic deeds of their pony.

Miners respected the sixth sense the ponies had, which allowed them to detect danger. Young miner, Eric Squires, relates such an incident with his pony, Ben.

> "He [Ben] backed off, then darted forward to within five or six yards of me before spinning and moving quickly away again… He was acting like a dog asking his master to follow. Suddenly as he turned to face me again, he screamed… I recall the icy shiver that went through me.
>
> Once again he screamed and I knew then that he wanted me to follow him. I did, dropping my snaptin [lunch pail], snatching up my lamp instinctively and racing towards him… The moment I started running there was a vicious crack above the junction, with thunderous rollings and boomings coming from above. The junction collapsed with a roar that shook the ground and gave me strength to run harder.

Hundreds of tons of hard grey rock crashed down on the place where the junction had been, mangling my snap-tin and dudley [thermos] into flat pieces of useless metal. Had I been still seated with my back to that prop I would have been crushed."

Squires, p. 47

But you are a chosen people, a royal priesthood, a holy nation, a people for God's own possession, to proclaim the virtues of Him who called you out of darkness into His marvelous light.

1 Peter 2:9

For you were once darkness, but now you are light in the Lord. Walk as children of light, for the fruit of the light consists in all goodness, righteousness, and truth.

Ephesians 5:8,9

In Him [Jesus] was life, and that life was the light of men. The Light shines in the darkness, and the darkness has not overcome it.

John 1:4,5

7

WALK YOUR HORSES

If we are saved, our lives will be different than they were before—and different from the world. For some people, this will be an immediate and dramatic change. In my case, I can pinpoint a specific day when I came to know Christ as my Savior. I have to confess I was a bit of a women's libber in my teen years (1970s). Although nothing extreme, I bought into some beliefs of that movement, but God dramatically changed my thinking. Many of my beliefs and views did a 180-degree turn immediately after I was saved. There was still a lot to learn, but I had a strong desire to please God.

The way we live as Christians is often referred to as our "walk." In fact, the Bible has a lot to say about walking, in terms of how, why, with whom, and where we are to walk.

"Walk your horses."

I've heard that command many times at horse shows. In a Western Pleasure class, horses perform three gaits—walk, jog (trot), and lope (canter). What a judge might consider a good walk in the show ring doesn't necessarily match what a trail rider considers a desirable walk. In the show ring, a slower, more controlled gait

might be preferred, while a rider that actually needs to go somewhere would rather have a faster, ground-covering stride.

When a horse walks, each leg moves independently, and the hooves hit the ground at different times. Not only is this four-beat gait the easiest for the horse to perform, it's easy on the rider as well.

At a walk, horses average four to five miles per hour, meaning a horse can walk a mile in twelve to fifteen minutes. Since it requires the least energy, over a full day of riding, most horses are capable of traveling farther by continually walking rather than using faster gaits.

While competitive endurance horses can cover fifty to one hundred miles in a single day, most horses are in no condition to do that. For the average horse, higher speeds deplete their energy, so they require frequent rests or they become so exhausted they can't continue at all. Eight hours of steady walking allows the most average of horses to travel thirty or more miles in a day.

In the Old Testament, the Hebrew word translated "walk" is usually "halak" or "yalak," meaning "to literally or figuratively walk" or "to behave." We are reminded to walk according to God's commandments, to obey Him. Those commandments aren't given to keep us from having fun. They come from a loving Father who wants to protect and guide us. We may not always understand the reason for His commandments, but we can be certain that following them will be best for us in the long run.

> You must walk in all the ways that the LORD your God has commanded you, so that you may live and prosper and prolong your days in the land that you will possess.
>
> *Deuteronomy 5:33*

> But be very careful to observe the commandment and the law that Moses the servant of the LORD gave you: to love the LORD your God, to walk in all His ways, to keep His commandments, to hold fast to Him, and to serve Him with all your heart and with all your soul.
>
> *Joshua 22:5*

> He who walks with the wise will become wise, but the companion of fools will be destroyed.
>
> *Proverbs 13:20*

In the New Testament, the Greek word used consistently for "walk" is "peripateo."

peripateo—to walk, to make one's way, to conduct oneself, to live

As in the Old Testament, we're urged to be obedient to God's commands (John 14:15 for example), but there are additional passages that describe more specifically what our Christian walk should look like.

Follow Jesus or Godly Examples

> Whoever claims to abide in Him must walk as Jesus walked.
>
> *1 John 2:6*

> Join one another in following my example, brothers, and carefully observe those who walk according to the pattern we set for you.
>
> *Philippians 3:17*

Walk in a Worthy Manner

Our walk should reflect the excellence or worth of the One we represent. When we're known as Christians, our behavior will be "read" by the unbelievers around us and will impact their understanding of God (for better or worse).

As a prisoner in the Lord, then, I urge you to walk in a manner worthy [axios] of the calling you have received:

Ephesians 4:1

…so that you may walk in a manner worthy [axios] of the Lord and may please Him in every way: bearing fruit in every good work, growing in the knowledge of God,

Colossians 1:10

axios—appropriately, suitably, in a manner worthy of

Walk in the Spirit.

As children of God, we are no longer controlled by our flesh or the world, but by the Holy Spirit.

You, however, are controlled not by the flesh, but by the Spirit, if the Spirit of God lives in you.

Romans 8:9

In Galatians 5:25, "peripateo" is not used. The word for "walk" here is "stoicheo" meaning to march or keep step.

Since we live by the Spirit, let us walk in step with the Spirit.

Galatians 5:25

Walk in the Light.

Horses have better night vision than humans do. It's believed horses can see as well on a moonlit night as we do in full daylight. Have you ever tried to walk in the dark? It's challenging physically and impossible spiritually. I'm glad God provided us with a light for our paths so we don't have to walk in darkness.

Your word is a lamp to my feet and a light to my path.

Psalm 119:105

I am the light of the world. Whoever follows Me will never walk in the darkness, but will have the light of life.

John 8:12

For a little while longer, the Light will be among you. Walk while you have the Light, so that darkness will not overtake you. The one who walks in the darkness does not know where he is going.

John 12:35

For you were once darkness, but now you are light in the Lord. Walk as children of light, for the fruit of the light consists in all goodness, righteousness, and truth.

Ephesians 5:8,9

If we say we have fellowship with Him yet walk in the darkness, we lie and do not practice the truth. But if we walk in the light as He is in the light, we have fellowship with one another, and the blood of Jesus His Son cleanses us from all sin.

1 John 1:6,7

Walk in Love

Be imitators of God, therefore, as beloved children, and walk in love, just as Christ loved us and gave Himself up for us as a fragrant sacrificial offering to God.

Ephesians 5:1,2

Walk in Truth.

I was overjoyed to find some of your children walking in the truth, just as the Father has commanded us.

2 John 1:4

For I was overjoyed when the brothers came and testified about your devotion to the truth, in which you continue to walk. I have no greater joy than to hear that my children are walking in the truth.

3 John 1:3,4

Walk in Wisdom

> Pay careful attention, then, to how you walk, not as unwise but as wise, redeeming the time, because the days are evil.
>
> *Ephesians 5:15,16*

The phrase "redeeming the time" has been my focus for the past few years. I find many things interesting. I will never understand people who are easily bored. But because I have so many interests, I often flit from one thing to the next, never finishing any of them. For example, I started this book years ago. While doing research for it, I got sidetracked by intriguing stories I discovered about various horses in history. I ended up writing the first *History on Horseback* book instead. Then, when researching the second *History on Horseback* book, I switched back to this one.

The *Outline of Biblical Usage* on the Blue Letter Bible website has an excellent definition for this phrase.

> **redeeming the time**—to make wise and sacred use of every opportunity for doing good, so that zeal and well doing are as it were the purchase money by which we make the time our own

> Act wisely toward outsiders, redeeming the time. Let your speech always be gracious, seasoned with salt, so that you may know how to answer everyone.
>
> *Colossians 4:5,6*

Walk in Faith

We need to trust in God and His word even when we can't see.

> For we walk by faith, not by sight.
>
> *2 Corinthians 5:7*

> Now faith is the assurance of what we hope for and the certainty of what we do not see.
>
> *Hebrews 11:1*

> And without faith it is impossible to please God, because anyone who approaches Him must believe that He exists and that He rewards those who earnestly seek Him.
>
> *Hebrews 11:6*

> So we fix our eyes not on what is seen, but on what is unseen. For what is seen is temporary, but what is unseen is eternal.
>
> *2 Corinthians 4:18*

Perform Good Works on the Journey

> Two words summarize the practicality of the Christian life: walk and work. The sequence is important: first wisdom; then walk; then work. I cannot work for God unless I am walking with Him, but I cannot walk with Him if I am ignorant of His will.
>
> *Warren Wiersbe*

> For we are God's workmanship, created in Christ Jesus to do good works, which God prepared in advance as our way of life.
>
> *Ephesians 2:10*

let your light shine before men, that they may see your good deeds and glorify your Father in heaven.

Matthew 5:16

So too, faith by itself, if it does not result in action, is dead.

James 2:17

Let us not grow weary in well-doing, for in due time we will reap a harvest if we do not give up. Therefore, as we have opportunity, let us do good to everyone, and especially to the family of faith.

Galatians 6:9,10

In addition to a walk, the Bible refers to the Christian life as a race. It's not a sprint, more like a marathon in which most of us have to pace ourselves so we can finish the race and not burn out.

let us throw off every encumbrance and the sin that so easily entangles, and let us run with endurance the race set out for us.

Hebrews 12:1,2

When you can't run, remember a slow and steady walk, in the long run, will cover more ground.

8

STUMBLING AND FALLING

People trip and fall at times. This rarely results in serious injury. In fact, often you're able to catch yourself and prevent a fall.

Did you know that tripping or stumbling can be a problem with horses, also? Since they have twice as many legs as we do, the chance that they will fall is lower, but it happens. Sometimes, they only go down to their knees in the front and recover before falling all the way down.

If you're on a horse that falls, it can be scary and potentially dangerous. I know. When I was fifteen, a horse I was riding fell. We were cantering in a grassy corral, and the ground was damp after a recent rain. Before I knew what was happening, the horse lost her footing and went down, rolling onto her side—on top of my left leg. When she scrambled back up, I was still in the saddle, but my leg and hip felt as if they were broken. Fortunately, they weren't.

As with people, an occasional stumble for a horse is nothing to worry about. But if he continues to stumble, it's important to discover what is causing it.

A variety of things may cause a horse to stumble or fall. Rocks or tree roots in the trail, uneven ground, loss of balance, injury to a hoof or leg, or slippery terrain. Horses may also stumble if the toe of their hoof is too long, literally tripping over their own feet. A good farrier will keep the hooves trimmed with the correct toe length and hoof angle.

If a horse stumbles with you, lean back and loosen the reins. Shifting weight away from his front end will help him regain his footing. Loose reins allow him to use his head and neck to rebalance himself. Kick your feet out of the stirrups in case you need to make a hasty dismount.

As a rider, you can help keep your horse from stumbling by keeping him focused on his work. A horse gawking all around will be more likely to stumble than one focused on where he is going. You can also practice leading or riding him over obstacles such as ground poles or railroad ties. This will teach him to be careful about picking up and placing his feet.

While a physical stumble or fall can be dangerous, stumbling spiritually is more serious. In Jude, we're reminded how we can keep from stumbling in our Christian walk.

> Now to Him who is able to keep you from stumbling and to present you unblemished in His glorious presence, with great joy—to the only God our Savior be glory, majesty, dominion, and authority through Jesus Christ our Lord before all time, and now, and for all eternity. Amen
>
> *Jude 24, 25*

Through the study of His word and prayer, God will help keep us from stumbling. Satan planted the first seed of doubt about God's word in the Garden of Eden.

> Now the serpent was more crafty than any beast of the field that the LORD God had made. And he said to the woman, "Did God really say, 'You must not eat from any tree in the garden?'"
>
> *Genesis 3:1*

We have to know and trust God's word. God never changes and neither does His word. It will never be old-fashioned or become outdated. Unfortunately, today, we have to be on our guard with some churches and with people who call themselves Christians, some of whom deny the infallibility of scripture or twist its meaning.

Jesus Christ is the same yesterday and today and forever.

Hebrews 13:8

Do not think that I have come to abolish the Law or the Prophets. I have not come to abolish them, but to fulfill them. For I tell you truly, until heaven and earth pass away, not a single jot, not a stroke of a pen, will disappear from the Law until everything is accomplished.

Matthew 5:17,18

Heaven and earth will pass away, but My words will never pass away.

Matthew 24:35

Woe to those who call evil good and good evil, who turn darkness to light and light to darkness, who replace bitter with sweet and sweet with bitter. Woe to those who are wise in their own eyes.

Isaiah 5:20,21

With all my heart I have sought You; do not let me stray from Your commandments. I have hidden Your word in my heart that I might not sin against You.

Psalm 119:10,11

Satan is a liar. He loves to cause us to believe his lies and to doubt God's word.

> You belong to your father, the devil, and you want to carry out his desires. He was a murderer from the beginning, refusing to uphold the truth, because there is no truth in him. When he lies, he speaks his native language, because he is a liar and the father of lies.
>
> *John 8:44*

Federal agents train to spot counterfeit money by studying genuine bills so intensely that they can easily spot a fake. The agents don't rely on sight alone; they also touch the bill, tilt it, and look through it. Each action detects characteristics of real money that are often absent in a counterfeit.

If we use a counterfeit bill, even unknowingly, we're responsible. We won't be arrested as if we created the counterfeit, but neither will we be compensated to replace the value of the fake.

The consequences of accepting false ideas about God are more serious than using fake money. The more we know about God's character and His word, the easier it will be for us to discern truth from errors or lies. Just as federal agents inspect dollar bills, we must inspect teachers and their teaching. We also need to examine our own beliefs and interpretations of scripture. As the agents have various methods in their examination process, so should we.

> Now the Bereans were more noble-minded than the Thessalonians, for they received the message with great eagerness and examined the scriptures every day to see if these teachings were true.
>
> *Acts 17:11*

Like the Bereans, we need to compare the things we read or hear to scripture. If they contradict the plain meaning of scripture, they must be wrong. Pray for God to reveal the truth to you. If you're still unsure, talk to knowledgeable and godly men or women.

If a teaching or belief contradicts historic Christianity, that should be a red flag. Not everything that has been historically taught about the Bible is true, but if something significant is presented as a newly discovered truth no one else has seen since the time of Christ, I would be skeptical.

Early in Jude's letter, we're reminded, "keep yourselves in the love of God." Jude 21

Our study of God's word shouldn't be merely an academic exercise. It's good to study scripture deeply and diligently, but God gave us His word because He loves us and wanted to show us how we should live.

Obedience doesn't mean we perform good works to earn His approval. Our obedience is the natural fruit produced when we love God and want to please Him.

9

CLOTHED WITH THUNDER

Have you given the horse strength?
Have you clothed his neck with thunder?
Can you frighten him like a locust?
His majestic snorting strikes terror.
He paws in the valley, and rejoices in his strength;
He gallops into the clash of arms.
He mocks at fear, and is not frightened;
Nor does he turn back from the sword.
The quiver rattles against him, The glittering spear and javelin.
He devours the distance with fierceness and rage;
Nor does he come to a halt because the trumpet has sounded.
At the blast of the trumpet he says, "Aha!"
He smells the battle from afar, The thunder of captains and shouting.

Job 39:19-25 NKJV

According to Genesis, horses were created on the sixth day, along with the other land animals. At the end of that day, God looked over His creation and pronounced it "very good."

And God looked upon all that He had made, and indeed, it was very good. And there was evening, and there was morning—the sixth day.

Genesis 1:31

After man, I think horses were one of God's favorite creations. If you count horses, mules, and donkeys together as equines, they are the second most frequently mentioned animal group in the Bible (after sheep).

Sheep: 212   Lambs: 203   Rams: 162   Total: 577

Horses: 166   Mules and Donkeys: 154   Total: 320

Goats: 172

Bulls: 171

Equines play important roles in scripture. Mary may have ridden a donkey to Bethlehem where she gave birth to Jesus. That ride is debatable, but Jesus definitely rode a donkey into Jerusalem the week of His crucifixion. Revelation depicts Jesus returning on a white horse with His army of saints following Him, also mounted on white horses.

In the third Sonrise Stable book, *Clothed With Thunder*, I explore the question of creation versus evolution. Rosie and her sister Carrie attend a 4-H meeting and have to sit through a demonstration by one of the club members on the evolution of the horse. Rosie is annoyed when this theory is presented as fact. She resolves that she and her sister will come up with a demonstration that gives the creation perspective.

Horses are the most frequently used animal to support evolution. You would be hard pressed to find a non-fiction horse book that doesn't present the evolution of the horse as a fact. Most contain drawings of the supposed progression over sixty million years from the five-toed, fox-sized Eohippus to Mesohippus, Merychippus, Pliohippus, and finally to Equus, the modern horse. Various other animals are sometimes

mentioned in that sequence. Although fossil remains show those animals lived in the past, no evidence indicates that any animal ever turned into another kind.

In *Clothed With Thunder*, rather than trying to disprove the evolutionary theory, I focused on the amazing design of the horse. That proves conclusively in my mind that horses were created by an intelligent designer—and not just any designer, but God Himself as stated in Genesis.

The girls are introduced to a concept called irreducible complexity. That phrase sounds complex in itself, but it's really not. It simply describes a system in which all the parts have to work at once or else the system doesn't work at all.

A good example is the digestive system. What if a horse's mouth "evolved" hundreds of years before his esophagus or stomach? If he ate grass, where would it go? In fact, how would he know what eating was? Or what he was supposed to eat? That would require a brain to give him signals and information as well as teeth with a jawbone to hold them, a tongue, a hinged jaw with muscles and tendons so he could chew—and it goes on and on. He'd need digestive juices to break down the grass into nutrients his body could use and a way to eliminate the unused parts, otherwise he'd keep swelling up like a balloon until something burst.

Irreducible complexity applies to just about everything in the horse's body. In fact, it applies to all living creatures, including people. The eye is another great example. Horses have the largest eyes of any land mammal. The precise placement of their eyes gives them nearly 360-degree vision.

The girls end up bombarded with so much information on the carefully designed features of the horse; they have a hard time deciding what to include, since their time will be limited.

At one point in their demonstration, Rosie, the artistic sister, shows a drawing of her horse, Scamper. The club members admire her skill in creating the realistic sketch. Then, Rosie pulls out a handful of colored pencils and drops them on a piece of paper. She shows the result—random marks on the page. Rosie asks the club members whether dropping the pencils enough times would eventually create a picture of a horse like her drawing. Of course, everyone thinks that's preposterous. You can't drop pencils on a paper and expect a sketch of a horse to appear.

Yet, many believe something more far-fetched occurred. A living, breathing, eating, reproducing horse appeared somehow by random chance accidents over millions of years. The complexity of a horse or any living being goes far beyond a paper sketch.

Here are some facts showing how horses are amazingly designed—from head to hoof. *(Chapter 14 has the horse parts labeled. Refer to that diagram if you're not familiar with the terms used below.)*

Hoof

The hoof is a complicated structure consisting of sole, frog, hoof wall, lamina, coffin bone, digital cushion, navicular bone, and short pastern bone. These parts work together to support the horse's weight and provide traction, shock absorption, and proper blood flow through the legs.

Pastern

The slope of the horse's shoulder, pastern, and hoof should all match. The horse's pastern serves an important role in absorbing shock as the horse moves.

Cannon

Although it averages a mere nine inches around, the cannon bone is crucial to the horse's anatomy since it is the primary weight-bearing bone in the leg. The cannon bone runs from the knee or hock to the fetlock.

Eyes

Horses' eyes are located on the sides of their heads, giving them a much larger field of vision than humans, about 350 degrees. Horses have small blind spots directly in front and behind; however, a slight shift

of the head brings those areas into view. They can see color, but not as well as humans. A horse's distance and night vision is better than that of humans.

Ears

In addition to hearing, horses use their ears to communicate with humans and other horses. Ears flattened against the horse's head indicate annoyance or anger. The funnel shape of the horse's ear captures and conducts sound to the inner ear. Horses can rotate their ears to hear sounds coming from different directions. Each ear can move independently up to 180 degrees. Ten different muscles control ear movement. Hairs inside the ear help keep dirt and insects out. Horses can hear higher-pitched sounds than humans, but not as high as those a dog or cat can hear.

Teeth

Horses have twelve incisors at the front of the mouth for grazing. Behind the front incisors is the inter-dental space, which contains no teeth. In the back of their mouth are twelve premolars and twelve molars used for chewing and grinding food. Some horses also have varying numbers of canine or wolf teeth. Horses' teeth never stop growing. They wear against the tooth above or below them. A horse's age can be roughly deter-mined by the number, size, shape, and angle of his teeth.

Tail

The tail is an extension of the horse's spinal column and serves as a very accurate fly swatter. It is also used for communication. Movement and position of the tail can indicate annoyance, fright, discomfort, and more.

Respiratory System

A horse cannot breathe through its mouth, only through its nostrils, because the nasal passages are separate from the oral cavity. The nostrils expand greatly during exercise to take in more air. Horses cannot pant. At rest, a horse normally breathes eight to twelve times per minute. Horses take in twice as much oxygen as humans for an equivalent body weight. At a canter or gallop, a horse's breathing is timed with his stride. The horse inhales when his front hooves are striding outward and exhales when all four legs come together.

Circulatory System

A horse's heart beats 28 to 45 times per minute at rest, but it can go up to 250 during strenuous exercise. The heart and blood vessels of the average horse contain approximately nine gallons of blood. The heart of an average horse weighs eight and a half pounds.

Digestive System

The horse's digestive tract is a complicated system, approximately 100 feet long. The esophagus carries food to the stomach. A one-way valve in the esophagus prevents horses from vomiting. After the food is processed in the stomach, it passes to the small intestine, the major organ of digestion in the horse. Digested food is absorbed through the walls of the small intestine into the blood stream.

Sense of Smell

Due to the length of the nasal cavity, the horse has a better sense of smell than humans. The flehmen response, a curling of the upper lip, allows horses to process scents through the Jacobson's organ located on the roof of their mouths.

Sleep

Unlike humans, horses don't need a solid, unbroken period of sleep. Most of their sleep occurs in short intervals, roughly fifteen minutes each, for a total of about three hours per day. A stay apparatus in their legs allows horses to enter light sleep while standing up.

Skin

The body of the horse is covered with a layer of panniculus muscles just under the skin. These muscles produce the twitching response used to remove flies that land on the horse. A horse's head and lower legs do not have these muscles, so horses stomp or toss their heads when flies land in those areas.

Winter and Summer Coats

Horses grow thick coats for warmth and shed them to smooth, sleek coats in warmer seasons. The changes in coat hair are not triggered by temperature, but by the number of daylight hours.

Velvety Muzzles

Is there anything softer than a horse's muzzle? There is nothing about a velvety-soft muzzle that would give the horse any evolutionary advantage, but God knew how soothing it would be for those who love horses to stroke that soft skin!

Belief in evolution means all the features of the horse's body happened randomly over millions of years. That is clearly impossible. Believing in evolution takes a lot more faith than believing the Bible's account of creation. An all-knowing, all-powerful God created horses in an instant, designing them in specific ways to make them useful to man and to maximize their chances for survival in a fallen world.

If you investigate, you'll discover all animals (and people) have their own set of remarkable features that could never have happened by accident or random chances.

The primary debate involves creation versus evolution, but almost as amazing as creation is the fact that God/Jesus sustains it all and keeps everything running smoothly. The sun rises each day to provide heat and light, the rains come, the crops grow, our hearts beat, and so much more!

> For in Him [Christ] all things were created, things in heaven and on earth, visible and invisible, whether thrones or dominions or rulers or authorities. All things were created through Him and for Him. He is before all things, and in Him all things hold together.
>
> *Colossians 1:16,17*

God made the beasts of the earth after their kind. *Genesis 1:25*

P.S. He did it in one day!

10

CHESTNUTS

What is your favorite color?

If you asked the average person that question, they would respond with something like red, blue, or purple. I've never been normal. Depending on the day, I might say buckskin or maybe bay roan.

Years ago, my oldest two daughters and I were at Marmon Valley Farm for a mother/daughter horse camp. We didn't have any horses at the time, so I was excited about being able to ride for the next few days. We were assigned to bunk in a remodeled chicken coop. After settling into our accommodations, we went to check out the herd of horses.

There were about a hundred of every size and color. Wranglers were busy catching the horses that would be used for our first trail ride. Everyone gathered at the barn, and Wrangler Matt assigned a horse or pony to each person. That would be our horse to ride and care for over the entire weekend. I was happy when he pointed out my horse—a beautiful, Paint gelding named Apache. My daughters were still young, so they were assigned small, brown ponies that looked very ordinary compared to my flashy Apache.

I saddled and bridled my horse, looking forward to our ride. When everyone in the group was ready, we mounted. The horses followed single file behind the trail guide. We rode through the woods and up into the hills. Everything was perfect—all that I had imagined it would be—until I heard the word that changed my entire weekend.

"Trot," the guide called out.

As the horse in front of me picked up speed, Apache walked faster and faster. When he realized the other horses were getting too far ahead of him, he broke into a trot. I guess it was a trot. I grew up riding horses, and that was the roughest gait I'd ever experienced. Being a Western rider, I'd never learned to post. That would have been a valuable skill to have. I stood in my stirrups as much as possible, but even that didn't eliminate the painful jarring of Apache's trot. I began silently begging our guide to slow back down to a walk.

In the midst of my bouncing, I glanced up ahead at my daughters. They were laughing with delight as their little mealy brown ponies jogged along.

Apache's beautiful coloring didn't mean much to me at that moment. I would have gladly traded him for the ugliest horse on the farm as long as it had a smooth trot. I survived that ride, but rather than looking forward to our remaining ones, I dreaded going out on the trails again.

God had an important lesson for me to learn that weekend. I was attracted to Apache at first because of his flashy appearance. I tended to judge horses primarily on what they looked like on the outside. But there were other things far more important than their external beauty.

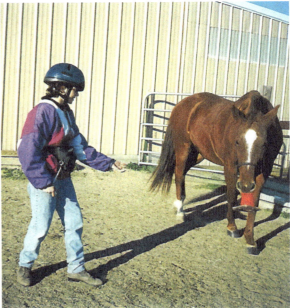

Although that weekend had a strong impact on me, I hadn't completely absorbed the lesson. It's one thing to mentally assent to a principle, but it's not truly learned until it changes your thoughts and behavior.

When I was able to buy my own horse a few years later, I was still too concerned about color and appearance. As I began my search, I dreamed of a beautiful horse with exotic coloring and a long, flowing mane and tail.

I heard about a Missouri Foxtrotter mare for sale that sounded like the kind of horse I wanted—smooth-gaited with extensive trail experience. When I arrived at the farm, the first thing I noticed was that she was a chestnut—my least favorite color.

I always assumed chestnut was the most common horse color. It seems I see chestnut horses everywhere. But according to my research, bay is the most common with chestnut in second place.

The Foxtrotter mare, Ginger, didn't have a long, flowing mane and tail either. In fact, she had a sparse mane and barely any forelock at all, just a few short, wispy hairs between her ears. On the positive side, Ginger had a smooth foxtrot and a wonderful little canter. Despite the fact that she didn't meet my standards for a beautiful horse, I decided to buy her.

When my middle daughter outgrew the pony, Ebony, we bought her a horse. The Racking Horse mare, Satin, was in foal when we purchased her. Satin was black, and the sire was a dark palomino. The foal would be mine to train as my future riding horse. While we waited for the baby to arrive, I imagined what color it might be—palomino, buckskin, or maybe a glossy black with bold white markings. Fortunately, I was there when the foal, Kezzie, was born. Guess what color she was?

Chestnut!

Foals begin to shed their fuzzy, baby coats at three or four months, sometimes turning a totally different color. I had convinced myself that when Kezzie shed her foal coat, she would be transformed into a gleaming palomino.

Kezzie was born in 2002. As of this writing in 2022, she is still a chestnut. She never morphed into a different color, but she did turn out to be one of the sweetest and gentlest horses I've ever owned.

I'm a slow learner sometimes, but I finally really got it. For horses, as well as people, what's on the outside doesn't matter as much as what's on the inside.

Now, whenever I see a chestnut horse, I'm reminded of 1 Samuel 16:7.

…the LORD does not see as man does. For man sees the outward appearance, but the LORD sees the heart.

It's easy to make hasty judgments about people based on their outward appearance. We do it in positive and negative ways. We are quick to assume a beautiful person is nice and a not-so-beautiful person is evil or mean. God wants us to get to know people's hearts. That's far more important than what someone looks like.

P. S.

In 2017, I purchased a driving pony at an Amish auction. Yep. He's a chestnut too, and I'm pleased to say I didn't think twice about his color. He's a sweet pony, much like our old Ebony. And, in 2022, Gemma joined the family. She's a Haflinger/Fjord cross. I guess she would be considered a chestnut as well, although her mane and tail are a unique color. The photo shows my two chestnuts when they first met.

11

A MOTHER'S LOVE

I mentioned Kezzie in the previous devotion. This is the story of her birth in the wee hours of April 8, 2002. My daughters and I were taking turns checking on Satin every four hours. The black Racking Horse mare was due to foal any day. Her foal would be my future riding horse. I was looking forward to raising and training it. I was scheduled to check on Satin at two in the morning, but around midnight I sensed I should head out to the barn early.

Sure enough, Satin was down in her stall, about to give birth. My heart pounded so loudly, it seemed I could hear it. I wanted to return to the house to wake everyone so they could join me in the barn. But I didn't want to leave Satin and miss the birth of the foal.

I ran to the house and pounded on a back window, not taking the time to go inside. I hoped that would be enough to wake someone. I raced to Satin's stall, making it back just as the chestnut filly was born. The rest of the family arrived soon after.

Something seemed wrong. The foal wasn't moving, and Satin showed no interest in her baby.

Had I waited this long only for the foal to be born dead?

I quickly cleared the filly's nostrils, so she could breathe, and grabbed a towel to dry her off. I rubbed her thin body until she began to twitch and move a little. She opened her eyes and blinked at me. Whew! The foal was going to be okay, after all.

I named her Keziah's Jubilee—well, not right then, but later. Jubilee appeared frequently in Satin's pedigree. Keziah was the name of one of Job's three daughters listed in Job 42:14. That was a big name for such a little girl, so she quickly became Kezzie. But back to her birth story.

We watched the foal attempt to stand. She was small and didn't seem very strong, but she was determined to get up. After a few failures, the little girl finally made it up on wobbly legs that seemed far too long for her body.

The foal instinctively moved to Satin's side. It was important for her to begin nursing. But Satin put her ears back and lifted a hind leg in warning. How dare this strange creature approach her!

This was not how things were supposed to proceed, according to the foaling books I had read.

Satin was not pleased with this filly who had somehow invaded her stall. It was now 3 a.m. I hated to wake my vet at that hour, but it seemed quite possible that Satin might hurt the foal.

Dr. Rings arrived within an hour and gave Satin a tranquilizer to calm the reluctant mother's nerves. Kezzie was then able to nurse. The vet left another tranquilizer with instructions to use it in several hours if Satin still hadn't accepted her foal.

My middle daughter and I spent the remaining early morning hours in the barn, keeping an eye on the mother and baby. When the effects of the tranquilizer wore off, Satin began to reject Kezzie again, so I gave the reluctant mama the second tranquilizer.

By noon, however, Satin had undergone a complete transformation. I couldn't believe she was the same horse that had nipped at and threatened to kick her foal a few hours earlier. Her motherly instincts finally kicked in, and she became very possessive and protective of Kezzie.

Several times in those first weeks, Satin charged at me with her teeth bared when I entered their pen. The mother who at first had tried to harm her own baby, now seemed determined to kill me if I came anywhere near her foal!

Just as most animal mothers have a fierce protective instinct when it comes to their young, God intended for human mothers and fathers to love, protect, and care for their children. Sadly, that doesn't always happen. It was bad enough that Satin, at first, rejected her foal. It's far worse when some human parents abandon, neglect, or harm their children.

Scripture assures us that even if we are rejected by our earthly parents, God is always there for us. And He loves us with an everlasting love.

> When my father and my mother forsake me, then the Lord will take care of me.
>
> *Psalm 27:10 NKJV*
>
> I have loved you with an everlasting love; therefore I have drawn you with loving devotion.
>
> *Jeremiah 31:3*

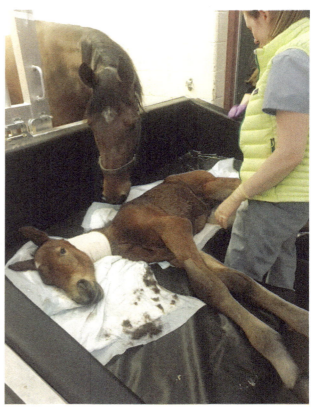

A neighbor raised a few Standardbred harness racing horses each year. I often took walks down the quiet, country road, and enjoyed watching the mares and foals in their pasture. One day, the owner happened to be outside and informed me one of his newborn foals had some abnormality with a back leg. The mare and foal had been taken to Ohio State Veterinary Hospital.

In contrast to Satin's initial dismal mothering skills, this mare showed an instinctive devotion to her foal. The mare patiently looked on as her baby was treated.

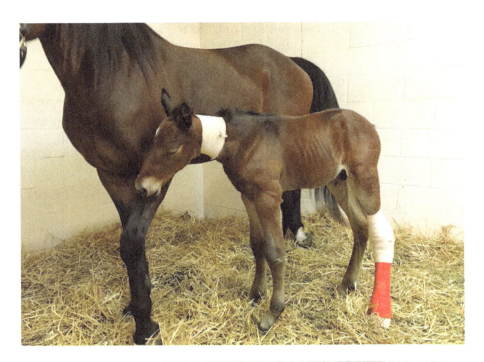

But when the treatment was complete, she hid the foal under the straw in her stall and kept watch over him.

Her look in the final photo seems to be a warning that she was taking charge of things now, and no one else better come near her baby—if they could find him!

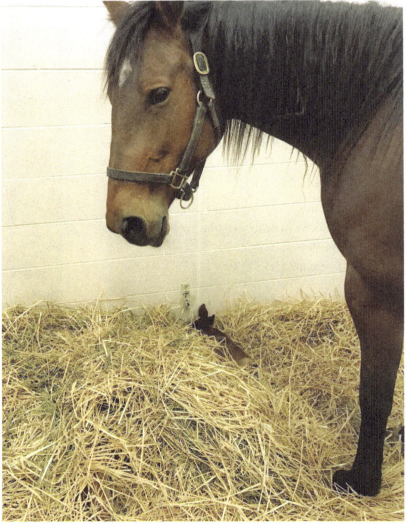

12

TWINS

It's not uncommon for goats to give birth to twin kids—sometimes even triplets, and more rarely, quadruplets. Sheep are also known to have twin lambs. However, the birth of healthy twin foals in horses is rare, about a 1 in 10,000 chance. Triplet foals are so rare, they're almost non-existent. I'm not aware of any record indicating triplet foals have all survived. In 1986, triplets were born to a buckskin Quarter Horse. The two fillies and a colt received intensive care at UC-Davis Veterinary Hospital in California. The foals ranged from twenty-eight to thirty-five pounds, while a typical foal weighs about fifty pounds.

The smallest of the foals died four days after its birth. The second was euthanized at twenty-four days because of a leg fracture. Although smaller than average, the third of the triplets was doing well at one year of age. I couldn't find any update on the horse after that.

A Mustang, Elsa, was one of those rare mares to give birth to live twins. The mare was part of a BLM (Bureau of Land Management) roundup. After the roundup, while in the BLM corrals, Elsa gave birth to her blue roan foals. Within months, the three were auctioned off to separate people in three different states. Fortu-

nately, all three were reunited when the owners of Elsa and her foals, Promise and Hope, turned them over to Skydog Ranch and Sanctuary, a 9,000-acre ranch near Bend, Oregon.

In 2005, a nine-year-old Belgian mare, Sally, bore twin mules, Dianna and Camilla. The twins were strong and healthy, needing no medical attention or special care. Destiny, an Irish Sport Horse, owned by Tania Mackee of GFS Sporthorses, had twin colts in 2018. The boys were named Shockwave and Aftershock. Amazingly, in February 2022, Destiny delivered a second set of twins, Pesky and Peakaboo, a colt and a filly. The chance of a horse giving birth to two sets of twins is about one in a million.

Twins are much more common in people than in horses. According to 2019 CDC statistics, 32 out of every 1,000 human births in the United States were twins. Fraternal twins are most common, while identical twins occur in roughly 4 out of 1,000 births.

The first-mentioned and best-known twins in the Bible are Jacob and Esau. Rebekah felt the boys struggling inside her before they were born. God explained what the struggle of these brothers meant.

> Two nations are in your womb, and two peoples from within you will be separated; one people will be stronger than the other, and the older will serve the younger.
>
> *Genesis 25:23*

Jacob was a quiet man who stayed at home and was his mother's favorite. Esau was a skillful hunter and was his father's favorite. (Genesis 25:27) Although the younger of the two, Jacob gained his father's birthright when Esau traded it to him for some stew. (Genesis 25:33) Jacob also received his father's blessing by tricking Isaac into thinking he was Esau. (Genesis 27)

The twins became fathers of two nations. Jacob's name was changed to Israel. His sons formed the twelve tribes of Israel, God's chosen people. Esau's descendants were the Edomites, a nation hostile to Israel.

Just as Jacob and Esau were very different men, children today, raised in the same family, may turn out quite differently. I won't pretend to understand how the process of salvation works in terms of election versus free will. But to some degree at least, I think God gives us enough free will to respond to Him when He pursues us.

I always believed there was a God, and I wanted a relationship with Him, even when I was young. But I had no idea how such a thing happened. The few people I knew who seemed to be Christians, never spoke to me about it. I floundered my way into adulthood with no spiritual guidance. When I reached a low point in my life, I resolved to read through the Bible for the first time. I didn't understand most of it, but I did read the whole thing. A verse that provided insight into my situation was Jeremiah 29:13.

> You will seek Me and find Me when you search for Me with all your heart.

I had never done that. I wanted God, but in addition to other things I was hanging onto. I had been willing to give God part of my heart but not all of it. That revelation was a turning point for me. There were things in my life I had to let go of in order to give God my whole heart. C. S. Lewis described this complete relinquishment of self in *Mere Christianity*.

> Give me all of you! I don't want so much of your time, so much of your talents and money, and so much of your work. I want you! All of you! I have not come to torment or frustrate the natural man or woman, but to kill it! No half measures will do. I don't want to only prune a branch here and a branch there; rather I want the whole tree out! Hand it over to me, the whole outfit, all of your desires, all of your wants and wishes and dreams. Turn them ALL over to me. Give yourself to me and I will make of you a new self—in my image. Give me yourself and in exchange I will give you Myself. My will, shall become your will. My heart, shall become your heart.

13

BEAUTIFUL SADDLES

One of the things I enjoy when I attend a horse exposition is browsing through western saddles in the vendor area. The smell of the leather, the intricately carved designs, rich colors, and silver or stitched ornamentation combine to make a beautiful piece of tack.

Years ago, when my daughters showed horses, we couldn't afford such fancy equipment.

Sometimes, I compared their well-worn, plain saddles to the expensive ones other kids had. I wished I could provide something nicer for my daughters. I had to remind myself the judges wouldn't select winners based on who had the most beautiful saddle.

In 1 Corinthians 12, Paul states that our bodies have many parts—eyes, feet, ears, mouth, and so forth. Each part is important and has its own role to play. They must all work together in order for our bodies to function properly. We wouldn't say that our heart is more important than our brain. Both are essential.

In that passage, Paul goes on to explain that the church is similar to our physical body. As Christians, we are members of the church body and have our own role and purpose. Each member of the body of Christ is important. It's not for us to say who has the greater role. We are all necessary to achieve God's purposes.

You may be wondering what this has to do with saddles. I didn't see a connection at first, either, but God has a way of reinforcing His truths through the everyday things in life.

When I'm struck by a saddle's beauty, it's the outward, most visible parts that catch my eye. However, there are important parts of a saddle that are very plain and partially or completely hidden from view. Are those parts unimportant? Could the saddle function just as well without them?

Absolutely not! A saddle is of no use without a girth. On a western saddle, this bland strap, usually black or brown, is hidden almost entirely by the stirrup fenders. The horse sweats all over it, and mud splashes on it. By the end of some trail rides I've been on, the girth was caked with mud. For that reason, neoprene girths are a great invention; just hose them off, and they're as good as new.

According to 1 Corinthians 12:26, "If one part suffers, every part suffers with it." I can almost guarantee if the girth breaks during a ride, the entire saddle will suffer, and most likely, the rider along with it. Assuming there was no back cinch, the saddle would fall off, and the rider would end up on the ground.

If a back cinch were present, that could be even worse. A rear cinch isn't fastened tightly enough to hold the saddle in place. Without the front girth, the saddle could flip under the horse's abdomen, but the rear cinch would prevent it from coming totally off. A calm horse may stand still and allow you to fix things. But horses are used to wearing saddles on their back not under their tummy. A flighty horse might freak out and cause a terrible wreck.

I had some personal experience with this when I was learning to ride years ago. While cantering up from the back pasture, I felt myself slipping sideways on the pony's back. The girth hadn't been tightened enough, and the saddle started to slide. This can be a problem with round, low-withered horses or ponies. A high wither helps hold the saddle in place. Someone caught the pony and grabbed me before I reached the point of no return.

Another example is the straps that hold the stirrups on. They're also hidden behind the fenders. Or the tree deep inside the saddle? It's totally covered with leather or a synthetic material. The only people who see the tree are the ones who create it or the saddle maker. But the tree is vital. It provides support and structure for the entire saddle.

The pieces of a saddle all work together. The more visible, beautiful parts and the underlying, plain ones combine to create a safe, useful piece of equipment.

If you've ever thought you're not important, remember this lesson about saddles. You and I may be one of those plain-looking pieces, like a girth, hidden beneath the fancier parts of the saddle. But our role, as small as it might seem, is still important in God's plan.

The body is a unit, though it is composed of many parts. And although its parts are many, they all form one body. So it is with Christ. For in one Spirit we were all baptized into one body, whether Jews or Greeks, slave or free, and we were all given one Spirit to drink.

For the body does not consist of one part, but of many. If the foot should say, "Because I am not a hand, I do not belong to the body," that would not make it any less a part of the body. And if the ear should say, "Because I am not an eye, I do not belong to the body," that would not make it any less a part of the body. If the whole body were an eye, where would the sense of hearing be? If the whole body were an ear, where would the sense of smell be?

But in fact, God has arranged the members of the body, every one of them, according to His design. If they were all one part, where would the body be? As it is, there are many parts, but one body.

The eye cannot say to the hand, "I do not need you." Nor can the head say to the feet, "I do not need you." On the contrary, the parts of the body that seem to be weaker are indispensable, and the parts we consider less honorable, we treat with greater honor. And our unpresentable parts are treated with special modesty, whereas our presentable parts have no such need.

But God has composed the body and has given greater honor to the parts that lacked it, so that there should be no division in the body, but that its members should have mutual concern for one another. If one part suffers, every part suffers with it; if one part is honored, every part rejoices with it.

1 Corinthians 12:14-26

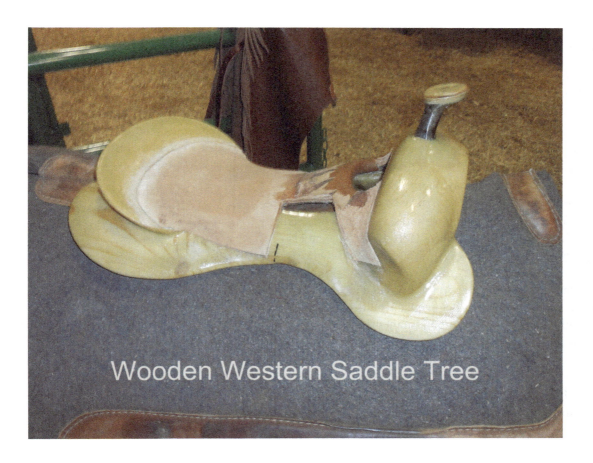
Wooden Western Saddle Tree

14

Body Parts

For as the body is one and has many members, but all the members of that one body, being many, are one body, so also is Christ. … If the whole body were an eye, where would be the hearing? If the whole were hearing, where would be the smelling? But now God has set the members, each one of them, in the body just as He pleased. And if they were all one member, where would the body be?

1 Corinthians 12:12,17-19

We looked at this passage in the previous chapter with respect to the parts of a saddle, but it applies to the parts of a horse's body as well. The point of the passage is that, as believers, each of us has a role to play in the optimal functioning of the body of Christ here on earth. One Christian can't claim to be more important than another. We are all important, regardless of how small our role might seem.

A horse's body is constructed of many parts. Most of them correspond to parts in humans, although they may function differently. The most likely reason for this similarity in structure is that God used the same overall blueprint when He made living creatures. Among the things we have in common with horses are eyes, ears, noses, legs, hearts, brains, muscles, bones, blood vessels, and much more.

Horses are wonderful evidence of a wise Creator, but in particular the structure of their legs. A horse's front legs carry over half (60%) of their weight. Horses have no muscles below their knees and hocks, only tendons and ligaments. Even more surprising, a horse's front legs are not attached to his skeleton by joints. The front legs are held to his body at the shoulder by strong muscles and ligaments.

Knowing the parts of a horse is important. How well a horse's parts match the standard (his conformation) determines to a great extent how the horse will be able to perform. That's an important factor when purchasing a horse or deciding what he could be used for. Knowing horse parts will also help you when purchasing and fitting tack. Properly fitting tack will function best and avoid injuring the horse or causing him discomfort.

When your horse is injured or sick, knowing the names of the parts allows you to describe symptoms or injuries accurately and will enable you to properly apply any treatment recommended by a veterinarian. For example, it would be impossible to ice a horse's hock if you have no idea what a hock is!

The importance of small, seemingly insignificant things is illustrated by the saying on the right that has been passed down for hundreds of years.

Its larger meaning is that we shouldn't overlook small problems, because they often grow into larger ones. It also highlights how important it is to properly care for a horse's hooves. There's a scene in Anna Sewell's *Black Beauty* where a man doesn't take action to correct a loose nail in one of Beauty's shoes. That negligence results in the man's death and Beauty's knees being permanently scarred.

> For want of a nail the shoe was lost.
> For want of a shoe the horse was lost.
> For want of a horse the rider was lost.
> For want of a rider the message was lost.
> For want of a message the battle was lost.
> For want of a battle the kingdom was lost.
> And all for the want of a horseshoe nail.

A horse's hooves are not flashy or glamorous in appearance. They're often muddy and can be smelly. When someone oohs and ahhs over a horse, I can almost guarantee it's not over how beautiful the animal's hooves are. Those who don't know horses well are typically impressed by a horse's coat color and sheen or maybe a long, thick mane and tail. A more experienced horse person might be in awe of an animal's near-perfect conformation and condition. About the only one who would pay special attention to a horse's hooves would be a dedicated farrier!

Poll

Crest

Withers

Forehead

Shoulder

Flank

Back Loin Croup

Point of hip

Muzzle

Cheek

Dock

Chin groove

Throat latch

Tail

Elbow

Barrel Abdomen

Thigh

Forearm

Gaskin

Stifle

Knee

Chestnut

Hock

Coronet

Cannon

Cannon

Ergot

Fetlock

Pastern

Pastern

Heel

Hoof

Their humble appearance doesn't reflect their importance in the horse's body. The full weight of the horse (often 1,000 pounds or more) rests on those four hooves. In the center of each hoof is a triangular or v-shaped pad known as the frog. Why it was given this peculiar name is unclear. If you let your eyes go a little fuzzy, I suppose you could imagine the frog as somewhat shaped like the amphibian it's named after.

If the hoof isn't known for its beauty, the frog is even less so. The grooves on each side of the frog are like a magnet for mud and muck that becomes embedded and can lead to infections like thrush if not regularly removed.

But the frog has several important jobs. It's constructed from a horn-like material similar to the hoof wall, but with a higher moisture content, making it somewhat spongy. The cushiony, elastic frog squishes or compresses under pressure. In most unshod horses, the frog will come in contact with the ground when the horse steps down. In this role, it helps provide traction and serves as a shock absorber, reducing wear and tear on the horse's joints.

The heart is a pump which circulates blood around the body. Since the heart is above a horse's legs, blood easily makes that downward journey. But that same blood has to return up to the heart. Remember, there are no muscles in the horse's lower legs, so muscular contractions can't help the blood move uphill.

Some have called the frog a horse's second heart. The frog isn't actually a pump, but it does serve a vital role in the movement of blood in a horse's legs. When the hoof lifts off the ground, the frog expands back to its normal size. This expansion and contraction of the frog works with internal structures of the hoof located above the frog to push blood back up the leg.

Glands in the frog which keep it moist and spongy seem to produce a scent, as well. When the frog contacts the ground, a scent unique to each horse is deposited. This allows horses to find each other. That scent can also be picked up by tracking dogs.

As you can see, the small, rather ugly, and mostly hidden frog in a horse's hoof has quite an important role to play.

The same goes for each member of the body of Christ. Just because your role isn't glamorous or well known, doesn't mean it's unimportant.

> Just as each of us has one body with many members, and not all members have the same function, so in Christ we who are many are one body, and each member belongs to one another. We have different gifts according to the grace given us. If one's gift is prophecy, let him use it in proportion to his faith; if it is serving, let him serve; if it is teaching, let him teach; if it is encouraging, let him encourage; if it is giving, let him give generously; if it is leading, let him lead with diligence; if it is showing mercy, let him do it cheerfully.
>
> *Romans 12:4-8*

If you're familiar with church history, you've probably heard of John and Charles Wesley, founders of the Methodist Church. Less well known is Susanna Wesley, the mother of not only John and Charles, but seventeen other children (nine died as infants). Susanna provided the early education for her children, which commenced when each child turned five. On the first day, they were expected to learn the entire alphabet. All but two of her children accomplished this.

> It is almost incredible, what a child may be taught in a quarter of a year, by a vigorous application, if the child has but a tolerable capacity, and good health.
>
> *Susanna Wesley*

As soon as the alphabet was mastered, Susanna began teaching the child to read using the King James Bible. They began with the first chapter of Genesis, spelling and reading a word, then progressing to a line, and then an entire verse. Additionally, the children were taught Latin and Greek.

It's easy to consider John and Charles Wesley important in the history of the church, but where would they have been without the early influence of their mother?

Another example involves Charles Haddon Spurgeon, known as the "Prince of Preachers." There are few who would recognize his godly mother, Eliza, or his father and grandfather who were both preachers.

Although those three gave Charles a strong foundation in the Christian faith, at the age of fifteen, he was still an unbeliever. At one point, Charles even doubted the existence of God.

> It was just when I wanted Christ, and panted after Him, that, on a sudden, the thought crossed my mind which I abhorred but could not conquer, that there was no God, no Christ, no Heaven, no hell; that all my prayers were but a farce, and that I might as well have whistled to the winds or spoken to the howling waves.

Autobiography, p. 87

An unknown and uneducated man was God's instrument to lead Spurgeon to salvation. One Sunday morning in 1850, Spurgeon set off to attend church. However, a severe snowstorm prevented him from reaching his intended destination. Instead, he turned down a side street and entered a Primitive Methodist Chapel. There were about fifteen people in attendance. Even the pastor had been unable to make it through the storm.

A thin man, a shoemaker or tailor, rose to speak in the pastor's absence. His text was Isaiah 45:22, "Look unto me, and be ye saved, all the ends of the earth: for I am God and there is none else."

The unprepared man, probably uncomfortable in this new role, focused primarily on the text. Even with frequent repetition, his message lasted at most ten minutes.

> My dear friends, this is a very simple text indeed. It says, "Look." Now lookin' don't take a deal of pain. It ain't liftin' your foot or your finger; it is just "Look!" Well, a man needn't go to college to learn to look. You may be the biggest fool, and yet you can look… A child can look. One who is almost an idiot can look. However weak, or however poor a man may be, he can look. And if he looks the promise is that he shall live. Many on ye are lookin' to yourselves. But it's no use lookin' there. You'll never find any comfort in yourselves. Some say look to God, the Father. No, look to Him by-and-by. It is Christ that speaks. I am in the garden in an agony, pouring out my soul unto death; I am on the tree, dying for sinners; look unto Me! I rise again. Look unto me! I ascend into heaven! Look unto me. I am sitting at the Father's right hand. O poor sinner look unto me! Look unto me! Some of ye say, "We must wait for the Spirit's workin'." You have no business with that just now. Look to Christ. The text says, "Look unto Me."

The man's brief, simple words spoke to Spurgeon's heart.

> I saw at once the way of salvation. I know not what else he said—I did not take much notice of it—I was so possessed with that one thought. Like as when the brazen serpent was lifted up, the people only looked and were healed, so it was with me. I had been waiting to do fifty things, but when I heard that word, "Look!" what a charming word it seemed to me.

15

STABLES AND CHURCHES

Secretariat is one of the most famous Thoroughbred racehorses of all time. When he began his racing career as a two-year-old in 1972, Secretariat's jockey wore the blue-and-white-checkered colors of the Meadow Stable.

Secretariat overshadowed another very successful Meadow Stable horse. Riva Ridge (shown below), a 16-hand bay stallion, was born in 1969, the year before Secretariat. In 1972, Riva Ridge won two of the three Triple Crown races—the Kentucky Derby and the Belmont Stakes. He finished fourth in the Preakness Stakes and earned over a million dollars in his racing career.

In January 1973, the founder of Meadow Stable, Christopher Chenery, passed away. After his death, Christopher's children owed high taxes on the estate. Her siblings urged Penny Chenery Tweedy to sell Meadow Stable. Instead, she decided to syndicate (sell shares of) their Thoroughbred stallions, Riva Ridge and Secretariat.

This was before Secretariat had won the Kentucky Derby, the first leg of the Triple Crown. No one could have predicted he would win all three of the top races that year. With the help of Seth Hancock of Claiborne Farm, Riva Ridge was syndicated for five and Secretariat for six million dollars, putting an end to the financial difficulties for Meadow Stable.

Although not mentioned at all in the movie, *Secretariat*, Riva Ridge played an equally important role in saving Meadow Farm. Chenery was disappointed that the horse who came before Secretariat was left out of the movie.

> I was disappointed in the movie because there were things in it that simply weren't true to life. But I just said to myself, "That's Hollywood." They couldn't have two heroes.

In fact, Riva Ridge had a special place in Chenery's heart. "Secretariat belonged to the people and Riva Ridge belonged to me. Secretariat had millions of people who cared about him. He didn't need me. But Riva Ridge only had me. He was my hero and I knew I meant something to him."

The Meadow Stable and Claiborne Farm are two of the best known Thoroughbred racing farms in the United States. When people speak of a racing stable, they don't mean the buildings but the famous horses it produced—or the owners, trainers, and jockeys associated with it.

Many Christians, if asked what church they attend, will respond with the name of a building. It's common for people to equate "church" with a building. But that isn't the biblical meaning of the word.

In Matthew 16, after Peter states that Jesus is "the Christ, the Son of the living God," Jesus responds,

> And I tell you that you are Peter, and on this rock I will build My church [ekklesia], and the gates of Hades will not prevail against it.
>
> *Matthew 16:18*

The Greek word "ekklesia" is an assembly or gathering of people. Ekklesia appears 118 times in the New Testament where it's consistently translated "church." At the time of Christ, an ekklesia wasn't necessarily a religious group. It was the term used for a general gathering of people.

When a riot occurred in Ephesus, the silversmiths realized their livelihood might dwindle because of Paul's preaching. If Paul convinced people to turn to the true God, they would stop worshiping the goddess Diana and would no longer buy statues of her. (Acts 19:21-41)

Although most in the crowd didn't know what was going on, they joined the riot, crying for two hours, "Great is Diana of the Ephesians!"

Eventually, the city clerk quieted them and advised them to take their complaints to the "legal or lawful assembly." That is the same word "ekklesia" that elsewhere is translated church.

> But if you are seeking anything beyond this, it must be settled in a legal assembly [ekklesia].
>
> *Acts 19:39*

Even the angry mob is referred to as "ekklesia" although translated again as "assembly."

> After he had said this, he dismissed the assembly [ekklesia].
>
> *Acts 19:41*

> With one accord they continued to meet daily in the temple courts and to break bread from house to house, sharing their meals with gladness and sincerity of heart, praising God and enjoying the favor of all the people. And the Lord added to their number daily those who were being saved.
>
> *Acts 2:46,47*

They did not add people to a building but to a group of believers, the "body" of Christ.

> And God put everything under His feet and made Him head over everything for the church [ekklesia], which is His body, the fullness of Him who fills all in all.
>
> *Ephesians 1:22,23*

Christ's body is all the people worldwide who have trusted in Him as their Savior. Many, or perhaps most, of the early Christians met in people's houses rather than a designated church building.

> When they arrived, they gathered the church [ekklesia] together and reported all that God had done through them, and how He had opened the door of faith to the Gentiles.
>
> *Acts 14:27*

> Aquila and Prisca greet you warmly in the Lord, and so does the church [ekklesia] that meets at their house.
>
> *1 Corinthians 16:19*

> To Philemon our beloved fellow worker, to Apphia our sister, to Archippus our fellow soldier, and to the church [ekklesia] that meets at your house:
>
> *Philemon 1:1,2*

The early Quakers took the meaning of "ekklesia" literally and opposed calling buildings "churches." They didn't believe a special building was necessary for gathering to worship. Instead, they met in each others' homes or, weather permitting, in the open air.

Amish communities continue this practice today, meeting in the houses or barns of families within their district. Home churches, by definition, limit the number of attendees, since most homes cannot accommodate hundreds of people. A typical Amish church consists of forty or fewer families. Meeting in homes doesn't limit the number of believers that can be added, but when a group reaches a certain size, it would need to split.

Is it wrong to worship in a church building today?

If your heart is right with God and your faith in Christ is sincere, you can worship anywhere. There are advantages and disadvantages to both home churches and church buildings with larger congregations.

Big churches typically have large budgets and can provide more ministry services and mission outreaches. However, it's easy to get lost in a large congregation and miss out on close fellowship with other believers. It's common for a large church to have subgroups to provide for this closer fellowship. These have a variety of names—home groups, discipleship groups, small groups, etc. These subgroups seem to match more closely what the early church practiced.

I've been part of two home churches. Advantages to a smaller gathering are closer connections and more accountability to other members. But because of that small size, there's no way to hide either. Personality clashes or differences of opinion on doctrine can be magnified and cause awkward conflicts.

Just as it's the horses that are what's important about a stable, we, the believers, are more important than our church buildings.

16

SIGHT AND EYES

Horses have the largest eyes of any land mammal. The position of their eyes toward the sides of their heads gives horses almost 360-degree vision. They can see nearly all the way around their bodies—except for small blind spots directly in front of and behind them. Because of the back blind spot, you should never approach a horse unannounced from the rear. This could startle him, causing him to kick.

Horses have both monocular and binocular vision. People see with binocular vision. Our eyes focus together on the same thing. We don't have monocular vision because our eyes are on the front of our heads rather than the sides. Predatory animals tend to have eyes more toward the front while prey animals have them at the sides of their heads. This gives the prey animal an opportunity to notice a predator while it's still at a distance, giving him a head start on escaping.

When looking forward, horses use binocular vision. When looking to the side, they see out of one eye. This monocular vision allows them to see with each eye separately—seeing something different with their right eye than their left. I can't imagine how that works, but apparently the equine brain sorts it all out.

Peripheral vision is what we see to either side of us. Hold your arm straight out from your shoulder to one side while looking straight ahead. Most likely, you won't be able to see your arm at all. In comparison, that arm held straight out to the side would be in the middle of a horse's monocular, peripheral vision. You'll have to move your arm forward for it to come into view.

This expanded peripheral or side vision allows a horse to quickly detect motion around him. As a prey animal, that motion may trigger his flight response before it even registers what is moving. This can be a problem when we're riding. We would rather be in charge of telling the horse when there's a need to run rather than the horse bolting at the sight of a harmless plastic bag.

Monocular vision can be the cause of a horse's fright over an object he's seen and accepted before. If the object moves to the other side or the horse turns around, he now sees it with the opposite eye and may not recognize it. He might decide it's some new, scary thing.

When a horse wants to see something better, he'll turn his head to focus on it with both eyes. Horses also raise or lower their heads to help them focus, depending on the distance of an object.

Cone cells in the retina of our eyes control how color is perceived. Tests have shown horses can see in color, although not exactly as humans do. Horses have only two types of cones versus three for people, so horses see greens and blues but not reds. Red objects aren't invisible to them, but their favorite red apples may be seen as a brown or greenish color.

Although they don't see color as well, horses have more rod cells and see approximately 50% better at night than people do. However, a horse's eyes do not adjust quickly to changes in lighting conditions—from bright to dim or vice versa.

Because of the size of their eyes, it's believed horses see close objects 50% larger than those objects appear to us. Horses cannot see fine details. For example, in reading material like this book, we must detect differences in tiny objects to distinguish letters. Horses can't see such small details.

The most common eye color for horses is brown. The rarest is green. Other colors include blue, amber, and hazel. A horse may have eyes of two different colors. One brown and one blue eye is a common combination, with the blue eye often found on the side of the head that contains a large white marking (as in the foal pictured on the left). There are no albino horses, so horses never have red or pink eyes.

Although physical sight is important, the Bible warns that not everyone who can physically see is able to understand.

> The mystery of the kingdom of God has been given to you, but to those on the outside everything is expressed in parables, so that, they may be ever seeing but never perceiving, and ever hearing but never understanding; otherwise they might turn and be forgiven.
>
> *Mark 4:12*

Some people believe Jesus taught in parables to make His messages easier to understand. Actually, the opposite is true. As stated in Mark 4:12, He used parables so only those who wanted to learn would pursue the truth and understand the deeper meaning.

Seeing is not necessarily understanding. We see physical things every day that we don't understand. Each spring, flowers and vegetables grow from seeds planted in the ground. I see them sprout and grow, but I have no idea how it works. On a simpler level, I use electronic devices, such as the computer I'm using to write these words. I see the text appearing on the screen and know bits and bytes get transferred electronically between various chips, but I don't have a complete understanding of how that happens.

The difference between seeing or hearing and understanding is even more pronounced in the spiritual realm. The Greek word for understanding or perceiving is "eido"—to know, be aware, or understand.

When Jesus taught, nearly all the people around Him could physically hear (unless they were deaf). But many didn't comprehend what He was saying. Although they heard the words, they didn't understand Him. Without that understanding, Jesus' words were misinterpreted or forgotten. To unbelievers, His parables were merely simple, or even nonsensical, stories.

Later, when the superficial listeners were gone, Jesus expanded on the parables and explained them to His closest followers. Once their meaning was understood, the story format of the parables helped His followers remember the teaching. Many of the stories involved things people of that time would encounter on a daily basis. Each time they saw those things, they were reminded of the parable and its meaning. For example, the lost sheep of Luke 15:4-7. Seeing sheep would remind them of the joy experienced in heaven when a sinner repents.

Unfortunately, the religious leaders of Jesus' day were the most spiritually blind.

In this passage in Matthew 15, the Scribes and Pharisees questioned why Jesus' disciples weren't following the tradition of ceremonial hand washing before meals. According to these religious leaders, Jesus and His disciples were unclean. Imagine the blindness that allowed these men to call the Son of God unclean!

Jesus responded that it's not what is on the outside that makes us unclean but what is in our hearts.

> They are blind guides. If a blind man leads a blind man, both will fall into a pit.
>
> *Matthew 15:14*

In order to lead a blind person, the guide must be able to see where he is going. If the guide cannot see either, he may lead them both into danger, like falling into a ditch. Although the religious leaders claimed to be guides, they were spiritually blind themselves. They knew scripture but couldn't grasp its true meaning. They valued man-made traditions over the word of God—and more than the Son of God who stood before them.

This spiritual blindness continued after Jesus was crucified and rose from the dead. While in a Roman prison, Paul spoke to some of the Jewish leaders. A few believed, but many did not. Paul quoted from Isaiah 6:9,10 about their spiritual eyesight.

> The Holy Spirit was right when He spoke to your fathers through Isaiah the prophet: Go to this people and say, "You will be ever hearing but never understanding; you will be ever seeing but never perceiving."
>
> For this people's heart has grown callous; they hardly hear with their ears, and they have closed their eyes. Otherwise they might see with their eyes, hear with their ears, understand with their hearts, and turn, and I would heal them.
>
> *Acts 28:25-27*

Sight and hearing are spoken of here, and both have willfully become dull. It says of their sight, "they have closed their eyes." No one forced their eyes shut. They closed them themselves.

> The wrath of God is being revealed from heaven against all the godlessness and wickedness of men who suppress the truth by their wickedness. For what may be known about God is plain to them, because God has made it plain to them. For since the creation of the world God's invisible qualities, His eternal power and divine nature, have been clearly seen, being understood from His workmanship, so that men are without excuse.
>
> For although they knew God, they neither glorified Him as God nor gave thanks to Him, but they became futile in their thinking and darkened in their foolish hearts. Although they claimed to be wise, they became fools, and exchanged the glory of the immortal God for images of mortal man and birds and animals and reptiles.
>
> *Romans 1:18-22*

According to Romans, spiritual blindness and unbelief are willful acts of sinners. Everyone has the evidence of God displayed to them every day through the wonders of creation.

Unbelievers have to work hard to avoid the truth of the existence of an all-powerful Creator (suppression). People who do that become spiritually stuck. They can't advance in their knowledge of God if they don't acknowledge Him as their Creator, the One to whom they owe everything.

17

BLIND FAITH

My daughter and I sat watching the Extreme Cowboy Race at Equine Affaire, a horse exposition in Columbus, Ohio. The participants competed, one by one, in a timed obstacle course. Each began by mounting her horse and running one lap at high speed around the coliseum.

A young woman and her Appaloosa, Stormy, were up next. Twenty-year-old Beka Setzer mounted and started her first lap. Rather than running, though, the gelding cantered leisurely around the ring.

Inwardly, I was thinking Stormy had no business being in the competition. I was eager to see more action. "Why are they going so slow?"

A woman behind me heard my complaint and said, "That horse is blind."

I was shocked. How could Stormy compete in the Extreme Cowboy Race if he was blind? The competition challenged even the best, sighted horses.

Beka and Stormy continued through the course, doing well at each obstacle. Then they approached a set of barrels. Stormy needed to jump three times over a series of barrels lying on their sides. By now, I was rooting for Stormy and Beka. But how in the world could the gelding jump over barrels he couldn't see?

Beka brought her Appaloosa up to the first set of barrels and slowed almost to a stop in front of them. I couldn't hear her from our seats up in the stands, but later I learned she was giving him a verbal command. "Up!"

Without hesitation, Stormy jumped. A back hoof grazed the metal barrel on his way down, making a loud, clattering sound. He hadn't cleared the jump, but it was a valiant effort. Stormy made the same courageous attempt at the next two jumps in unquestioning obedience to Beka's commands.

After completing all the obstacles, the contestants took a final lap around the coliseum. This time, Stormy really moved out, galloping sightlessly, guided solely by the rider he loved and trusted.

When they crossed the finish line, the entire audience stood and cheered for their incredible performance. Tears filled my eyes, and I don't think I was the only one crying. What an inspiration Beka and Stormy were!

May our faith in our Master be as bold and unwavering.

For we walk by faith, not by sight.

2 Corinthians 5:7

Stormy and Beka are featured in the fifth book in the Sonrise Stable series, *Outward Appearances*. Stormy went blind, suddenly and completely, as a result of equine recurrent uveitis (ERU), a disease that causes inflammation in the eyes. It occurs more often in Appaloosas than any other breed.

When Beka was fourteen and Stormy was ten, she exhibited him at a county fair. Just a day after successfully showing in a jumper class, Stormy crashed into a jump. A medical examination determined that Stormy had lost his sight overnight. The veterinarian concluded Stormy would no longer have a useful life and recommended he be put down.

Beka obviously disagreed, and her commitment to Stormy paid off. She was able to retrain him to do everything they had done together before he lost his sight.

18

SLEEPY TOM

In 1879, Sleepy Tom set a pacing record of 2:12 1/4 for the mile. The horse's record stood for two years until another pacer, named the Little Brown Jug, beat it. Racing records are often set and beaten. What made this achievement special?

Sleepy Tom was totally blind.

A stone blind horse setting speed records? It sounds impossible, but many contemporary newspaper articles confirm the racing career of Sleepy Tom.

> The fact that Sleepy Tom was stone blind and ugly only tended to increase the public interest in him. He was about the toughest looking piece of horseflesh ever seen on a speed ring and was generally the laughing stock of spectators who were not familiar with his marvelous powers of speed.

> *The Boonville Enquirer, Boonville, Indiana - September 3, 1887*

PUBLISHED BY CURRIER & IVES   COPYRIGHT, 1879, BY CURRIER & IVES, N.Y.   115 NASSAU ST. NEW YORK

The Pacing Wonder **SLEEPY TOM,** the Blind Horse,
WITH PHILLIPS HIS DRIVER COAXING HIM TO "GO ON AND WIN."

The chestnut colt with bold, white markings was foaled in the village of Bellbrook, Ohio, on June 22, 1868. Sleepy Tom's name was chosen because of his laziness as a foal. At three, Tom was trained for harness. Charley Dingler first raced him in Columbus, Ohio.

During his years with Dingler, Tom was worked hard. Some claim Dingler drove a hot and lathered Tom into a river to cool him off. The abrupt change in temperature may have damaged the horse's health. Others say Tom developed a severe cold, which settled in his eyes. Whatever the cause, Tom began to lose his sight and was totally blind by the age of seven.

Considering Tom's racing days over, Mr. Dingler sold him in 1875. The blind horse was ill-treated and passed between several owners before being purchased by a harness racing trainer.

Stephen C. Phillips, aware of Tom's early racing days, purchased Sleepy Tom for $7.50 and a jug of whiskey. Other accounts say a pint of whiskey and $5. Either way, Phillips wouldn't be out much if Tom proved unusable.

With good care and additional training, Phillips restarted the horse's racing career. The new team hit the track in 1878 and started to win. In fact, Sleepy Tom was one fourth of a famous quartet of Standardbred pacers that attracted great crowds in their day. The other three included Mattie Hunter, Lucy, and Rowdy Boy. The four often met and competed against each other in a series of races known as the Grand Circuit.

On July 27, 1879, in Chicago, Illinois, Sleepy Tom set his world record for the mile pace.

The Star Tribune described the blind horse's amazing performance, referring to Tom as "Sleepy Tom, the blind whirlwind of the Buckeye state."

> To a blind horse, there is necessarily more in the human voice than one with sight. It is sound and not object that claims his attention. For a blind horse to be a successful racer, he must have absolute confidence in his driver. Let once a serious mishap befall him; let him once feel that he is liable at any moment to rush upon an accident, and his usefulness is gone. With the sense of sight closed, those of feeling and hearing are necessarily quickened, and, as it is by these he must be guided, it is needless to say that they should never be deceived or abused.
>
> Between Tom and his driver there is the closest of friendship, and so long as the horse hears the kindly voice close to his ears he knows all is well, and it is the tone of that voice that literally guides his action. It indicates to him whether he can take his ease or whether he must do his utmost, and it was by speaking to him all along in a kindly but anxious tone that such terrible speed was got out of him.
>
> *Star Tribune Minneapolis, Minnesota - July 28, 1879*

Much as Sleepy Tom had other senses that allowed him to trust his driver and run full speed around a track he couldn't see, Christians also have an ability to "see" the unknown. This spiritual sight produces faith and understanding that non-believers don't have and cannot understand.

> This is why I speak to them in parables: Though seeing, they do not see; though hearing, they do not hear or understand.
>
> *Matthew 13:13*

Unbelievers see physically, but they do not understand the meaning behind the things of God.

> "No one is so blind as he who will not see, the one who thinks he has 'all truth' and there is nothing more for him to learn."
>
> *Warren Wiersbe*

Our spiritual sight gives us confidence that God will do all He has promised. There is more to this life than the things we see around us. Something better awaits us.

> Now faith is the assurance of what we hope for and the certainty of what we do not see.
>
> *Hebrews 11:1*

So we fix our eyes not on what is seen, but on what is unseen. For what is seen is temporary, but what is unseen is eternal.

2 Corinthians 4:18

The fact that Sleepy Tom raced blindly around a track at full speed inspires me to trust God and keep moving forward in my Christian journey, even when it sometimes feels as if I'm stumbling around in the darkness.

The Grey Mare **LUCY**, the Pacing Queen.
OF THE FAMOUS QUARTETTE OF 1879.

19

BLIND HORSES

In my book, *Outward Appearances*, I featured Beka Setzer and her blind horse, Stormy. In the book, I changed their names to Hannah and Dusty. After seeing the pair compete in the Extreme Cowboy Race at Equine Affaire in Columbus, I saw a connection between the horse's trust in his master and how we should trust God.

The disease Stormy had, Equine Recurrent Uveitis (ERU), is the leading cause of blindness in horses. It's sometimes referred to as "moon blindness" because, in the past, people believed the moon somehow caused the condition. Today, veterinarians don't agree on what causes ERU. Because the cause hasn't been pinpointed, diagnosis may be delayed and treatment is often ineffective, resulting in the horse losing sight in one or both eyes.

But as I portrayed in *Outward Appearances*, as well as the *Blind Faith* and *Sleepy Tom* devotions, blind horses aren't useless. Horses may also lead productive lives with a single eye. One of the most prominent was a Thoroughbred named Patch, who ran in the 2017 Kentucky Derby.

The bay colt was born at Calumet Farm on March 18, 2014, to a mare named Windyindy, a great grand-daughter of Secretariat. His sire was Union Rags. Patch's name isn't related to the loss of his eye, since they named him as a foal.

As a two-year-old, the colt's eye became infected and swelled shut. A veterinarian treated Patch with antibiotics but several weeks later, when the infection hadn't cleared up, they decided his eye needed to be removed. The cause of the infection was never determined.

Patch's trainer, Todd Pletcher, hoped the colt could still race, but he and the owners weren't sure how Patch would react to the loss of vision on his left side.

The colt took it all in stride and adjusted quickly to his vision loss. He didn't race as a two-year-old while recovering from his surgery. In 2017, he ran three races prior to the Derby. He won one and finished second twice.

Patch was a crowd favorite for the Derby. Ridden by Tyler Gaffalione, the one-eyed colt finished fourteenth out of twenty entrants in the race—definitely not a good race for the brave horse. He was also entered in the Belmont Stakes the following month, finishing a respectable third in that race. Patch ran seven more races over his career, winning one and finishing no lower than eighth in the others.

oldfriendsequine.org

After racing for three seasons, Calumet Farm donated Patch to Old Friends, a Thoroughbred retirement farm in Kentucky where he will live out the rest of his days.

Many blind horses, like Beka Setzer's Stormy, can continue to be ridden and lead productive lives even though they cannot see. Nationally recognized horse trainer, John Lyons, owned an Appaloosa, Bright Zip, who went blind in his twenties after an allergic reaction to medication. Lyons continued to use Zip for years in his training seminars and clinics. He thought the Appaloosa might have assumed all horses went blind as they got older, and Zip just accepted it.

Too often, people assume a blind horse can no longer lead a useful life but will at best serve as an expensive pasture ornament. As Beka experienced with her veterinarian, they may be advised to put the horse down.

Sissy Burggraf, founded Lost Acres Horse Rescue and Rehabilitation in Chillicothe, Ohio. Over the years, she has gained an appreciation for blind horses through her extensive experience of caring for these special animals. As of this writing, twenty-one of her thirty-one horses are blind. (October 2022)

Sissy shares some of her insights in the following interview.

How have you seen people respond when their horse goes blind?

Unfortunately, the general attitude of people toward blind horses is not good. I'm always puzzled when people aren't willing to give these horses a chance. A blind dog or cat often receives sympathy and compassion, but the first response to a horse becoming blind is often to want to get rid of it. People may consider a blind horse to be dangerous.

You mean blind horses aren't dangerous?

As with people, losing sight is a frightening experience. Horses can be most dangerous while in the process of losing their sight. During this time, they only see shadows or partial objects. They may spook more easily because they know something is out there, but they can't tell what it is.

Horses that have recently lost their sight will need time to adjust. Some adjust quickly, others may take a few months, and rarely, a horse won't adjust at all. Thankfully, this is rare, as the horse that cannot accept his blindness should be humanely euthanized.

What's different about handling a blind horse?

If your horse was asleep when you entered the stall, the first thing you would do is speak to him so you don't startle him. Then, you would approach him. That's the same thing you do with a blind horse. Except with blind horses, you speak to them when approaching from any direction. After speaking, if you're close enough, reach out and touch them.

Do I have to keep my blind horse in a stall to keep him safe?

At LAHRR, we keep our blind horses in a field with a run-in shelter. They only come into the barn to eat. When feeding, I go to the gate, call to them to get their attention, and clap my hands to give them the direction they need to come. I open the gate, they come in, and each goes to his own stall. When they've finished eating, I lead them back to the gate where they return to the pasture and usually head straight to the watering trough.

Horses often communicate by using physical gestures, like flattening the ears or snaking their head at another horse. A blind horse will miss those signals. Make sure your horse isn't turned out with a horse that will bully him.

What characteristics are required for the owner of a blind horse?

Patience is the major ingredient needed to care for blind horses. Until a blind horse fully trusts you, they may be slower in their actions, hesitating to follow you or go to an unfamiliar place. Once you earn that trust, however, what a beautiful reward!! Your horse will come to you when called, follow you as you walk, and what wonderful riding horses they can become!

You mean I can ride my blind horse?

Blindness doesn't affect horses' intelligence, their desire to please their owner, or their ability to be useful. If you rode your horse before, there is generally no reason why you can't continue to do so after he has become blind. As with handling the horse on the ground, it's important to use your voice to communicate with him. Training your horse to respond to voice commands like "whoa" and "step up" is important.

You may find your blind horse will go places and do things some sighted horses won't. They can't see what the sighted horse fears; things like going through mud or water, over obstacles, and crossing bridges. As your horse's confidence increases, you'll be able to enjoy the faster gaits—cantering or even a gallop!

Given the chance, a blind horse can be a wonderful, faithful, companion and riding horse. They thrive on attention, love to be loved, and love to give love.

The photo below shows two LAHRR horses. Willow, the buckskin on the left, is twenty-four. She has been at the rescue for eleven years. Willow is totally blind. Her pal, Elvis, on the right, is nineteen. His left eye was removed due to an infection, prior to his arrival at LAHRR, where he has lived for six years. Elvis, a registered Hackney horse, does have sight in his right eye.

I will lead the blind by a way they did not know; I will guide them on unfamiliar paths. I will turn darkness into light before them and rough places into level ground. These things I will do for them, and I will not forsake them.

Isaiah 42:16

20

HEARING AND EARS

There are so many things we take for granted in this world and don't give much thought to. Have you ever wondered what sound is and how our ears work?

Sounds are waves traveling through some material, most commonly air. When a sound is produced, it causes vibrations which disturb the surrounding air particles. Those particles disturb the particles next to them and so forth, causing the sound to travel in a wavelike form.

Sound waves must be captured by a person or animal in order to be heard. That's what our ears are for. The hearing process is nearly identical for humans and horses. Since this isn't a biology text, I'll give you a simplified version of how this works.

The outer ear (auricle or pinna) "captures" the sound waves and funnels them inward through the auditory canal to the eardrum. Those waves cause the eardrum to vibrate.

Three small bones in the middle ear amplify the vibrations. The malleus (hammer) is connected to the eardrum. When the eardrum vibrates, it moves the malleus, which in turn moves the incus (anvil), which then moves the stapes (stirrup). (The stapes resembles a stirrup of an English saddle.)

Satin

Ginger

Maggie

Ebony

Note the horses' ears. It's hard to get four people and four horses looking happy at the same time.

The other end of the stapes connects to the spiral cochlea of the inner ear. Vibration of the stapes creates waves in the cochlea's fluid, which mimic the pattern of the sound wave. Thousands of tiny hairs in the cochlea convert the fluid waves into electrical signals that are carried by the cochlear nerve to the auditory cortex of the brain, where they are interpreted as sounds.

This overview level is complicated enough, but the complete details of sound and hearing are much more complex. I marvel that anyone can believe in evolution—that this entire system of sounds and hearing simply happened by chance.

How does the hearing of horses compare to that of humans?

One difference that's immediately noticeable is the outer ear. While human ears are relatively small and close to our heads, horse's ears are large, furry, funnel-like appendages. Horses have muscles that allow them to move each ear independently up to 180 degrees to focus on the source of a sound and improve its reception. This way they can determine the direction a sound is coming from far better than humans can.

Horses also make use of this wide range of ear movement for communication. If a horse has both ears flat back, look out!

Marwari horses from India and Pakistan have the most distinctive ears of any horse breed. When in an upright position, their long ears often curve inwardly so much that the tips meet. Related breeds with similarly shaped ears are the Kathiawari and the Sindhi.

Once past the outer ear, the functionality and structure of human and horse ears is amazingly similar. Coincidence? Or the same designer?

People's hearing ranges from wave frequencies of 20 hertz (lowest pitch) to 20,000 hertz (highest pitch). I found conflicting numbers for horses. Some claim humans have a lower range. Other sources said horses do. All agreed that horses can hear higher pitches than humans, up to 33,500 hertz. It also seems horses can pick up vibrations from the ground through their hooves, teeth, or jawbone. These vibrations are also processed as sounds. As prey animals, good hearing is essential for horses in the wild as it gives them a head start against predators who might attack them.

Like humans, horses may experience some hearing loss with age. However deafness in horses is rare. Paint horses with blue eyes and coat patterns with extensive white (splashed white) are more at risk for deafness. The theory is that the gene which causes the loss of pigment affects the sensitive hairs in the cochlea, impairing their ability to transmit sound. Deafness in domestic horses isn't a huge handicap and may actually make them less spooky.

The deafness connection with Paint horses appears to be related to a similar problem in pure white cats. Eighty percent of white cats with two blue eyes are deaf. If a white cat has only one blue eye, the chance of deafness drops to thirty or forty percent. And if neither eye is blue, the chance of deafness for a white cat is ten percent.

Jesus often used the phrase, "He who has ears to hear, let him hear." Matthew 11:15; Mark 4:9, 23

It's like a call to attention. Listen up now. A notification to pay particular attention to what He is about to say or has just said. Jesus made it clear there is a difference between those who have ears (most of us) and those who understand His word.

Not everyone who hears, understands or takes to heart what is being said. If they did, they would take action on it. This is clearly illustrated in the parable of the sower.

> Listen! A farmer went out to sow his seed. And as he was sowing, some seed fell along the path, and the birds came and devoured it.
>
> Some fell on rocky ground, where it did not have much soil. It sprang up quickly because the soil was shallow. But when the sun rose, the seedlings were scorched, and they withered because they had no root.
>
> Other seed fell among thorns, which grew up and choked the seedlings, and they yielded no crop.

Still other seed fell on good soil, where it sprouted, grew up, and produced a crop—one bearing thirty-fold, another sixtyfold, and another a hundredfold.

Then Jesus said, "He who has ears to hear, let him hear."

Mark 4:3-9

The seed is God's word. The recipients represented by the soils in the parable all had ears, but only one of the types understood and responded properly.

Wayside: Satan quickly snatched the word away.

Stony ground: They received the word gladly, but it took no root, and they didn't last through difficult times.

Thorns: The things of this world choked out the word.

Good ground: The word produced fruit.

Only those with ears to hear and soft, receptive hearts truly receive the word and allow it to transform them.

> they may be ever seeing but never perceiving, and ever hearing but never understanding; otherwise they might turn and be forgiven.
>
> *Mark 4:12*

Similar warnings are given to us in Revelation.

> Revelation 2:7, 11, 17, 29—He who has an ear, let him hear what the Spirit says to the churches.
>
> Revelation 3:6, 13, 22—He who has an ear, let him hear what the Spirit says to the churches.
>
> Revelation 13:9—He who has an ear, let him hear.

Although we can't turn our ears around to focus on different sounds as horses do, we can control the things we allow into our minds. The best thing we can listen to or read is God's word. We should strive to understand scripture and how we can apply it in our lives, so we continue to become more like Christ.

> Do not be conformed to this world, but be transformed by the renewing of your mind. Then you will be able to test and approve what is the good, pleasing, and perfect will of God.
>
> *Romans 12:2*

> I will set no worthless thing before my eyes. I hate the work of those who fall away; it shall not cling to me. A perverse heart shall depart from me; I will know nothing of evil.
>
> *Psalm 101:3,4*

Other input should be wholesome, god-honoring material. When you're in doubt, Philippians 4:8 is a good test as to what you should be reading or listening to.

> Finally, brothers, whatever is true, whatever is honorable, whatever is right, whatever is pure, whatever is lovely, whatever is admirable—if anything is excellent or praiseworthy—think on these things.
>
> *Philippians 4:8*

21

SLEEP AND SLOTH

Most people sleep in one continuous stretch, averaging about eight hours each night. The sleep pattern of horses differs greatly from ours.

If horses were to lie down and sleep for hours at a time, they would be vulnerable to attack. An interesting feature of horses is their ability to enter a light sleep while standing—without falling over. By resting in an upright position, they can quickly run away if they sense a predator. Horses in a group or herd won't all sleep at the same time. They rest in shifts. Those who are awake stand watch, ready to sound an alarm at the first sign of danger.

Foals, from birth to three months, may sleep up to twelve hours a day. Adult horses only require, on average, two to five hours of rest per day. And much of that comes while dozing in an upright position.

Horses are able to sleep standing up because of an intricate anatomical system known as the stay apparatus. This system consists of muscles, tendons and ligaments which allow the horse to lock their front and back legs in place so they can stand with little muscular effort. Only one hind leg will lock, so the horse's weight rests on three legs. They cock the other hind leg, resting the toe on the ground. When dozing in this manner, the horse's head will be low, his ears relaxed, and his lower lip may droop. Be careful not to walk up behind a horse while he is resting like this, as your sudden appearance may startle him and cause him to kick.

Horses also lie down to rest. They may lie down in a more upright position—on their chest with their legs folded up close to their body. This position is known as sternal recumbency.

But to enter a deep sleep (REM, rapid eye movement), a horse needs to lie flat out on his side. Horses sleep deeply like this for periods of ten to twenty minutes at a time, almost always at night, and only if they feel safe and comfortable. Like humans, horses seem to dream while in these cycles of deep sleep.

Because of their size and weight, the pressure exerted on their bodies while lying down makes it difficult for them to breathe and for blood to circulate properly. A horse needs only thirty to forty minutes of REM sleep each day, usually split into two or three sessions. If down for too long, the horse's nerves or internal organs may be damaged.

Although there is nothing wrong with people requiring more sleep than horses, the Bible cautions us against being lazy or a sluggard.

> Go to the ant, you sluggard! Consider her ways and be wise, Which, having no captain, Overseer or ruler, Provides her supplies in the summer, And gathers her food in the harvest. How long will you slumber, O sluggard? When will you rise from your sleep? A little sleep, a little slumber, A little folding of the hands to sleep—So shall your poverty come on you like a prowler, And your need like an armed man.
>
> *Proverbs 6:6-11 NKJV*

In this passage from Proverbs, we're warned not to be lazy, but to work and prepare for the future as ants naturally do. Proverbs has much to say about the dangers of laziness. Here are a few samples.

> The slacker craves yet has nothing, but the soul of the diligent is fully satisfied.
>
> *Proverbs 13:4*

> Laziness brings on deep sleep, and an idle soul will suffer hunger.
>
> *Proverbs 19:15*

> The slacker does not plow in season; at harvest time he looks, but nothing is there.
>
> *Proverbs 20:4*

The craving of the slacker kills him because his hands refuse to work.

Proverbs 21:25

As a door turns on its hinges, so the slacker turns on his bed.

Proverbs 26:14

Slothfulness today doesn't just mean extra sleep. It can be wasting time by frivolous things such as too much game playing, TV watching, social media, or internet surfing. Although perhaps not bad in themselves, it becomes a problem if we engage in those activities when there are more important things we should be doing. God has a purpose for each of us while we're here on earth. If we sleep too much or waste our time, we can't be as effective in serving Him or the people around us. Redeeming the time means we will use our time wisely, making the best use of the days God gives us.

For we are His workmanship, created in Christ Jesus for good works, which God prepared beforehand that we should walk in them.

Ephesians 2:10 NKJV

Whatever you do, work at it with your whole being, for the Lord and not for men, because you know that you will receive an inheritance from the Lord as your reward. It is the Lord Christ you are serving.

Colossians 3:23,24

Pay careful attention, then, to how you walk, not as unwise but as wise, redeeming the time, because the days are evil. Therefore do not be foolish, but understand what the Lord's will is.

Ephesians 5:15-17

22

EVIL COLD

I've lived in Ohio all my life. Although the weather is milder than at the North Pole, it gets COLD here in the winter! Caring for horses in near zero or below zero temperatures is much more work than in warm weather.

The water trough I fill once a week in the summer often becomes a solid brick of ice in winter, so the horses require daily watering. At extreme temperatures, the water faucet freezes. Too often, I've had to fill water buckets from the bathtub and carry them to the barn. Even the manure freezes, often to the ground, making it impossible to clean outdoor pens.

In this area, I've seen horses blanketed at temperatures as warm as forty degrees. For most horses, there's no need for that. In fact, a horse may get hot and sweaty under his blanket at those temperatures.

People seem to think that if they're cold, their horse must be also. But God designed horses with the ability to grow a long, thick coat to keep them warm in winter. The decreasing amount of daylight hours initiates the growth of the winter coat. By the time the extreme cold arrives, that long, winter hair is able to trap pockets of air, providing insulation comparable to us wearing a thick, down coat. Putting a heavy, winter blanket on your horse flattens his hair, decreasing its natural insulating properties.

A horse's coat contains oil that helps make it waterproof. The horse can stay warm even though light snow may melt and freeze on the outer surface of his coat if that frozen crust never reaches his skin.

Prolonged wet snow or rain can soak down to the skin, though, and chill the horse. Wind makes things even worse. In those conditions, the horse needs shelter out of the weather or a waterproof blanket to stay warm.

An adult horse in good condition can stand temperatures as low as -40 degrees Fahrenheit as long as he has adequate shelter and food. It's important to increase a horse's feed in extreme cold. Plenty of hay is best. The process of digesting roughage produces heat, which helps the horse stay warm.

I once read there is no such thing as "cold." According to that theory, it's the removal of heat that causes the feeling or sensation we call "cold." Molecular motion generates heat in objects. As heat is removed, the molecules move more slowly. The theoretical point at which all heat is removed is called absolute zero, -273 degrees Celsius. At absolute zero, no heat is present, meaning there is no molecular movement at all. It is impossible to get any colder than that. Fortunately, absolute zero is impossible to reach outside of a laboratory.

It's fall as I write this. As the temperature in Ohio continues to drop, I'll keep reminding myself that there is no such thing as cold!

While this dissertation on the meaning of cold may seem like a random rabbit trail, it corresponds to a belief of some theologians that there is no such thing as evil. Just as cold is the absence of heat, some claim evil is the absence or removal of good. That's not to say that both cold and evil don't have real, perceivable effects, only that neither has a tangible, objective existence. In a similar sense, darkness can be viewed as the absence of light.

When God created Adam and Eve and placed them in the Garden of Eden, everything was theirs to enjoy, except for one thing.

> You may eat freely from every tree of the garden, but you must not eat from the tree of the knowledge of good and evil; for in the day that you eat of it, you will surely die.
>
> *Genesis 2:16,17*

Notice the name of the tree they were not to eat from, "the tree of the knowledge of good and evil." At that moment, Adam and Eve lived in a perfect world. All they knew was good. There was no sin, sadness, illness, or death. The animals didn't kill each other, and they lived at peace with Adam and Eve. There was nothing positive to be gained by eating from the forbidden tree. They already possessed the knowledge of good. All their disobedience would give them was the knowledge of evil.

If evil is a self-existent thing, where did it come from? Who created it? The only One who can create something out of nothing is God. While I'm not saying it's impossible, I have a hard time believing God created evil.

> I am the LORD, and there is no other. I form the light and create the darkness; I bring prosperity and create calamity [ra]. I, the LORD, do all these things.
>
> *Isaiah 45:6,7*

In that verse, the King James Version translates "ra" as evil. Other translations use words like calamity, disaster, and woe.

In his commentary on this verse, Matthew Henry states, "'ra' is not the evil of sin (God is not the author of that), but the evil of punishment."

This concept of evil as the absence of good may be the answer to the origin of evil. Augustine's position was that evil is the absence of good or God. "Evil does not exist except as privation from, or absence of, God. When humans freely chose to reject God, committing Original Sin, they thus introduced evil into the world."

In Mark 10:18, Jesus responds to the rich young ruler.

> Why do you call Me good? No one is good except God alone.

According to Jesus' words, it isn't possible for us, as God's creations, to be completely good. Only God is absolutely good. There can be no evil (or absence of good) in Him. However, there is evil in us, at least while we're on Earth.

In that passage, Jesus isn't denying His own divinity. The young man doesn't comprehend that Jesus is God, and he's not ready for that revelation.

This theory of good and evil is speculative, designed to get you to think. It's not essential to our salvation to understand or even accept this perspective on evil. Maybe it's not possible for our finite minds to understand the origin of evil.

The fact that even unbelievers call some actions good and others evil is a strong argument for God's existence. Everyone is born with an innate sense of right and wrong, recognizing to varying degrees the absolute standard of morality established by God. Without God's moral standard, as revealed in the Bible, everyone is free to create their own definition of good and evil behavior. And who is to say that one person's definition is better than another?

I'll stick to the standard God revealed to us in His word.

Love must be sincere. Detest what is evil; cling to what is good.

Romans 12:9

23

HORSE AROMAS

Smell is one of the five senses humans share with horses—sight, sound, smell, taste, and touch. Smell is an olfactory sense. Various particles float around in the air. When horses inhale those particles, they are trapped in their nasal tissues. Olfactory nerves send signals to the olfactory bulbs in a horse's brain where they are interpreted as distinct smells.

Since horses' nostrils are large and positioned at the sides of their head, they can pick up smells from a wider area than humans. A horse's nostrils can also flare or become larger to draw in more air, and therefore, more scents. A herd of "wild" horses can detect the scent of a predator and gallop away to avoid danger.

Each horse has a unique scent. New horses greet each other nose to nose, taking in the aroma of the other horse. Foals can locate their mothers in a herd by using their sense of smell. Horses use this sniffing approach when meeting humans as well. They stretch out their muzzle to take in the person's scent. The best approach is to hold out the back of your hand and let the horse sniff you until they are satisfied. Offering the back of your hand prevents the horse from mistaking your fingers for carrots.

Horses cannot breathe through their mouths. They are known as "obligate nose breathers." Their extensive nasal passages not only provide them with plenty of space for airflow, they also allow for a multitude of olfactory receptors that pick up scents for processing.

Besides the olfactory bulbs, horses, along with some other animals, have a vomeronasal (VNO) organ, also known as Jacobson's organ, that processes smells. This organ is located between the horse's nasal cavity and the roof of his mouth.

Horses don't smile or laugh, but you may have seen a horse that looked like he was. His head will be raised with his top lip curled up, exposing his teeth. His nostrils will briefly close. This behavior is known as the flehmen response. Rather than finding something humorous, the horse has encountered an unusual scent and is trapping particles inside his nasal passage to be processed by the VNO organ.

All horses use the flehmen response, but it's most often seen in

stallions when they detect a mare's scent. It's commonly believed that horses can sense when a person is afraid. If true, perhaps the person gives off a scent that is detected by the horse's VNO organ.

Some may assume dogs have the best sense of smell, since dogs are the most common tracking animals. It's difficult to rank an animal's ability to process smells. You can find various lists that rank them in different orders.

The strength of the sense of smell may be connected to the number of receptors lining the nasal cavity. If that is true, it's not surprising, considering its long trunk, that the elephant would have one of the most highly developed senses of smell.

Dogs, particularly Bloodhounds, rank high for their scent abilities, but some place both bears and elephants higher than dogs.

Horses definitely have a better sense of smell than humans, but it's probably less than that of dogs. However, we may have underestimated the sense of smell in horses. Horses have long been used by mounted search and rescue teams to locate people lost in remote areas. Some trainers are experimenting with using horses as scent-tracking animals, as well.

Horses have a few advantages over dogs as tracking animals. Their height, when combined with their excellent vision, gives them a much wider view of the search area. Since the tracking horses are ridden, the rider is in an excellent position to survey the area. A horse's nose is higher than a dog's, and he can pick up scents from both sides of his body. Also, horses are faster and can cover the same territory in less time.

Just as all dogs are not good at tracking, not all horses take to it either. A good prospect for a tracking horse is one who is independent, with a large dose of natural curiosity. When entering a search area, the rider loosens the reins and allows the horse to move out on his own. Time will tell whether horses prove as useful as dogs when it comes to tracking.

> Rosie enjoyed spending time in the barn with the horses. The previous summer, she had overheard someone at the county fair complaining about the smell in the horse barn. That didn't make sense to her. She loved everything about her grandmother's barn: the worn and faded boards, the smells— leather, grain, and the hay stacked in the hayloft. But most of all, she loved the smell of the horses themselves.

Those words from *Rosie and Scamper* reflect my sentiments. If the barn hasn't been cleaned all winter, that's a different story, but in general, I find the mingling of the smells associated with horses produces a pleasant aroma. However, I know that others find those same odors unpleasant, and they try to avoid them.

The Bible describes a difference in the perception of aromas in 2 Corinthians 2:14-16.

> But thanks be to God, who always leads us triumphantly as captives in Christ and through us spreads everywhere the fragrance of the knowledge of Him. For we are to God the sweet aroma of Christ among those who are being saved and those who are perishing. To the one, we are an odor of death and demise; to the other, a fragrance that brings life.

Those verses aren't talking about the fragrance of horses. Instead, they refer to how you and I smell. I have a friend who is allergic to horses. She can pick up the scent on people and knows when someone has been around an equine.

Are you a "fragrant" Christian? Can those around you pick up the scent of Christ on you? People should not be near us very long before they detect we have been around Christ. His fragrance should rub off on us and be noticeable to others.

Just as some people can't wait to get out of the horse barn and away from its distinctive smell, there are people who can't stand the fragrance of Christ. Second Corinthians 2:16 says we are the aroma of death to them.

The fragrance of Christ makes them aware of their sinfulness. It reminds them they are dead in their sins. Whether they think those exact thoughts, the aroma of a Christian produces an uncomfortable feeling they want to avoid.

People don't have to like the aroma of horses, but the fragrance of Christ needs to become a pleasant one to them—an aroma that leads them from death to life.

Your mission is to become a fragrant Christian so others can detect the aroma of Christ on you.

24

CLEANLINESS NEXT TO GODLINESS?

You may have heard people attribute the saying "cleanliness is next to godliness" to the Bible. However you won't find that expression in scripture.

In 1605, Sir Francis Bacon wrote, "Cleanness of body was ever deemed to proceed from a due reverence to God." And in 1791, John Wesley used the expression in one of his sermons, "Slovenliness is no part of religion. Cleanliness is indeed next to Godliness."

Cleanliness was an important part of the Jewish ceremonial law. A laver, a large basin or bowl, was present at the tabernacle and Solomon's Temple. Priests used the laver for washing their hands and feet before their service.

> He placed the basin between the Tent of Meeting and the altar and put water in it for washing; and from it Moses, Aaron, and his sons washed their hands and feet. They washed whenever they entered the Tent of Meeting or approached the altar, just as the LORD had commanded Moses.
>
> *Exodus 40:30-32*

Another example of cleanliness is Jesus' washing of the disciples' feet.

> So He [Jesus] got up from the supper, laid aside His outer garments, and wrapped a towel around His waist. After that, He poured water into a basin and began to wash the disciples' feet and dry them with the towel that was around Him.
>
> *John 13:4,5*

When Peter objected, Jesus said to him, "Whoever has already bathed needs only to wash his feet, and he will be completely clean. And you are clean, though not all of you." John 4:10

More than external cleanliness, God is concerned with the internal—what is in our hearts. Jesus called the Pharisees hypocrites because they focused on outward appearance but neglected their hearts.

> Woe to you, scribes and Pharisees, you hypocrites! You are like whitewashed tombs, which look beautiful on the outside, but on the inside are full of dead men's bones and every kind of impurity. In the same way, on the outside you appear to be righteous, but on the inside you are full of hypocrisy and wickedness.
>
> *Matthew 23:27,28*

Unlike some animals, such as cats, who are fastidious about keeping themselves clean, horses aren't concerned with cleanliness. In fact, many of them seem to enjoy being dirty. If you turn most horses loose after a bath, they'll almost certainly find the dustiest spot in the pasture to drop down and roll.

Rolling may be a minimal form of self grooming as it can help remove a shedding winter coat. It also seems quite satisfying to itchy horses. Adding a layer of mud or dirt may serve as a natural insect repellent. When the horse stands up after rolling, he will typically give a full-body shake, creating an equine cloud of hair and dust. Like yawning with people, rolling seems to be contagious among horses. If a horse sees another one roll, he may soon do the same.

Horses also love to rub against things—a fence post, barn wall, tree, etc. This may not be grooming either but simply scratching themselves. The same goes for two horses "grooming" each other. They sometimes use their teeth on each other's backs, usually in the area of the withers. This may not be grooming at all but scratching or communicating friendship.

Although not fond of bathing themselves, in the 1800s, horses played a critical role in the bathing of humans.

For people who lived near a coast, especially in England, it was common to bathe in the sea. The sea not only cleansed one, many believed sea water had health-giving powers. But public bathing was problematic for women. Standards of modesty were much higher then. Women's bathing suits of modern times would not only have been considered immodest but immoral. How could women bathe in the sea while preserving their modesty?

Horses helped solve this dilemma.

Bathing machines became popular in the 1800s in coastal areas. These machines date back at least to 1735 at Scarborough Beach in North Yorkshire, England. From their name, it sounds as if these "machines" might have mechanically scrubbed people until they were shiny and clean.

In reality, a bathing machine was merely a specially designed wagon used to transport bathers, primarily women, into the sea so they could bathe in privacy. That's where the horses came in. They provided the power to transport the bathing machines into and out of the water.

The "machine" resembled a miniature cabin on wheels with doors at each end. The carts averaged six feet long, five feet wide, and eight feet tall. The wheels lifted the cabin four feet off the ground. Holes drilled into the floor allowed water to drain out. A large number was painted on the cabin, and advertisements or the name of a resort often covered the sides. Some had lavish interiors, but most bathing machines were more spartan.

The woman entered via steps at the back, closed the door behind her, and in the privacy of the cabin, changed into a bathing costume. This woolen swimwear covered her body from neck to ankles. A horse then towed the bathing machine into the water until the cabin floor was at sea level. At that point, the horse was unhooked from the cart.

The bather opened the door at the sea end and plunged into the cold water. If she couldn't swim or the waves were strong, a stout female attendant, known as a dipper, tied a rope around the woman's waist, attaching the other end to the bathing machine, so waves wouldn't sweep the bather out to sea.

Fifteen minutes later, the dipper hoisted the bedraggled woman back into the cabin. Since men were not permitted to see the female bathers in their swimwear, even though it covered nearly the entire body, dippers were women. The additional weight of the bulky, waterlogged swimwear required dippers to be exceptionally strong.

Once inside, the woman changed from her wet bathing attire back into her everyday clothes. The horse was reconnected and plodded to shore where a line of bathers awaited their turn in the machine.

Just as dirt on our bodies makes us feel unclean on the outside, sin makes us unclean on the inside. God is more concerned with our inner cleanliness and purity than with our outward appearance.

In Psalm 51, David recognized that his sin had left him impure, and he asked God to cleanse him.

Purify me with hyssop, and I will be clean; wash me, and I will be whiter than snow. … Create in me a clean heart, O God, And renew a right spirit within me.

Psalm 51:7,10

Hyssop is a small, bushy plant. The Israelites used it during the first Passover to sprinkle blood from the slain lambs onto their door posts. That was the sign that caused the angel of death, sent to kill the firstborn of the Egyptians, to pass over those houses.

Then Moses summoned all the elders of Israel and told them, "Go at once and select for yourselves a lamb for each family, and slaughter the Passover lamb. Take a cluster of hyssop, dip it into the blood in the basin, and brush the blood on the top and sides of the doorframe. None of you shall go out the door of his house until morning.

When the LORD passes through to strike down the Egyptians, He will see the blood on the top and sides of the doorframe and will pass over that doorway; so He will not allow the destroyer to enter your houses and strike you down.

Exodus 12:21-23

The lamb's blood on the doorpost was a picture of the blood of Christ on the cross that would be shed, not for temporary protection, but for eternal salvation and cleansing from sin.

When Christ said "I thirst" on the cross—

A jar of sour wine was sitting there. So they soaked a sponge in the wine, put it on a stalk of hyssop, and lifted it to His mouth. When Jesus had received the sour wine, He said, "It is finished." And bowing His head, He yielded up His spirit.

John 19:29-30

This presence of hyssop during Christ's death on the cross provides another connection with the Passover.

Many varieties of soap will get us clean on the outside, but only the blood of Christ purifies us from the uncleanness on the inside.

But if we walk in the light as He is in the light, we have fellowship with one another, and the blood of Jesus His Son cleanses us from all sin.

1 John 1:7

25

HUNGRY AS A HORSE

It's amazing that a large animal like a horse can survive by eating grass. God's provision of food for every kind of animal should make even the most stubborn unbeliever ponder the wonders of creation.

The Mustangs out West graze primarily on grass, however, during the harsh winter months, they may be forced to eat shrubs to survive. Did you know the Mustangs are not "wild" horses? There are no wild horses in the U.S. The Mustangs that are frequently called wild are actually feral horses. At some point back in their history, they were tame animals that were either released or escaped into the "wild." Originally, they date back to horses from the Spanish explorers in the 1500s. The bloodlines have been diluted over the years. The Kiger Mustangs in Oregon are the most closely related to those early Spanish horses.

The only true wild horse in existence today is Przewalski's horse, native to Asia, particularly the area of Mongolia.

Domestic horses eat grass—or the dried version of it—hay. Variations include timothy, orchard grass, bermuda, oat, and alfalfa. Horses may also eat smaller quantities of concentrates—grains like oats, corn, beet pulp, bran, and barley.

Of course, horses enjoy treats in small quantities, including a variety of fruits and vegetables, the most common being carrots and apples. They may also like strawberries, watermelon, cantaloupe, pears, and bananas.

In addition to food, a salt and mineral block provides valuable nutrients. And, last but not least—water. Fresh, clean water is vital to a horse's health, typically five to ten gallons per horse each day.

Horses have small stomachs relative to their size. They prefer to eat frequently throughout the day. Their digestive system works best with food moving through it almost continuously. But for the convenience of people, horses may only be fed once or twice a day.

The amount of feed a horse needs to maintain a healthy weight depends on his size, activity level, metabolism, and the quality of the feed. Active, working horses need to eat more than sedentary ones.

Did you know people were originally vegetarians? Not only were people vegetarians, animals were also. We had to be, since in the beginning there was no death. Sometimes, I detect a level of animosity between vegetarians and those who eat meat as if one group is superior to the other. According to the Bible, God permits both today. However it wasn't that way in the beginning.

> Then God said, "Behold, I have given you every seed-bearing plant on the face of all the earth, and every tree whose fruit contains seed. They will be yours for food. And to every beast of the earth and every bird of the air and every creature that crawls upon the earth—everything that has the breath of life in it—I have given every green plant for food." And it was so.
>
> *Genesis 1:29,30*

Even after Adam and Eve sinned by eating from the one forbidden tree—the Tree of the Knowledge of Good and Evil—they remained vegetarians.

> …cursed is the ground because of you; through toil you will eat of it all the days of your life. Both thorns and thistles it will yield for you, and you will eat the plants of the field.
>
> *Genesis 3:17,18*

It wasn't until after the flood that God gave man permission to eat animals.

The fear and dread of you will fall on every living creature on the earth, every bird of the air, every creature that crawls on the ground, and all the fish of the sea. They are delivered into your hand. Everything that lives and moves will be food for you; just as I gave you the green plants, I now give you all things. But you must not eat meat with its lifeblood still in it.

Genesis 9:2-4

It's interesting that at this same time, God made the animals fear man. Before that, no animals were afraid of people. By giving them a fear of man, God increased their chances for survival. They would avoid man and the possibility that they might be killed for food. In the Millennium, it seems we will all return to being vegetarian.

The wolf will live with the lamb, and the leopard will lie down with the goat; the calf and young lion and fatling will be together and a little child will lead them. The cow will graze with the bear, their young will lie down together, and the lion will eat straw like the ox.

Isaiah 11:6,7

Today, whether vegetarian or meat eater, Jesus emphasized we need more than physical food to sustain us.

The tempter came to Him and said, "If You are the Son of God, tell these stones to become bread."

But Jesus answered, "It is written: 'Man shall not live on bread alone, but on every word that comes from the mouth of God.'"

Matthew 4:3,4, Jesus quoted Deuteronomy 8:3

After Jesus was baptized by John the Baptist, He fasted for forty days in the wilderness and was then tempted by Satan. Although He must have been extremely hungry after forty days without food, Jesus refused to turn stones into loaves of bread. More important to Him than physical food was being obedient to the will of God and trusting in God's provision in God's time—not Satan's.

In fact, Jesus relied on the word of God to counter all three of Satan's temptations. And, each time, Jesus quoted from the book of Deuteronomy. (8:3, 6:16, and 6:13)

> How sweet are Your words to my taste—sweeter than honey in my mouth!
>
> *Psalm 119:103*

> God's Words are meat, drink and food—and if bodies live not upon words—souls and spirits feed upon the Words of God, and so are satisfied and full of delight!
>
> *Charles Haddon Spurgeon*

Spurgeon goes on to say that tasting or eating is something we must each do for ourselves. This is true in both a physical and spiritual sense.

> But tasting, surely, is a personal business—there is no possibility of my eating for you! If you choose to starve yourself by a long fast of fifty days, so you must. If I were to sit down and industriously attempt to eat your portion of food, and my own, too, it would not help you in the least! You must eat for yourselves and there is no knowing the value of God's Word till you eat it for yourself. You must personally believe it, personally trust to it, personally receive it into your innermost spirit, or else you cannot know anything about its power to bless and to sustain!
>
> *Sermon #2340, December 24, 1893*

I mentioned previously that the pastor of the first church I attended refused to have a Bible study, despite me begging him to do so. Spurgeon's words remind me of that time. "There is no knowing the value of God's word till you eat it for yourself."

If things had gone differently then, I may have been content to have a pastor spoon feed me God's word.

As it turned out, I was forced to dive in and study scripture for myself.

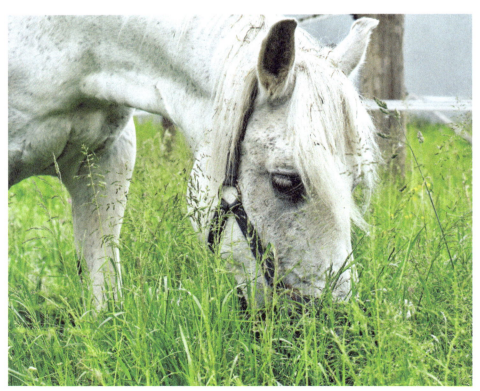

26

OLD AGE

When Enoch was 65 years old, he became the father of Methuselah. And after he had become the father of Methuselah, Enoch walked with God 300 years and had other sons and daughters. So Enoch lived a total of 365 years. Enoch walked with God, and then he was no more, because God had taken him away.

When Methuselah was 187 years old, he became the father of Lamech. And after he had become the father of Lamech, Methuselah lived 782 years and had other sons and daughters. So Methuselah lived a total of 969 years, and then he died.

Genesis 5:21-27

Genesis 5 gives us a bit of the story of Methuselah. His father was Enoch, a righteous man who did not die but who was taken to heaven by God at the age of 365.

Methuselah had a son, Lamech, who was the father of Noah. Methuselah was still alive when his grandson, Noah, built the ark. Perhaps Lamech and Methuselah helped with the building project.

Enoch->Methuselah->Lamech->Noah was God's chosen line to preserve humanity and the animal kingdom through the flood. It seems Lamech and Methuselah would have been righteous men given the godly character of both Enoch and Noah.

Lamech died a few years before the flood at the age of 777. Methuselah died in the same year as the flood. Many believe he died shortly before the rains came rather than being destroyed in the flood.

The following Old Testament men lived to be over 900 years old.

Adam 930   Seth 912   Enosh 905   Cainan 910   Jared 962   Methuselah 969   Noah 950

Some may be skeptical of these ages. However, considering God created man to live forever, I don't find the long ages surprising.

Methuselah was the oldest man in the Bible. After the flood, something changed, causing the life span of people to decrease. Noah's son, Shem, lived to be 600. And Abraham died at 175. The reason for this decrease in life spans is uncertain. Perhaps it was because of a major shift in the climate after the cataclysmic flood, combined with increasing genetic abnormalities.

Today, the average human life span in the United States is approximately eighty years. Most horses live twenty-five to thirty years. Ponies tend to live a little longer.

How does a horse's age correspond to that of a human?

Some recommend multiplying the horse's age by three to get a human equivalent. That works reasonably well except for the first five years. The correlation between human and horse ages is not as simple in the early years. Human infants walk on average at a year old, but most foals do that within an hour of birth. Early growth and development occur much more rapidly in horses than humans, and ponies mature even faster than horses.

Equine Resources International came up with the following correspondence. It's not perfect, since a yearling horse is self-sufficient, while a 6.5-year-old human is not.

Horse—human ages in years:

1—6.5 | 2—13 | 3—18 | 4—20.5 | 5—24.5

According to Guinness World Records, the oldest verifiable age for a horse is sixty-two—a brown English horse called Old Billy. Well, the "Old" part was probably tacked onto his name after a considerable number of years. Multiply Billy's age by three for his equivalent age in human years!

Billy was born in 1760 in Woolston, Lancashire, UK and died on November 27, 1822.

Could a horse really live that long? Is Billy's age reliable?

It seems so. Billy was raised by Edward Robinson, a farmer in Woolston. At the age of two, Billy was trained by seventeen-year-old Henry Harrison to be a plow horse.

William Bradley, a portrait artist, painted Old Billy in his retirement in 1821, the year before the horse's death. Henry Harrison is also pictured in that portrait. They included the following description with copies of the painting.

> This print exhibiting the portrait of Old Billy is presented to the public on account of his extraordinary age. Mr. Henry Harrison of Manchester, whose portrait is also introduced, has nearly attained his seventy-sixth year. He has known the said Horse Fifty Nine Years and upwards, having assisted in training him for the plough, at which time he supposes the Horse might be two years old. Old Billy is now playing at a farm at Latchford, near Warrington, and belongs to the Company of Proprietors of the Mersey and Irwell Navigation, in whose service he was employed as a Gin horse until May 1819. His Eyes and Teeth are yet very good, though the latter are remarkably indicative of extreme age.

Harrison was given the job of caring for Old Billy in his retirement, which didn't last long. Amazingly, the horse worked until he was almost sixty years old.

Although as a young horse, Billy was trained for farm work, at some point he was purchased by the Mersey and Irwell Navigation Company. Some accounts claim he was a barge horse, pulling boats along the canals. That may have been a seasonal job, but he also worked as a "gin" horse—gin being the short form of engine. In the days before electricity and steam engines, horses provided the power for many tasks through gins. The horse walked around and around, rotating a central drum connected to a system of cables and pulleys. Billy likely worked a gin used to raise goods from the decks of ships.

Until he reached the age of fifty, Old Billy had a bad temper,

> particularly shown when, at the dinner hour or other periods, a cessation of labor took place; he was impatient to get into the stable on such occasions and would use, very savagely, either his heels or his teeth (particularly the latter) to remove any living impediment… that happened, by chance, to be placed in his way…

Another artist, Charles Towne, painted Billy in June, 1822.

> At that time, Billy had "the use of all his limbs in tolerable perfection, lies down and rises with ease; and when in the meadows will frequently play, and even gallop, with some young colts, which graze along with him. This extraordinary animal is healthy, and manifests no symptoms whatever of approaching dissolution."

But five months later, the old horse passed away. Oddly enough, Old Billy's skull is on display at England's Manchester Museum, while his stuffed head, with its white blaze on a brown coat and a set of false teeth, is exhibited at the Bedford Museum. The fact that Billy worked so long and served his owner so faithfully, reminds me we are never called to retire from our faith. We should serve God in some capacity as long as we are able. It's a shame that in today's world, youth is worshiped, and the elderly are often forgotten or dismissed as old-fashioned.

> O God, You have taught me from my youth, and to this day I proclaim Your marvelous deeds. Even when I am old and gray, do not forsake me, O God, until I proclaim Your power to the next generation, Your might to all who are to come.
>
> *Psalm 71:17,18*

Two people who continued to serve God into their old age were Simeon and Anna, who ministered at the time the baby Jesus was brought to the temple. (Luke 2:25-38)

Gray hair is a crown of glory; it is attained along the path of righteousness.

Proverbs 16:31

The painting of Old Billy below shows that his ears were cropped. Cropped ears were considered fashionable at one time. This was also called "foxing."

This consists of depriving a horse of a portion of his ears, for the purpose of improving his looks. An easy mode of performing the operation is to take a small paintbrush and with paint in contrast in colour to the horse, mark the ears of the shape and length required: then place a switch on the horse's nose, at the same time holding up a fore foot; with a sharp knife cut the ears in the line made by the paint. Wash the wound with salt and water once a day for a week, after which apply sweet oil until healed. Those horses only which have small, thin, delicate heads, are improved by foxing.

New Family Encyclopaedia, or Compendium of Universal Knowledge, Charles Goodrich 1831

"Vanity of vanities," says the Preacher; "Vanity of vanities, all is vanity."

Ecclesiastes 1:2 NKJV

27

THE SACRIFICES OF GOD

I readily acknowledge that God is God, and I am not. However, as an animal lover, I always found it difficult to understand why the God who created animals also commanded the sacrifice of them. It seemed cruel. Then, I discovered verses like:

> For You do not delight in sacrifice, or I would bring it; You take no pleasure in burnt offerings. The sacrifices of God are a broken spirit; a broken and a contrite heart, O God, You will not despise.
>
> *Psalm 51:16-17*

That confused me. Did God want sacrifices or not?

As I studied and tried to figure this out, I realized I didn't understand how much God hates sin. There is very little hatred of sin today. The world indulges freely in sinful activities. People joke about sin and flock to movies where they are entertained by it.

God, however, takes sin very seriously. The penalty for sin is death (Romans 6:23). That death penalty began in the Garden of Eden when Adam and Eve first disobeyed God.

> And the LORD God made garments of skin for Adam and his wife, and He clothed them.
>
> *Genesis 3:21*

Wait a minute! Skin? Where did that come from?

Most Bible scholars believe that was the first occurrence of death on earth. One or more animals were killed to provide the skins that covered Adam and Eve.

I began to understand the way the sacrificial system was supposed to have worked—not that God got it wrong—the people did.

At that time, we had two horses and a pony. My daughters and I loved all three of them—Maggie, Ginger, and Ebony.

What if the next time I sinned, one of our horses had to pay for my disobedience with his life? Even worse, what if I had to kill that horse myself? It was so horrible I didn't want to think about it.

God's instructions were that the sacrifice must be the owner's best, most perfect animal. I couldn't even choose the horse I liked the least. It had to be the best one.

If I really had to sacrifice one of my horses when I sinned, it would force me to take my behavior more seriously. That was the purpose of the sacrificial system. It was intended to be a grim reminder of how awful sin is and the price that must be paid for it. When people had to kill a perfect, innocent animal in order to atone for their own sinful behavior, it should have caused them to be obedient to God.

In Isaiah 1:11, God says He is not pleased with the people's sacrifices.

> "What good to Me is your multitude of sacrifices?" says the LORD. "I am full from the burnt offerings of rams and the fat of well-fed cattle; I take no delight in the blood of bulls and lambs and goats."

The Israelites lost sight of the fact that their sinful behavior caused the death of those animals. They began to believe the dead animals pleased God. Sacrifices were callously presented as a mindless ritual that had no impact on their behavior. They continued to live however they pleased. Their ritualistic sacrifices didn't take away their sin; they added to it.

What God really wants has to come from inside us—a broken spirit, a broken and contrite heart. Wouldn't it break your heart to know that your horse or favorite pet was killed because of something you had done?

God hates sin because He is perfectly holy. He knows how harmful it is for us to disobey His laws. Sin enslaves us and draws us away from God. It causes pain and suffering for us, and its consequences spill over and hurt those around us as well.

The sacrificial system showed us the seriousness of sin and the dreadful penalty that had to be paid for it. I couldn't even imagine killing one of my horses, but God sacrificed His precious Son so that we could have eternal life. Unlike the animal sacrifices, Christ's death was once, for all, the perfect Lamb of God who took away the sins of the world.

Since Jesus was the perfect sacrifice, God no longer asks us to sacrifice animals, but He still wants our heartfelt love and obedience. He now asks each of us to offer ourselves to Him as a living sacrifice. He wants it all—our heart, soul, mind, and strength. Are you willing to make that sacrifice?

> Therefore I urge you, brothers, on account of God's mercy, to offer your bodies as living sacrifices, holy and pleasing to God, which is your spiritual service of worship.
>
> *Romans 12:1*

> Now one of the scribes had come up and heard their debate. Noticing how well Jesus had answered them, he asked Him, "Which commandment is the most important of all?"
>
> Jesus replied, "This is the most important: 'Hear O Israel, the Lord our God, the Lord is One. Love the Lord your God with all your heart and with all your soul and with all your mind and with all your strength.' The second is this: 'Love your neighbor as yourself.' No other commandment is greater than these."
>
> *Mark 12:28-30*

28

RAINBOW BRIDGE

Just this side of heaven is a place called Rainbow Bridge. When an animal dies that has been especially close to someone here, that pet goes to the Rainbow Bridge. There are meadows and hills for our special friends so they can run and play together. There is plenty of food, water, and sunshine and our friends are warm and comfortable.

All the animals who had been ill and old are restored to health and vigor; those who were hurt or maimed are made whole and strong again, just as we remember them in our dreams of days and times gone by. The animals are happy and content, except for one small thing; they each miss someone very special, someone who was left behind.

They all run and play together, but the day comes when one suddenly stops and looks into the distance. His bright eyes are intent; his eager body begins to quiver. Suddenly, he breaks from the group, flying over the green grass, faster and faster.

You have been spotted, and when you and your special friend finally meet, you cling together in joyous reunion, never to be parted again. The happy kisses rain upon your face; your hands again caress the beloved head, and you look once more into those trusting eyes, so long gone from your life, but never absent from your heart.

Then you cross the Rainbow Bridge together…

Author Unknown

The Rainbow Bridge presents someone's idea of how God has provided for the pets we've loved when they pass from this life. It's a beautiful picture of how we might be reunited with them one day. I've been surprised by the number of people who insist our pets will not be in heaven or on the new earth.

I think they're wrong—for a variety of scriptural reasons. After all, whose idea was it to create these wonderful creatures in the first place?

God's, of course. Animals were in the Garden of Eden with Adam and Eve. Since sin and death weren't present in that paradise, people and animals were created to live forever. And they would have, if Adam and Eve hadn't eaten from the forbidden tree. Their sin resulted in death and a curse on all of creation.

Some argue that because the Bible doesn't explicitly state animals will be in heaven, they will not be there. That is an *argumentum ex silentio*—an argument from silence. The absence of a statement cannot be considered a proof.

On the contrary, many scriptures show how much God values animals. When He looked at the animals He'd created, God "saw that it was good."

> God made the beasts of the earth according to their kinds, the livestock according to their kinds, and everything that crawls upon the earth according to its kind. And **God saw that it was good.**
>
> *Genesis 1:25*

God gave Adam the task of naming each of the animals.

> And out of the ground the LORD God formed every beast of the field and every bird of the air, and He brought them to the man to see what he would name each one. And whatever the man called each living creature, that was its name.
>
> *Genesis 2:19*

The intelligence and power of God is revealed through His creation, which includes the animals He made. Every species has features and abilities that go far beyond what could have occurred by mere chance. They point to an intelligent designer and creator.

> For since the creation of the world God's invisible qualities, His eternal power and divine nature, have been clearly seen, being understood from His workmanship, so that men are without excuse.
>
> *Romans 1:20*

Remember Noah and the worldwide flood? Not only were Noah and his family saved from the ravages of the flood waters, God directed Noah to preserve creatures that would repopulate the animal kingdom. God gave the rainbow as a sign of the covenant He made with man not to destroy the earth again by a flood. God made that covenant not just with Noah and his descendants but with the animals also.

> Behold, I now establish My covenant with you and your descendants after you, and with every living creature that was with you—the birds, the livestock, and every beast of the earth—every living thing that came out of the ark.
>
> *Genesis 9:9,10*

Read Genesis 9:8-17 for all the details. God must have considered animals important, since He included them in that covenant. God's concern extends to creatures as insignificant as a sparrow.

> Are not two sparrows sold for a penny? Yet not one of them will fall to the ground apart from the will of your Father.
>
> *Matthew 10:29*

Romans 8 describes how all of creation is under the curse of sin. It continues to tell of the future deliverance of the whole creation from that curse. Next to people, it seems animals are the second most important part of God's creation. It makes sense they will be part of the promised deliverance from the curse.

> For the creation was subjected to futility, not by its own will, but because of the One who subjected it, in hope that the creation itself will be set free from its bondage to decay and brought into the glorious freedom of the children of God. We know that the whole creation has been groaning together in the pains of childbirth until the present time.
>
> *Romans 8:20-22*

John Wesley, founder with his brother Charles, of the Methodist Church, has an interesting sermon addressing animal immortality, titled *The Great Deliverance*. The outline of the sermon follows.

I. What was the original state of the brute creation?

Wesley supposes that in their original state, both man and animals had higher intelligence and superior faculties than they do today. According to Wesley, the biggest difference between man and animals is, "Man is capable of God; the inferior creatures are not. We have no ground to believe that they are, in any degree, capable of knowing, loving, or obeying God."

II. In what state is it at present?

As stated in Romans 8, the entire creation is currently under a curse, which affects animals as well as man.

III. In what state will it be at the manifestation of the children of God?

When the curse on creation is lifted, Wesley believes, "The whole brute creation will then, undoubtedly, be restored, not only to the vigour, strength, and swiftness which they had at their creation, but to a far higher degree of each than they ever enjoyed. … No rage will be found in any creature, no fierceness, no cruelty, or thirst for blood."

Wesley's description sounds similar to passages from Isaiah. Whether those refer to the Millennial Kingdom, the New Earth, or both isn't clear, but the behavior of the animals differs greatly from that of today.

> The wolf will live with the lamb, and the leopard will lie down with the goat; the calf and young lion and fatling will be together, and a little child will lead them. The cow will graze with the bear, their young will lie down together, and the lion will eat straw like the ox.
>
> *Isaiah 11:6,7*

> The wolf and the lamb will feed together, and the lion will eat straw like the ox, …
>
> *Isaiah 65:25*

These verses indicate animals will return to being vegetarians. What about horses specifically? They are apparently one of God's favorite animals.

Horses transported Elijah up to heaven.

> As they were walking along and talking together, suddenly a chariot of fire with horses of fire appeared and separated the two of them, and Elijah went up into heaven in a whirlwind.
>
> *2 Kings 2:11*

The four horses of Revelation 6 are most likely symbolic, but Christ returns on what seems to be an actual horse in Revelation 19.

> Then I saw heaven standing open, and there before me was a white horse. And its rider is called Faithful and True.
>
> *Revelation 19:11*

The saints who return with Christ are also riding white horses.

> The armies of heaven, dressed in fine linen, white and pure, follow Him on white horses.
>
> *Revelation 19:14*

Do I know for certain animals will be in heaven or the New Earth? No. But for the reasons mentioned, I believe they will.

God is more loving and compassionate than any human could ever be. In fact, 1 John 4:8 says that God *is* love. If we care about what happens to animals we have loved here, I believe God cares even more. It seems He would have provided for their future as He has for ours. If God will create a perfect, eternal body for us, can't He do the same for animals?

> Behold, I am the LORD, the God of all flesh. Is anything too difficult for Me?
>
> *Jeremiah 32:27*

29

IDOLATRY

Hernando Cortez was a Spanish conquistador who sailed for the New World in 1504. He landed in the Caribbean on an island known then as Hispaniola. After conquering the Aztecs in Mexico, Cortez traveled south with his men and ninety horses to Honduras in Central America. His personal mount was a black stallion named El Morzillo (from the Spanish morcillo—black with reddish hairs).

While traversing the rough terrain, Morzillo was injured and unable to continue. Cortez left his favorite horse in the care of Mayan natives from a local tribe at Lake Peten Itza. In a letter, the explorer wrote:

> I was obliged to leave my black horse with a splinter in his foot. The chief promised to take care of him, but I do not know that he will succeed, or what he will do with him.

The natives didn't want to incur the wrath of Cortez who had promised to return later for Morzillo, but they had no idea how to care for a horse. They stabled El Morzillo in their temple and fed him delicacies of fruits, nuts, chicken and other meats, all topped with flowers. Whether because of his unusual diet or his foot injury, the stallion apparently didn't live long. Cortez never returned for his favorite horse. The conquistador died in Spain in 1547.

When Spanish missionaries visited Peten Itza in 1618, they found a strange sight—a statue of the stallion in the temple. The stone Morzillo was seated on his hindquarters with his forelegs stretched out in front of him. The Mayans knew him as Tzimin Chac, the God of Thunder. In the years since Cortez had left his horse, El Morzillo was worshiped as a weather god. The missionaries considered the stone horse a pagan idol and destroyed it.

Many would find it amusing that the Mayans worshiped the statue of a horse, but this is how John ends the final chapter of 1 John.

> Little children, keep [phylasso] yourselves from idols [eidolon]. Amen.

Unlike the Mayans and their horse weather god, I don't know anyone who worships a horse statue. We don't seem to have a problem with idol worship today.

Or do we?

Perhaps we should dig deeper into John's warning.

phylasso—to watch, be on guard, beware, avoid

eidolon—an image for worship, a heathen or false god, whatever represents the form of an object, either real or imaginary

The word "phylasso" implies action on our part. We need to be diligent in protecting our relationship with God so that nothing becomes more important to us than Him.

Though we are unlikely to worship a physical statue, the word "eidolon" indicates there are other forms of idolatry just as dangerous. Anything we devote a lot of time and attention to can become an idol in our lives—even horses—for those of us who love them.

The Amplified and Living Bible paraphrases of 1 John 5:21 give us additional insight into what idolatry encompasses.

> Little children (believers, dear ones), guard yourselves from idols—[false teachings, moral compromises, and anything that would take God's place in your heart]. AMP

> Dear children, keep away from anything that might take God's place in your hearts. TLB

Charles Haddon Spurgeon expands on the things idolatry may include.

- This speaks against obvious, visible idols.
- This speaks against worshiping yourself. We can do this by overindulgence in food or drink, by laziness, or by too much concern about how we look or what we wear.
- This speaks against worshiping wealth.
- This speaks against worshiping some hobby or pursuit.
- This speaks against worshiping dear friends or relatives.

Horses definitely fall into Spurgeon's fourth category—a hobby or pursuit. Have we allowed our horses to become idols? If asked that point-blank, most would deny it. Intellectually, we may admit horses aren't more important to us than God, but would our daily lives reflect that affirmation?

I've found the following questions are a good way to identify potential idols.

- What do I devote my time to?
- What do I spend my money on?
- What do I get excited about?
- What do I often think or talk about?

Horses can be an expensive and time-consuming hobby, especially if you show or compete in other types of events. Many of those competitions are now scheduled on Sundays or over entire weekends, so you face the choice of whether to go to a horse event or a worship service.

God doesn't expect us to spend all our waking hours in prayer and Bible study, but it should be a warning flag if we schedule God around our hobbies rather than the other way around. If other interests consume us to the extent that we have little or no time for God, it will be difficult to maintain a close relationship with Him.

For some people, horses or other animals do not come close to approaching the level of an idol. For them, idolatry may take other forms—pursuing wealth, fame, or power—basically the worship of oneself. Anything we value more than God can take His place in our hearts.

If our hobbies are wholesome ones, I believe God is often the author of those interests. I can't remember not loving horses—long before I owned or was even around them. There seems to be no explanation for my passion for horses other than God planting it in me.

Much as Jesus used the things around Him as object lessons to illustrate God's nature and scriptural principles, we can use our hobbies and interests to share the Good News with others. It's what I try to do in the books I write.

Not everyone is a writer, but the insights about God and faith you gain through whatever your interests are, can be a natural way to steer conversations with unbelievers toward spiritual matters.

For example, if someone asks what I do, it's easy to say I write Christian horse books for kids. If the conversation continues, I explain the stories are based on experiences I had with horses that allowed me to better understand my relationship to God. My answer may spark further interest or the person may shut down the topic, but at least I've attempted to initiate a conversation about God.

In the past, and across cultures, horses have been buried along with their owners. Several Viking burial sites in Iceland have revealed stallions buried with wealthy, powerful men.

An extreme case is that of Chinese ruler, Duke Jing of Qi (547 to 490 BC). In 1964, archaeologists found his tomb and uncovered the skeletons of more than 200 horses. It's believed when excavation is complete, the tomb may contain as many as 600 horses.

The presumption is that horses were buried with people either to transport them to the afterlife or for the person's use once they arrived there.

In Norse mythology, Sleipnir was the eight-legged horse ridden by the god Odin.

30

FOLLOWING A PATTERN

I run in the path of Your commandments, for You will enlarge my heart.

Psalm 119:32

The entirety of Psalm 119 is about how precious the word of God is and how we should be obedient to it. This obedience doesn't come from a grudging sense of obligation or duty but from a heart full of love for God and appreciation for all He has done for us. I found these insights from several commentators valuable.

> Those who know and love the law of the Lord, desire to know it more, and love it better. Those that are going to heaven, should still press forward. God, by his Spirit, enlarges the hearts of his people when he gives them wisdom.
>
> *Matthew Henry*

> I will not merely keep them—which might be expressed by "I will walk in them," but I will hasten to keep them; I will do it with alacrity, as when one runs to accomplish an object. I will devote to them all the energies of my life.
>
> The phrase "to enlarge the heart" means to make it free; to deliver it from all hindrances to what is right; to fill it with noble and holy purposes; to stimulate and animate it. The heart is contracted or made narrow by selfishness, pride, vanity, ambition, covetousness; it is made large by charity, love, hope, benevolence. Sin narrows the soul; religion enlarges it.
>
> *Barnes' Notes on the Bible*

> I will run the way of thy commandments, … Not only walk but run in it; which is expressive of great affection to the commands of God, of great readiness and cheerfulness, of great haste and swiftness in the way of them, and of great delight and pleasure therein; when thou shall enlarge my heart; with the knowledge of God, his word, ways, worship, and ordinances; with his love more fully made known, and with an increase of love to him;
>
> *Gill's Exposition of the Entire Bible*

Psalm 119:32 reminds me of a horse event that requires a lot of heart on the part of both the horse and rider and involves adhering to a course or pattern—barrel racing.

It's a timed event over a triangular pattern created by three fifty-five gallon barrels. An electronic device keeps the time which begins when the horse and rider gallop down the alley and cross the start/finish line.

Competitors may choose to approach either the right or left barrel first. Most make the right turn first. After making a tight clockwise circle around that barrel, the horse must do a flying lead change in order to make a left circle around the second barrel. From there, they circle the third barrel at the tip of the triangle, going left around that barrel also, then run straight back across the start/finish line. The resulting pattern resembles a cloverleaf.

Taking the first barrel to the right makes sense because about seventy percent of horses are "left-handed," meaning they prefer going to the left and are more coordinated in that direction. That sounds contradictory, but by taking the right barrel first, they circle the remaining two barrels to the left or counter-clockwise. A horse that is "right-handed," about twenty percent of horses, may prefer to take the left barrel first. The remaining ten percent of horses work equally well in either direction.

Winning times at the professional level are in the range of thirteen to sixteen seconds, depending on the length of the course. A horse that doesn't complete the course within sixty seconds is disqualified. Going off course or missing a barrel entirely also results in disqualification. There is no penalty for hitting a barrel—as long as it doesn't tip over. Knocking a barrel down incurs a five second penalty added to the team's time. Competitions typically consist of three rounds.

Barrel horses are rated by their speed. One D horses are the fastest. The ratings go from 1D to 4D, fastest to slowest. A top 1D horse may sell in the range of $25,000 to $35,000 with the elite in that range going even higher.

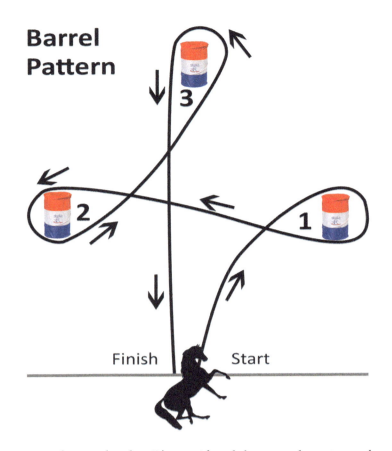

Barrel racing is the only women's event in professional rodeo. It's considered the second most popular event after bull riding. Though men compete at amateur and youth levels, it's women only at the professional level.

Barrel racing started in Texas in the 1920s and early 30s as a figure-eight pattern and was not timed. Winners were chosen based on their horsemanship skills. By 1935, the event began switching to the current cloverleaf pattern.

To help riders remain seated at high speeds with sharp, sudden turns, special Western saddles are used. These lightweight but strong barrel saddles have high pommels and cantles, with tall, slim horns. Reins are a single loop so they can be easily recovered if dropped during a run. Protective boots are usually worn on the horse's legs to help prevent injury.

Charmayne James, born in 1970, won her first of eleven world championships at the age of fourteen. James was the first barrel racer to earn a million dollars (1990). Now, she trains barrel horses and holds barrel-racing clinics.

Almost as famous as James was her barrel horse, Gills Bay Boy, known as Scamper. The bay Quarter Horse gelding was an unlikely champion. When twelve-year-old James first saw the horse, he was used for sorting cattle at a feedlot. He'd ended up there after bucking off and injuring his previous owner. Charmayne purchased him for $1200.

The gelding had probably never seen a barrel, but in 1982, after only two weeks of training, the pair won their first local competition. Gills Bay Boy was given his nickname for the way he scampered around the barrels. Scamper and James went on to win the WPRA World Championship every year from 1984 through 1993.

An incident in 1985 showed the amazing ability of both the horse and rider. While waiting to enter a race, Scamper bumped his head against a wall, breaking a screw that held the bridle's headstall together. By the time James noticed the bridle dangling from Scamper's head, they had already started their run. At first, the bit remained in the horse's mouth, but he spit that out while circling the third barrel. At that point, Charmayne had no control over him. Rather than panicking, she tapped him with her bat for more speed. The horse, so accustomed to the pattern, didn't need to be steered. Even without a bridle, the two ended up winning the round.

Scamper retired from competition in 1993 and was later inducted into the Pro Rodeo Hall of Fame. In 1998, Breyer created a model of Scamper. Charmayne James had the horse cloned in 1999 at a cost of $150,000. The procedure resulted in a colt she named Clayton, who was used as a breeding stallion. James hoped to produce more horses with the qualities Scamper possessed. Scamper died on July 4, 2012, at the age of thirty-five.

Like a good barrel horse, we need to stick to our pattern. We're called to run the course God has set out for us, following His commandments because we love Him and don't want to disappoint our heavenly Father.

> Join one another in following my example, brothers, and carefully observe those who walk according to the pattern we set for you.
>
> *Philippians 3:17*

31

HANDICAP RACES

It's not surprising that carrying more weight slows a runner. That concept is used in some horse races in an attempt to give all the entrants an equal chance at winning. This type of race is called a handicap.

The best-known handicap in the United States is the Santa Anita Handicap held in Arcadia, California. One of the most famous handicaps in the world is the Melbourne Cup in Australia.

In these races, weight is added to that of the jockey, saddle, and saddle pad to match an amount predetermined for each horse in the race. Each pound added is believed to slow the animal by one horse length per mile. The weights may be in the form of lead bars inserted into pockets in the saddle pad or by using weighted saddle pads. Faster or more successful horses are assigned higher weights. That seems unfair, but the intent is to make the race more interesting to spectators by leveling out the competition and making the outcome less predictable.

Thoroughbred jockeys average between 4'10" and 5'6" in height and weigh between 108 and 118 pounds. The saddle and saddle pad contribute another seven pounds. If a 113-pound jockey rides in a handicap race requiring his horse to carry 130 pounds, ten pounds of additional weight would be required to reach the assigned 130 pounds. (113 + 7 + 10)

In 1970, a mare named Ta Wee (Sioux for Beautiful Girl) was so successful in previous races that they assigned her a weight of 142 pounds for the Interborough Handicap in New York. Ta Wee won the race despite carrying twenty-nine pounds more than the horse and rider who finished second.

Therefore, since we are surrounded by such a great cloud of witnesses, let us throw off [apotithemi] every encumbrance [ogkos] and the sin [hamartia] that so easily entangles [euperistatos], and let us run with endurance [hypomone] the race [agon] set out for us [prokeimai]. Let us fix [aphoraō] our eyes on Jesus, the author and perfecter of our faith, who for the joy set before Him endured the cross, scorning its shame, and sat down at the right hand of the throne of God.

Hebrews 12:1,2

This passage in Hebrews speaks of our life's journey as a race. Rather than adding weight when racing, the Bible recommends removing it. The principle remains the same as in horse racing—additional weight slows us down or holds us back. You may have never considered yourself a racer or even a runner, but according to the Bible, all believers are. Each of us is running a special race or course God has laid out for us.

apotithemi—lay aside, put away, cast off, throw off

ogkos—mass, burden, hindrance, bulk, encumbrance

hamartia—missing the mark, offense, wrong

euperistatos—ensnare, beset, thwart, entangle, surround in every direction

hypomone—endurance, patience, continuance, steadfastness, constancy

agon- conflict, contest, fight, race, course, struggle

prokeimai—set before us, to be appointed or destined

aphoraō—to turn the eyes away from other things and fix them on something

Unlike in a handicap horse race, people don't carry lead bars that slow us down. Two things hinder us in our race—sin and weight. It's easy to see that outright sin is something every Christian should avoid. Disobedience to God harms us as well as others in our lives, and it damages our witness to non-believers. We should repent from known sin, and with God's help, keep from returning to it.

But there's a more subtle factor that can slow us in our race. Sometimes, the decisions we make in life aren't as obvious as a choice between right and wrong. They often involve a choice between what is acceptable and what is best or excellent. Something might not be sinful but may distract us from achieving the goals God has set for us. Getting rid of the excess bulk that slows us down may involve throwing off some good things in order to reach our best running weight.

Horses run at a fast and furious pace for a short distance, but the race of life occurs more slowly. Rather than speed, the most important ingredients for success in our race are endurance, patience, and a steadfast constancy in going the right direction. Our race is a marathon rather than a sprint. We have to keep going, putting one foot in front of the other, even when we may not feel like it.

Huge crowds attend the top horse races, loudly cheering on their favorites. While we can't hear their cheers, we can find encouragement from "a great cloud of witnesses" who have already completed their races. A few of those examples of the faith are listed in Hebrews 11—Abel, Enoch, Noah, Abraham, and Moses among others. Their faith enabled these men to persevere through difficulties, trusting God would keep His promises, even though they didn't always see results in their lifetimes.

Even better, we have the example of Jesus, who endured the pain and shame of the cross for us. When we become tired and discouraged, we should remember all that Christ endured because of His love for us.

Not that I have already obtained all this, or have already been made perfect, but I press on [diōkō] to take hold of that for which Christ Jesus took hold of me. Brothers, I do not consider myself yet to have taken hold of it. But one thing I do: Forgetting what is behind and straining toward [epekteinomai] what is ahead, I press on [diōkō] toward the goal to win the prize of God's heavenly calling in Christ Jesus.

Philippians 3:12-14

epekteinomai—to stretch one's self forward to

diōkō—to run swiftly in order to catch a person or thing, to run after. Interestingly, this same word is frequently translated as "persecute(d)" as in Matthew 5:10, Blessed are those who are persecuted because of righteousness, for theirs is the kingdom of heaven.

If our eyes are "fixed on Jesus" and we're "pressing toward the goal," we won't look back. In the middle of a race, a person or horse never turns around and looks backward. The focus is always ahead, toward the finish line.

> I have fought the good fight, I have finished the race, I have kept the faith. From now on there is laid up for me the crown of righteousness, which the Lord, the righteous Judge, will award to me on that day—and not only to me, but to all who crave His appearing.
>
> *2 Timothy 4:7,8*

It's interesting that the actual leg motion of the horse at the gallop wasn't known for certain until the advent of the camera. The positions shown in many early prints, such as the one above, are not accurate. The horse on the right shows the front and back legs all fully extended and off the ground. That never happens with a real horse.

32

ENLARGE MY HEART

I have chosen the way of truth; I have set Your ordinances before me. I cling to Your testimonies, O LORD; let me not be put to shame. I run in the path of Your commandments, for You will **enlarge my heart**.

Psalm 119:30-32

We looked at this passage previously in the sense of staying on course, as in following a barrel racing pattern. Now we'll look at the phrase in verse 32, "enlarge my heart."

The physical heart is the organ in our chest that pumps blood throughout the body. It's not good for people to have an enlarged heart. This condition is called cardiomegaly and occurs when the heart muscles thicken or a chamber of the heart widens. Cardiomegaly usually means the heart cannot function as efficiently as it did before.

In horses, though, a larger than normal heart can be an advantage. It's believed something known as the X-Factor determines whether this condition is present in a horse. The factor was named because the gene that may be responsible for the large heart is located on a horse's X chromosome. The X-Factor is most common in Thoroughbreds and traces back to Eclipse through the mare Pocahontas, foaled in 1837.

In 1969, stable owners Ogden Phipps and Penny Chenery met at the New York Racing Association for a coin toss. Chenery assumed the operation of the family farm, Meadow Stable, when her father's health declined. The winner of the coin toss would receive a foal born that year to Hasty Matelda, sired by Bold Ruler. The loser would receive a foal the following year, also from Bold Ruler, but by a different mare, Somethin-groyal.

That day, everyone considered Phipps the winner of the toss, but time would reveal Penny Chenery was the real winner. In 1970, Somethingroyal gave birth to Chenery's foal—a chestnut colt with three white socks—Secretariat. That wasn't the first choice for his name, though. Initial ideas were Sceptre, Royal Line, Something Special, Games of Chance, and Deo Volente (God Willing). As he grew and developed, Secretariat came to be known around the stable as Big Red.

No one was particularly impressed with the colt, including Eddie Sweat, who became the horse's groom.

I didn't think much of him when we first got him. I thought he was just a big clown. He was real clumsy and a bit on the wild side, you know. And I remember saying to myself I didn't think he was going to be an outstanding horse.

But outstanding he was, proving it in 1973 by becoming the ninth horse to win the Triple Crown. He not only won the three races, but set records in each that still stand today.

Kentucky Derby (1 1/4 miles): 1:59 2/5 (Rich Strike's winning time in 2022 was 2:02.61)

Preakness Stakes (1 3/16 miles): 1:53

Belmont Stakes (1 1/2 miles): 2:24.

The Belmont Stakes was the most astounding of Secretariat's Triple Crown wins. The race announcer, Chic Anderson, expressed the thoughts of many as Secretariat seemed to effortlessly increase his lead over the other four horses in the race. "He is moving like a tremendous machine!"

Secretariat won the Belmont by an amazing thirty-one lengths.

After his racing career, the great horse was retired to Claiborne Farm in Paris, Kentucky. As a trial run, he was mated with an Appaloosa mare, Leola, producing his first foal in 1974. That chestnut colt, First Secretary, had three stockings and a white blanket covering his hindquarters. Secretariat would go on to sire 663 Thoroughbred foals. None of his offspring achieved the racing success of their father, however Secretariat was considered a leading broodmare sire.

In 1989, at the age of nineteen, Secretariat developed a severe case of laminitis, and he had to be euthanized. Dr. Thomas Swerczek, the veterinarian who performed an autopsy on Secretariat, was shocked by the size of the horse's heart.

> We just stood there in stunned silence. We couldn't believe it. The heart was perfect. There were no problems with it. It was just this huge engine.

Although Swerczek didn't weigh Secretariat's heart, he estimated it to have been close to twenty-two pounds, over twice the size of an average Thoroughbred's heart (eight and a half pounds).

Considered by many to be the greatest racehorse of all time, Secretariat's success can't be attributed solely to the size of his heart. The horse's conformation was perfect for racing. His chest was so large he required a custom-made girth. His powerful hindquarters produced a 24' 11" stride. Additionally, his temperament, intelligence, training, owners, handlers, and jockeys all contributed to the horse's success.

Let's return to the phrase in Psalm 119—"enlarge [rahab] my heart [leb]." Of course, it isn't referring to horses or even physical hearts. It's speaking of heart in a spiritual sense.

> **rahab**—to broaden, make room, make open, grow wider, enlarge
>
> **leb**—inner man, mind, will, heart, understanding

How can our spiritual hearts be enlarged? And why would we want that to happen?

As we come to know and love God more by studying and obeying His word, our hearts will figuratively be enlarged so we can begin to love as He loves.

Just as Secretariat's big, strong heart allowed him to run faster than other horses, an enlarged heart will help us "run the course of His commandments."

In the Gospels, we see that Jesus was often "moved with compassion."

> And Jesus, when He came out, saw a great multitude and was moved with compassion [splagchnizomai] for them, because they were like sheep not having a shepherd. So He began to teach them many things.
>
> *Mark 6:34 NKJV*

> **splagchnizomai**—to be moved as to one's bowels, hence to be moved with compassion (the bowels were believed to be the seat of love and pity)

Jesus' compassion went beyond just a feeling; it led Him to action, reaching out to the lost and needy. With enlarged spiritual hearts, we'll have an increased capacity for love and compassion toward those around us. That compassion won't stop at just a feeling but will cause us to take action. An enlarged heart will also help us love the things God loves and hate the things He hates. Our hearts will break over the things that break God's heart. A verse I ran across a few years ago keeps coming back to me. It doesn't seem to be well known.

> "Go throughout the city of Jerusalem," said the LORD, "and put a mark on the foreheads of the men sighing and groaning over all the abominations committed there."
>
> *Ezekiel 9:4*

After the marks were applied, God commanded that all those who did not have the mark, who did not mourn over the abominations in Jerusalem, were to be killed.

Many today seem to believe we must be happy all the time. The verse from Ezekiel indicates that is not how God views things. It tells about a vision given to Ezekiel of a coming judgment from God. It's unclear whether the markings and killings were actually carried out at that time. The vision may refer to the eventual capture of Jerusalem by the Babylonians but the principle remains. The people God approved of were those who mourned over the sinful behavior of the people.

> Have you been crying out to God because of all the abominations that fill the land? Have you been on your face before the Lord weeping because of the iniquity in the land, or has your pursuit of your own pleasure given you a careless disregard of the abounding evil? Those who sighed over the conditions, and cried out to God because of their great concern over the abominations, were the ones that the Lord marked for protection from the judgment of the Lord.
>
> *Chuck Smith*

Mourning is also presented as a good thing in the Sermon on the Mount. Mourning can show that you care about the things God cares about.

Blessed are those who mourn, For they will be comforted.

Matthew 5:4

Cleanse your hands, you sinners, and purify your hearts, you double-minded. Grieve, mourn, and weep. Turn your laughter to mourning, and your joy to gloom. Humble yourselves before the Lord, and He will exalt you.

James 4:8-10

Create in me a clean heart, O God, And renew a right spirit within me.

Psalm 51:10

I will give you a new heart and put a new spirit within you; I will remove your heart of stone and give you a heart of flesh.

Ezekiel 36:26

The LORD is near to the brokenhearted; He saves the contrite in spirit.

Psalm 34:18

God doesn't want us to go around being gloomy all the time, either. But when you realize the extent of the evil and suffering in this world, the only way to maintain a constant, lighthearted happiness is by ignoring the pain of others. Rather than happiness, Christians have a deep-seated joy, knowing that God is in control, working all things for the good of believers. We have the assurance that one day,

He will wipe away every tear from their eyes, and there will be no more death or mourning or crying or pain, for the former things have passed away.

Revelation 21:4

33

THE FIRST SHALL BE LAST

In Matthew 19, a rich, young ruler approached Jesus, asking how he could obtain eternal life. Jesus sensed the man's riches were far too important to him.

> Jesus told him, "If you want to be perfect, go, sell your possessions and give to the poor, and you will have treasure in heaven. Then come, follow Me."
>
> When the young man heard this, he went away in sorrow, because he had great wealth.
>
> *Matthew 19:21,22*

This led to a question from Peter. He wondered what reward awaited the disciples since they had left everything to follow Christ. Jesus assured them they would receive a reward, but then He added this curious statement.

> But many who are first [protos] will be last [eschatos], and the last will be first.
>
> *Matthew 19:30*

This statement is repeated in Matthew 20:16 when Jesus tells the parable of the laborers. The men who worked all day were surprised when the workers who joined them at the end were paid the same amount.

> **protos**—first in time or place, first in rank or honor
>
> **eschatos**—last in time or place, or of the lowest rank or worth

Jesus is illustrating that the way things are valued in this world doesn't always match the value system of heaven. In this world, we hold in high regard people who are wealthy, famous, or those in positions of power. Based on Jesus' statement, the people who are first here on earth may well be last in heaven.

I was reminded of this "first shall be last" concept when I learned about a horse named Rich Strike. The Thoroughbred was born on April 24, 2019, at Calumet Farm in Kentucky. The chestnut sports a blaze and two socks on his back legs. As a two-year-old, he finished last out of ten horses in his first race—not a great start on a racing career.

On Sept. 17, 2021, Rich Strike was entered in a claiming race at Churchill Downs. He won the race by an amazing seventeen lengths. Trainer Eric Reed claimed the colt for owner Richard Dawson for $30,000. That might sound like a lot of money, but it pales when compared to many racehorses. At Keeneland's Thoroughbred yearling sale in September 2021, a sale for untrained, unraced Thoroughbreds, the average price was nearly $400,000, with a high sale of $1,400,000.

All the horses in a claiming race are offered for sale. The price varies depending upon the caliber of the race. The person who wants to buy or "claim" one of the horses submits a written form, before the start of the race, for the horse he wants. If more than one person submits a claim for the same horse, the winner is determined by a random drawing known as a shake. Technically, the claimer owns the horse once the race starts, but the claim can be voided if the horse dies, is injured during the race, or tests positive for drug use. Anything the horse wins during the claiming race goes to the owner who entered him in the race, not to the new claimant.

Claiming races are often a way for owners or trainers to unload horses who are not performing up to their expectations, which is why Rich Strike was entered in one. After his win in the claiming race, Rich Strike continued running for his new owner Richard Dawson, finishing third three times, fourth once, and fifth once. Rich Strike's less than spectacular performance seemed to match the misfortune of his trainer.

Eric Reed and his wife, Kay, experienced a tragic barn fire in December 2016 at their Mercury Equine Center in Lexington, Kentucky. Reed and his employees saved thirteen horses by leading them out of the burning barn, but twenty-three Thoroughbreds died in the fire thought to be caused by lightning. They would have lost fewer horses, but the fire department, located just five minutes away, didn't arrive until forty minutes after the first call for help. The tragedy made Reed consider leaving horse racing.

> The next morning when we saw the devastation—because this happened in the middle of the night—I just thought of all the years and all the stuff we had done to get this beautiful farm. And to have this happen, that something might be telling me it's the end of the line.

Overwhelming support from his friends and others in the racing industry convinced Reed to rebuild and continue training. It was after that fire that Reed claimed Rich Strike and began working with the colt.

Reed's experience with the barn fire reminds me of a question I've thought about often—how do you know when obstacles you face in life are Satan blocking you or God redirecting you? Is the obstacle something we need to push through and overcome as Eric Reed chose to do? Or is God nudging us in a different direction? I don't have an easy answer for that. The best thing I can advise is to pray about each obstacle and try to determine which way God is steering you.

Back to Rich Strike, or Richie, as his new owner, Richard Dawson, calls him. Although his racing career hadn't been remarkable, he'd earned enough points to qualify for the Kentucky Derby as a three-year-old in 2022. However, the field for the race was full. Richie was first on standby in the "Also Eligible" list in case any of the entrants dropped out of the race (scratched).

At 8:45 a.m. on Friday, the day before the race, Reed was informed there were no scratches. Disappointed, the trainer began calling his clients and friends to inform them that Richie wouldn't be racing. But fifteen minutes later, Reed received a call. A horse named Ethereal Road had scratched at the last possible moment—Rich Strike was in the Derby, after all!

As a virtually unheard of horse, Rich Strike was given eighty to one odds of winning the race. In other words, he was an extreme long shot or an underdog. No one, other than Richie's owner and team, thought the horse would do anything but fill the empty slot created when Ethereal Road dropped out of the race.

Fortunately, Rich Strike was unaware of everyone's low opinion of him.

There were twenty horses in the race. The favorites were Epicenter and Zandon. As the last entry, Rich Strike was in the twentieth position at the far outside of the track, wearing number twenty-one. Running from the outer positions means covering a longer distance, so it's important for the outside horses to move quickly to the inside of the track. But doing so guarantees they will encounter a pack of horses it's difficult to get around or through.

Rich Strike's jockey, Venezuelan Sonny Leon, was as well known at the Kentucky Derby level of racing as his mount, that is—unknown. Leon began racing at fifteen in Youngstown, Ohio. Prior to the Derby, his experience was limited to the Ohio area horse-racing world. Before the start of the race, Leon insisted he wasn't nervous, only excited.

The Derby is a one and a quarter mile race. For most of the early race, Richie ran at the back of the pack. At a half mile, he was in eighteenth place. At the mile mark, with only a quarter mile to go, he was fifteenth. Then, Sonny Leon maneuvered the horse toward the rail, and the pair began expertly weaving in and out, passing horses in the pack who were tiring.

The race announcer was so focused on the battle between the leaders, Epicenter and Zandon, he missed the freight train that was Rich Strike coming up from behind. Richie pulled ahead of the favorites to win by three-quarters of a length over Epicenter with Zandon in third. Rich Strike lived up to his name that day, winning $1.8 million. He became the first claimed horse to win the Kentucky Derby.

A *Sports Illustrated* article described the underdog's victory perfectly, stating that no one saw Rich Strike coming. "Not until the very end, when this nobody of a horse, with a nobody trainer and nobody jockey and nobody owner, came knifing along the rail a few strides before the wire to launch himself into history."

Richie matched the meaning of "eschatos" or "last" in several ways.

- He was the last horse accepted into the race.

- He raced from the last position at the outside of the track.

- He ran in nearly last place for most of the race.

- Because of his past racing record, he was considered the least worthy entrant in the race.

- His team—owner, trainer, and jockey were unknown at that level of racing.

But Richie flipped all that upside down, proving that even in this world, sometimes the last can be first!

I'm not a horse racing fan, but I had to watch the ending of Rich Strike's winning Kentucky Derby run repeatedly. It was spectacular on the part of both the horse and the jockey.

Owner Richard Dawson decided to skip The Preakness, the second race in the Triple Crown, run just two weeks after the Derby. He didn't feel that was enough time for Richie to rest.

Rich Strike was entered in the Belmont Stakes on June 11, the third Triple Crown race. The horse finished a disappointing sixth out of eight entries in the Belmont. Trainer Eric Reed took the blame for Richie's poor performance, claiming he gave the jockey bad instructions for their racing strategy.

Even if Rich Strike never wins another race, no one can take away his amazing come-from-behind victory in the 2022 Kentucky Derby.

34

CANDY AND FROSTY

When I was nine, my neighbor, Candy, got a pony. Her gelding was a stocky, strawberry roan named Frosty.

No. I'm not making those names up.

Frosty was smaller than my bay pony, Dolly, but he was so calm you could do just about anything with him. Dolly was a little more temperamental.

Candy didn't have a saddle, so she always rode bareback. We often rode double on Frosty. At times, we had as many as four of us on him. Frosty patiently endured all of our foolishness. When he got tired, he would head for the closest tree. Walking under a low branch was a tried-and-true way to get us off his back in a hurry!

At that time, we lived in a small, one-story house. A sidewalk led to our front door and into the kitchen. One summer day, Candy came over with Frosty. We stood near the front of our house talking when suddenly a mischievous sparkle appeared in Candy's eye. "I bet Frosty would walk into your house."

I did some quick thinking. I knew my mom was inside, and I doubted she would consider a pony in our house a good idea—but it would be funny.

Then, Candy said the words that clinched my decision. "You're afraid to do it, aren't you?"

Me, afraid? In my youthful foolishness, I was eager to prove I wasn't afraid of anything. I grabbed Frosty's lead rope, and Candy opened the door. Remember when I said Frosty would do anything? The pony viewed this as just another one of our adventures. He didn't hesitate but marched through the doorway into the kitchen. So far, Mom was nowhere to be seen. When we reached the end of the long, narrow kitchen, we made a left turn into the living room.

I took a deep breath. There she was! Mom sat in a recliner, reading. The noise of Frosty's hooves clip-clopping across the floor got her attention, and she looked up from her book. The expression on her face told me that Frosty in our living room was about the last thing she'd expected to see!

Maybe I imagined it, but I thought I saw a hint of a smile cross her face, before she yelled at us to get that pony out of the house. Frosty seemed to enjoy his visit and wanted to stay. With Candy pushing and me pulling, we got him turned around and led him back outside.

Taking Frosty into our house wasn't the worst thing I've ever done in my life. And I have to admit it was funny. The worst part was how easy it was for Candy to convince me to do something I knew I shouldn't. Friends have a powerful influence on us for good or bad.

Some of our pranks just become amusing stories we can tell as adults, but foolish actions may result in harm or injury to ourselves or others. Bad decisions can start us down a wrong path with lifelong consequences.

According to Proverbs 13:20, He who walks with the wise will become wise, but the companion of fools will be destroyed.

Here are some tips for good decision-making I wish I'd known and followed when I was younger. They're relevant even for adults.

- Be careful who you choose as your friends.
- Think for yourself.
- Don't always go along with what everyone else is doing.
- Study your Bible. It's God's primary way to communicate His wisdom to us.
- Walk with the wise. Since wisdom often comes with age, listen to those who are older than you.

35

MONKEY SEE MONKEY DO

When we were younger, my three siblings and I gave our mother many opportunities to use the expression, "monkey see monkey do" as we tried out the latest "cool" thing we'd seen other kids do.

One neighbor, Lila, was a couple of years older than me. She could run up behind her palomino, Trouble, plant both hands on his hindquarters, and vault onto his back. I thought that was the neatest thing. Of course, I had to try it with my pony, Dolly. When my younger sister saw me doing it, she wanted to try as well.

We weren't as good at vaulting as Lila—or maybe Dolly wasn't as patient as Trouble. Perhaps it was a little of both. When my sister almost got kicked in the face during one of her attempts, my mom put a stop to that trick.

One day as an adult, I was reminded of the "monkey see, monkey do" behavior. While cleaning stalls in the barn, I glanced out the back door. Two of our horses, Ginger and Carmel, stood side by side under a tree in the pasture. We' recently replaced some fencing, and I'd left a partial roll of farm fence in the field.

Carmel pawed at the roll with one of his front feet. I made a mental note to remove the fencing as soon as I finished in the barn. But as I continued cleaning, Ginger began to paw at the roll. It was as if she had watched Carmel do it, and pawing the fence looked like so much fun, she had to try it.

There was a problem, though. Ginger had shoes on her front feet. As she pawed the fence roll, the edge of one of her shoes hooked over a strand of the wire. When placed her hoof back on the ground, the fence was stuck to it. That scared her, and she tried to move away from the roll. The fencing was firmly attached to her shoe and followed her.

I watched in horror. If Ginger had taken off at a mad gallop, it could have been disastrous. I hurried out of the barn as quickly as I could without scaring her more. Fortunately, Ginger had the good sense to stop after she'd gone only a short distance. She stood, waiting for me to come and rescue her. I unhooked the wire from the shoe, and freed her from the fence roll.

When I thought about what might have happened to the mare if she hadn't stopped and stood still, I heaved a sigh of relief. Then, I was angry at myself for leaving the fence roll in the pasture.

Having three daughters, I was aware of how easy it was for children to imitate bad behavior, but that was the first time I'd seen such an obvious case of it with horses. When performed by animals, this imitation is known as allelomimetic behavior. The term comes from two root words:

allele—the variants of a single gene

mime—to mimic or imitate

Allelomimetic behavior occurs in all animals and is an important form of learning for their young. A foal learns how to be a horse by imitating the behavior of his mother and any other horses around him. They may also learn unacceptable behavior by imitation. For example, the foal of a nervous, temperamental mare may pick up her bad habits by observing and imitating his mother's behavior.

But imitation can be a good thing. In fact, the Bible calls us to be imitators. The crucial point is who or what we are imitating. We should be imitators of Christ/God or godly people—not imitators of foolish or evil people.

One of the verses I find the most challenging is 1 Corinthians 11:1.

Imitate [mimetes] me, just as I also imitate Christ. *NKJV*

In that short verse, Paul encourages the Corinthians to imitate him as he imitated Christ. The second "imitate" in that verse is implied but not actually present in the original Greek. It literally reads,

> Followers of me become ye, as I also am of Christ.
>
> *YLT*

mimetes—to imitate or follow. The word is always used in a positive sense in the New Testament.

Rather than following Paul's pattern of being an example to others, Christians today are quick to offer excuses such as, "No one's perfect."

That is undoubtedly true and shouldn't need to be stated. If someone believed they were perfect, they would be guilty of the sin of pride, thereby making them imperfect. Regardless of our current imperfection, the Bible still calls us to be holy.

> but as He who called you is holy, you also be holy in all your conduct, because it is written, "Be holy, for I am holy."
>
> *1 Peter 1:15,16*

Is your life the kind others should imitate? If not, don't make excuses for yourself. Strive to be a godly person worthy of imitation. These verses also use the word "mimetes" or the related word "mimeomai."

> For though you might have ten thousand instructors in Christ, yet you do not have many fathers; for in Christ Jesus I have begotten you through the gospel. Therefore I urge you, imitate [mimetes] me.
>
> *1 Corinthians 4:15,16*

> Therefore be imitators [mimetes] of God as dear children.
>
> *Ephesians 5:1*

And you became followers [mimetes] of us and of the Lord, having received the word in much affliction, with joy of the Holy Spirit,

1 Thessalonians 1:6

For you yourselves know how you ought to follow [mimeomai] us, for we were not disorderly among you; … not because we do not have authority, but to make ourselves an example of how you should follow [mimeomai] us.

2 Thessalonians 3:7,9

And we desire that each one of you show the same diligence to the full assurance of hope until the end, that you do not become sluggish, but imitate [mimetes] those who through faith and patience inherit the promises.

Hebrews 6:11,12

Beloved, do not imitate [mimeomai] what is evil, but what is good. He who does good is of God, but he who does evil has not seen God.

3 John 1:11

A helpful exercise is to make a drawing of who you are imitating and who may look to you as an example. Stick figures will work if you're not artistic. If you're young, don't think you aren't an example. Except for the extremely young, everyone has someone watching them.

- In your drawing, place God/Jesus at the top as the One we all should imitate.
- Place yourself in the center.
- Between you and God, put those who are in a position of authority over you—parents, grandparents, pastor, older godly siblings, friends, or others.
- Below you, draw anyone who is younger or younger in their faith and knowledge of God. These are the people who are watching you and forming ideas of what it means to live a godly life.
- To the sides, draw your peers. Although they are at roughly the same phase in life as you, you can still be a positive influence on them.

I had my girls memorize the following poem by an anonymous author when they were young. It was originally written as "brother," so you can switch back to that if it's more applicable for you.

The only line I have a slight quibble with is, "The bad in me she must not see."

That makes it sound as if you should do your bad things in secret to hide them rather than not doing them at all! The poem doesn't apply just to older brothers or sisters. It applies to everyone, parents especially. Except for infants, we all have someone observing us and potentially imitating our behavior.

A Little Sister Follows Me

A careful girl I want to be
A little sister follows me.
I do not dare to go astray
For fear she'll go the selfsame way.

I cannot once escape her eyes;
Whate'er she sees me do, she tries;

Like me she says she's going to be—
That little sister following me.

She thinks that I am good and fine
Believes in every word of mine.
The bad in me she must not see—
That little sister following me.

I must remember as I go,
Through summer's sun and winter's snow
I'm building for the years to be
That little sister following me.

36

FOLLOW OUR LEADER

Imitating and following are closely related behaviors. Imitating may be the stronger word, but following is important, as well. In my book, *Follow Our Leader*, the grandmother reminds the kids that "Who you follow determines where you will go."

In the horse world, there is a related practice called ponying. Despite the name, this doesn't involve just ponies. In fact, it's used more often with horses. It involves a person on horseback leading a second horse. Ponying allows two horses to be exercised at once, but it's also used for training younger or less experienced horses. Thoroughbred racehorses are ponied to and from the track to help keep them calm.

Ponying isn't something just anyone can do. The rider needs to be experienced. He will need to handle the reins to control the horse he's riding (the pony horse) while holding the lead rope attached to the horse being led (the ponied horse). A western saddle is often used. The rider may wrap the lead rope of the ponied horse once around the horn, although it should not be tied.

A strong, reliable animal with an unflappable, spook-free disposition is used as the pony horse, since the horse being led may act up. The rider has to guide the pony horse with a single hand on the reins, so the animal should neck rein well. Geldings are most often used for ponying as they tend to be more even-tempered than mares.

The ponied horse should have been taught ground manners. He needs to understand what it means to be led, to have a rope touch him all over, and to be comfortable being close to another horse. The ponied horse is positioned close to the ridden horse's right side with his nose between the rider's leg and the pony horse's head. If he gets too far ahead or behind, the rider will have less control over him.

If you don't know what you're doing, ponying can be dangerous. With two horses so close together, it's easy to imagine all the things that might go wrong—the ponied horse may shy, rear, try to bolt, or kick or bite the pony horse or rider. The lead rope may become wrapped around his head, under his tail, or around a rider. That's why you don't tie the lead to the saddle horn. You don't want to be connected to a panic-stricken animal. In a worst-case scenario, it's better to let the ponied horse go rather than to risk injury to the horses or riders.

When it works as intended, the pony horse serves as a good example and role model for the ponied horse. The less experienced or more nervous horse gains confidence from the calm behavior of the other horse. This allows him to be introduced to new experiences or obstacles he might find frightening if he had to face them alone.

A similar technique is used when training harness horses. A horse who has completed the preliminary training and is ready to be driven is paired in harness with an experienced horse. Anna Sewell describes Black Beauty's harness training in chapter three of her book.

> And now having got so far, my master went on to break me to harness; there were more new things to wear. First, a stiff heavy collar just on my neck, and a bridle with great side-pieces against my eyes called blinkers, and blinkers indeed they were, for I could not see on either side, but only straight in front of me; next, there was a small saddle with a nasty stiff strap that went right under my tail; that was the crupper. I hated the crupper; to have my long tail doubled up and poked through that strap was almost as bad as the bit. I never felt more like kicking, but of course I could not kick such a good master…

> My master often drove me in double harness with my mother, because she was steady and could teach me how to go better than a strange horse. She told me the better I behaved the better I should be treated, and that it was wisest always to do my best to please my master;

A young horse who spooks could bolt and run off with a carriage or wagon. But it would be more difficult or impossible to pull another horse along with him. He may try to take off, but the weight of the other horse resisting him and the fact that the more established horse isn't bothered will calm the younger one.

In the Bible, we're told to imitate Christ or godly people in our lives. That Greek word is "mimetes"—to imitate or follow.

There are other words that mean to follow. One of them is "akolouthos" meaning a follower or companion, one going in the same way. "Akolouthos" is used over seventy times in the Gospels in the sense of following Christ. When Jesus called Peter and Andrew, Matthew 4:20 says, "They immediately left their nets. and followed Him."

However, not everyone who followed Christ was a genuine believer.

> Great multitudes followed Him—from Galilee, and from Decapolis, Jerusalem, Judea, and beyond the Jordan.
>
> *Matthew 4:25*

The multitudes followed Jesus in a physical sense, but they had no desire to imitate Him and did not continue with Him when things became difficult.

> From that time many of His disciples went back and walked with Him no more.
>
> *John 6:66*

As believers, we are called to follow Christ in a more serious way than those who simply followed Him physically in order to be healed from sickness or to receive free food.

When He had called the people to Himself, with His disciples also, He said to them, Whoever desires to come after Me, let him deny himself, and take up his cross, and follow Me.

Mark 8:34

According to Warren Wiersbe, "We deny self when we surrender ourselves to Christ and determine to obey His will."

True believers will not follow Jesus only when it's easy. We'll follow Him wherever it takes us in life, doing our best to be obedient to His will.

As the horse who is ponied or driven in double harness discovers, it's easier to follow the example of his more steady partner than to fight and try to go his own way.

37

MEEKNESS

What do you think of when you hear the word "meek"? Today, if you called someone meek, they might not consider it a compliment. Many believe that to be meek means you are weak or a coward. Word meanings change over time and across cultures. The Greek word translated "meek" is "praus." Here's one definition I found:

> Biblical meekness is not weakness. It refers to exercising God's strength under His control, demonstrating power without undue harshness.

It's believed this concept of "strength under control" goes back to the armies of ancient Greece. The Greeks would locate wild horses and bring them in for training. After working with the animals, they decided what each was best suited for. The horses were then separated into categories for further training—whether farm work, pulling heavy loads, racing, or general transportation. They selected the strongest and bravest for use as war horses. A war horse had to be fearless in the chaos of battle. He had to remain focused so he could respond to the slightest command of his rider.

When the war horse's training was complete, they described him as praus—meek. He was no longer wild, rebellious, and unmanageable, but could be trusted to obey his master instantly in the heat of battle. His training hadn't made the horse weak; he still possessed the same power and strength. But that strength was now under control and could be used for his master's purposes.

For hundreds of years, Lipizzan horses were trained to perform special maneuvers called the "airs above the ground." These were designed so that, in battle, a horse could protect his rider from the enemy. The capriole is one such maneuver. In this move, the horse leaps up, and while still in the air, kicks his hind legs back. Lipizzans are no longer used in wars, but the difficult maneuvers they perform under the control of their rider are a good example of praus.

Today, we don't use the word "praus" to describe a well-trained horse, however, we use a similar word—"gentle". Rather than "breaking" horses, it's preferable to gentle them. The idea is the same as that of the ancient Greeks. A trainer's goal is to bring the power of the horse under control, so he will be useful for our purposes.

The average horse weighs a thousand pounds and is much stronger than any man. If they chose to, horses would never have to submit to training. Surprisingly, there aren't many that remain rebellious. Those few untamable horses are of no use to people and can often be dangerous.

Another way of saying "strength under control" is that we "harness" the strength and power of the horse.

In 2017, I bought a pony, Toby, who was harness trained by the Amish. Toby, although only 10.3 hands or 43" tall, is quite strong. His Amish trainer did a wonderful job training him to pull a cart, but he still needs more work to become praus.

Throughout the New Testament, Jesus gave visual illustrations of lessons for His disciples. Look at that bush, tree, door, sheep, etc. I remember scriptural principles much better when I connect them with an object or story. Each time I get Toby's harness out to hook him to his cart, I'm reminded of this concept of praus—harnessing power.

In Matthew 5:5, Jesus said, "Blessed are the meek, For they shall inherit the earth."

Jesus wasn't talking about meek horses; He meant us. He didn't want us to be weak, wimpy doormats that people walk all over. In a sense, we're like those war horses, soldiers in God's army. Praus doesn't mean submission to everyone. A war horse would be of no use in battle if he obeyed the commands of the enemy. The same applies to us.

Meekness means we submit to our Master. God asks us to use our strength for His purposes. When we're meek, we haven't lost our strength; we've agreed to let God control it.

Jesus was the ultimate example of meekness. God, the Creator of the universe, became man and came to Earth, allowing people to abuse and crucify Him. Jesus had the power to destroy everyone who opposed Him, but He didn't use it. Instead, He chose to be obedient to His Father's plan for our salvation.

> Take my yoke upon you, and learn of me; for I am meek and lowly in heart: and ye shall find rest unto your souls.
>
> *Matthew 11:29 KJV*

> Tell the daughter of Zion, 'Behold, your King is coming to you, lowly (meek), and sitting on a donkey, a colt, the foal of a donkey.'
>
> *Matthew 21:5 NKJV*

38

TRAIN UP A CHILD

A few of the horses we owned over the years had been abused by previous owners. I blamed some of their less-than-desirable behaviors on the poor treatment they received early in life. One of those was a Racking Horse mare, Satin, who was in foal when we purchased her.

> Train up a child in the way he should go: and when he is old, he will not depart from it.
>
> *Proverbs 22:6*

I thought about that principle from Proverbs and resolved to "train up" Satin's foal in the way he or she should go. Fortunately, I was there when Satin gave birth to her filly—both for the foal's safety and the advantage of being able to handle her as early as possible.

Using a process called imprinting, I began to train Kezzie from the moment she was born. When the foal was just a few days old, one of my daughters would lead Satin, while I led Kezzie behind them. We groomed and handled the foal frequently. She became accustomed to being touched all over and learned to stand quietly while her feet were picked up. We also put a lot of things on and around Kezzie: shirts, blankets, and ropes to prepare her for carrying a saddle and rider when she was older.

Kezzie's training continued daily throughout her early years. She developed a wonderful, calm temperament. When she was old enough to ride, Kezzie readily accepted a saddle and rider—never once rearing, bucking, or bolting. There's no way to tell for certain whether that was because of her early handling or whether Kezzie was simply born with an easy-going personality. But early, consistent training is important for horses just as it is for children.

I missed out on that myself, since I didn't become a Christian until I was almost thirty. At that time, I was nearly biblically illiterate. When my first daughter was young, she attended a Christian preschool a few mornings each week. She listened to Bible stories and memorized verses. When I picked her up from preschool, she would ask me questions about the Bible—questions I didn't always have answers for.

I joined a Bible study and began devouring commentaries so I could learn the answers my daughter—and I—both needed. By daily seeking God's wisdom and guidance, He helped me grow spiritually, enabling me to "train up my children in the way they should go."

Proverbs 22:6 is a maxim or principle not a guarantee. Even a properly raised child who is taught God's word and His ways can choose to rebel. That rebellion isn't so much against the parents—it's against God. Even Adam and Eve had a rebellious son, Cain, who killed his brother, Abel.

Training a horse may sound like something only professional trainers can do. But every time you do anything with your horse, you're training him—to behave better or worse. For example, if you allow him to rub his head against you, you're teaching him he doesn't need to maintain a proper distance out of respect for you. Rubbing against you might seem like affection, but horses don't operate the way humans do. A horse lower in the pecking order of his "herd" would never walk up and rub his head on a horse higher in rank than himself.

Just as horses are learning every day, so are we. Everything that enters our mind through various channels impacts and shapes our thoughts, character, and behavior. Be careful who your friends are and what you listen to, watch, or read.

> These words I am commanding you today are to be upon your hearts. And you shall teach them diligently to your children and speak of them when you sit at home and when you walk along the road, when you lie down and when you get up.
>
> *Deuteronomy 6:6*

Many home educators could point to this verse as their motivation for educating their children at home. Those words were definitely an inspiration to me. God's desire is for us to transmit our faith and knowledge of Him to our children. We can't rely on Sunday schools, church sermons, or youth groups to do that. God has entrusted us with that responsibility. And we can't do it unless we first have God's word in our own hearts.

God doesn't say we are to have His word in our minds. We should do that, of course, but it can't stop there. It has to be in our hearts. If it's only knowledge rattling around in our heads, our children will sense that it doesn't mean much to us. If it's in our hearts, it will be obvious in our attitudes, words, and behavior.

Just as I worked frequently with Kezzie, with a clear purpose and goal in mind, Deuteronomy 6:6 calls parents to teach their children diligently. That doesn't mean whenever we feel like it or whenever it's convenient. There's nothing more important we can teach our children than God's word, His character, and how much He loves them.

If you're young or don't have children, you can still share your faith with whomever happens to be in your life. Having gotten a late start, I put myself through a crash course to catch up, spending about fifteen years obsessively reading commentaries and doing in-depth Bible studies. I was homeschooling my girls during those years, so fortunately I had time to study. It wasn't a chore; I loved it! I just wish I'd known the Bible when I was younger.

I haven't stopped studying the Bible, however I do allow myself to read (or write) an occasional fiction book now.

39

GOD IS LOVE

God is love. A loving God would never send anyone to Hell.

God is angry, waiting to catch us doing something wrong so He can punish us.

I often hear opinions that reflect these two extreme views of God—an imaginary god who either won't punish anyone or one who delights in punishing everyone.

People holding either of these views miss the true God. Usually it's because they don't know scripture well. They've picked up these ideas based on someone's faulty teaching or from a few verses rather than by reading the whole Bible to get the complete picture.

The reality is He is a God of love, but He is also a just God who abhors evil. His justice requires that He punish those who do not repent, come to Christ, and accept the payment Jesus made for our sins on the cross. If someone ends up in Hell, it's not because God delights in sending people there. In fact, He wants us all to come to repentance.

> The Lord does not delay [as though He were unable to act] and is not slow about His promise, as some count slowness, but is [extraordinarily] patient toward you, not wishing for any to perish but for all to come to repentance.
>
> *2 Peter 3:9 AMP*

People often quote John 3:16 about God loving the world and sending His son to give us eternal life, but if you continue reading, verse 18 states:

> Whoever believes in Him is not condemned, but whoever does not believe has already been condemned, because he has not believed in the name of God's one and only Son.

God gave us one way to heaven, through His son, Jesus.

> I am the way and the truth and the life. No one comes to the Father except through Me.
>
> *John 14:6*

The reality that some people refuse to accept God's free offer and therefore end up in Hell, doesn't make God hateful or mean, it shows that sinners are prideful and stubborn—lost people who love their sin more than they love God. The idea that a loving God would never send anyone to Hell proves that people today don't understand the definition of love.

> Whoever does not love does not know God, because God is love.
>
> *1 John 4:8*

It's interesting that the verse doesn't say God is a loving God. It says that He IS love. Love is the essence of His very being. We can't apply our man-made definition of love to God. God defines love for us through His character.

The word for "love" in that verse is the Greek "agape." There are several types of love mentioned in the Bible, but agape refers to an unselfish, intentional love that desires the greatest good for others. Agape love isn't based on feelings or emotions—at least not primarily. It's a love demonstrated by deliberately chosen actions with no expectation of anything in return.

When Jesus told us to love God with all we are, He used that same Greek word, "agape."

> Love the Lord your God with all your heart and with all your soul and with all your mind and with all your strength.
>
> *Mark 12:30*

First Corinthians 13 provides the most complete description of what love looks like in practice. It's an active love.

> Love is patient, love is kind. It does not envy, it does not boast, it is not proud. It is not rude, it is not self-seeking, it is not easily angered, it keeps no account of wrongs. Love takes no pleasure in evil, but rejoices in the truth. It bears all things, believes all things, hopes all things, endures all things. Love never fails.
>
> *1 Corinthians 13:4-8*

Most non-Christians today seem to believe love means God overlooks and tolerates any type of sinful behavior. By definition, if God loves us, He cannot overlook our sin. Sin is harmful, not only to us but to those around us. For God to overlook sin would not be loving, anymore than it is loving for a parent not to correct misbehavior in their children. Agape love wants the best for the object of its love, and that may require discipline.

Sometimes the actions of agape love may seem harsh, but ultimately they are the most loving of all. I can't think of anything more loving than helping a lost sinner find his way off the broad road leading to destruction and onto the narrow path that leads to life.

One of my pet peeves in horse books, particularly those written for children, is also based on a misunderstanding of love. Too often in these books, a young girl loves her horse in a sentimental way, and believes the horse returns her love in the same manner. All that needs to happen to transform an unruly, dangerous horse into a safe, obedient one is for the horse to feel the love his new owner has for him.

I get emotionally attached to my horses and certainly take actions that look out for their good—feeding, cleaning, training, medical interventions, etc. In that sense, I love my horses. But I am under no illusion my horses love me in the same way. Sure, they whinny when they see me coming. However, the reality is they would learn to whinny for anyone who consistently fed them. If sold to another kind owner, it wouldn't be long before they felt just as comfortable in their new home.

Horses don't operate on the same emotions as people. It's a mistake for a horse owner to think they do. Being tolerant of a horse's improper behavior so he will "like us" can put us in dangerous situations.

As I mentioned previously, some think a horse is showing affection when he rubs his head against his handler's shoulder. Trust me; it's not a sign of love. The horse is merely itchy and views his handler as a convenient substitute for a fence post. Rather than love, his rubbing is a sign of disrespect. In the interest of safety, we should teach horses to respect our space. If you've ever been stepped on by a horse, no further explanation is needed.

I'm not saying horses don't bond with people—some do, but their connections aren't based on our sentimental conceptions of love. Horses work on a dynamic of trust and respect. If you watch horses in a group, there will be a clear leader, the one at the top of the pecking order. The horse at the bottom of the pack would never casually approach the lead horse to scratch against her. The lower horse is always careful to keep a respectful distance. That respect even contains an element of fear, much as the Bible reminds us to fear God.

> The fear of the LORD is the beginning of wisdom; all who follow His precepts gain rich understanding.
>
> *Psalm 111:10*

Abused or neglected horses benefit from a kind owner's loving care. However, what they need, rather than a mushy sort of love, is to know they can trust the new owner. Over time, kind, consistent care will show the horse he is in different hands, and he will no longer be abused.

Mistreated horses have had to protect themselves against cruel people. Anyone who wants to gain an abused horse's trust and respect must gradually earn it. As long as the horse considers himself the leader in that relationship, the actions he takes will be based on self-preservation.

If he believes he needs to escape danger, whether real or imaginary, and you happen to be in the way, he may run over you. Until he trusts you, his first thought will always be to look out for number one!

The horse will never mistake a human for a fellow equine, part of his "herd." The goal is for him to learn to trust and respect us in a new horse-human relationship and to accept our leadership.

A misconception of love in horse relationships may never cause you any problems, but it is a serious problem, with potentially eternal consequences, to misunderstand God's love.

God's love doesn't mean a tolerance or acceptance of continual, willful, sinful behavior as many today seem to believe.

This is why horses need to respect our space! Imagine if this were a horse rather than a pony.

40

PRESSURE AND RELEASE

Understanding the concept of pressure and release can make training a horse easier. This technique doesn't apply just to horses. The method works with dogs and other animals, even with people. It's technically known as negative reinforcement. That sounds bad, but there doesn't have to be anything harsh or mean about the process.

Pressure is applied in order to produce a desired behavior. As soon as the behavior is exhibited, the pressure is released. Pressure doesn't only mean pressing somewhere on the horse; it can be anything the horse finds unpleasant or makes him uncomfortable.

A simple example is training a horse to lead. After attaching a lead rope to his halter, you step forward. Assuming he stands still and doesn't walk with you, you pull on the rope to apply a little pressure. The instant he steps forward, you put slack in the rope, releasing the pressure on his head.

Timing the release is crucial and the hardest for those new to this concept to master. The more consistent you are in releasing the pressure at the proper time, the faster the horse will learn. When you first begin training, reward the horse for even a slight approximation of the desired behavior.

For example, when teaching a horse to lead, if he only moves one leg forward, consider that a correct response. Give him a brief break, then ask for forward movement again, gradually building up the distance.

Do not release when he is misbehaving. The release tells the horse that what he did at the moment of release was correct. If you're trying to teach a horse to lead, but you release pressure on the rope when he is

moving backwards or sideways, you've rewarded him for disobeying, and he will repeat that incorrect behavior. The concept is the same whether from the saddle or on the ground. When riding, if you want the horse to stop, apply pressure by pulling back gently with both reins. As soon as he stops, release the pressure on his mouth.

The same applies for turning (using direct, two-handed reining). Apply pressure on the right rein to turn right. When the horse starts in that direction, release the pressure. Releasing the pressure at the proper time on a turn seems difficult for beginning riders to grasp. Keeping the pressure on too long results in the horse turning around in a circle rather than going the direction the rider intended.

Even if you've never thought about pressure and release before, you should see other ways it's used when riding. Want the horse to go forward? Squeeze both legs into his sides. When he moves, stop squeezing. Want him to back up? Use backward pressure on the lead or the reins—always remembering to release pressure when the horse responds correctly.

An experienced rider will use the least amount of pressure required to achieve the desired response, always beginning with very light pressure. Think of a mother who wants her child to clean his room. She starts by asking him to do so. If the child doesn't obey, she increases the pressure. What that increased pressure looks like will depend on her parenting style. Maybe the first increase will be a raised voice. Then if the child still doesn't comply, a loss of privileges.

With horses, non-compliance means you gradually increase the physical pressure until the horse responds. Remember, initially, accept any attempt by the horse to comply with your request. In most cases, he's not being rebellious. He's probably uncertain about what you want him to do. Don't expect him to do something perfectly the first time or maybe not the first fifty times!

Horses learn from the release—not from the pressure. Not removing pressure when the horse is complying will confuse and frustrate him, leading to more inappropriate behavior.

For example, if a rider keeps a tight grip on the reins, constantly pulling on a horse's mouth that pressure no longer means stop. (see photo on the right) The horse may respond violently by rearing or trying to run off to escape the pain. A more submissive horse will somehow learn to endure the pain caused by the harsh pressure from the bit. If the horse is always ridden this way, he will become "hard-mouthed."

This hardness may be physical—toughened gums or deadened nerves, but it's also a psychological hardness.

The horse expects to be pulled on constantly, so it no longer means anything to him. Hard-mouthed horses are difficult to steer, slow, and stop.

What can we learn from this pressure-release training technique that applies to our own lives?

People also respond to pressure. Unlike with horses, the pressure we feel sometimes comes from within. Each of us has been created with a conscience (Greek syneídēsis). This is a God-given capacity planted within us that tells us what is right and wrong. Our conscience prompts us to do what is right or morally good and tries to keep us from doing what is bad or morally wrong.

We don't experience these promptings as external pressure like that used when training a horse, but it is pressure just the same. If you've ever felt that inner voice whispering that you should—or shouldn't—do something, you know the mental and emotional pressure our conscience exerts on us is very real.

To keep our conscience clear and active, we should respond to it at the slightest prompting—like the horse trained to respond to light signals, ones imperceptible to a bystander.

When we don't respond but ignore our conscience, we harden ourselves. We become like that hard-mouthed horse, no longer sensitive to what our conscience is trying to tell us. The Bible calls this a seared conscience.

In 1 Timothy 4:2, false teachers are described as having such a conscience.

> influenced by the hypocrisy of liars, whose consciences are seared with a hot iron.

Just as a horse can pick up bad habits if pressure is released incorrectly, the same is true for people. We should find our release from inner conflict through obedience to God rather than from inappropriate means. The best example that comes to mind is people using drugs or alcohol to numb feelings they don't know how, or don't want, to deal with.

It's important to be sensitive to the promptings of our conscience and respond to them in a timely manner. You need to have a good understanding of the Bible, so you aren't misled into taking actions or making decisions contrary to scripture. God will never ask us to do something, through our conscience or otherwise, that goes against His word. The more we love God and His word, the more sensitive we'll be to His promptings through our conscience.

According to the wisdom of this world, feelings of guilt or shame are a bad thing. The world encourages us to believe we are inherently good, and we should do whatever makes us happy. That advice goes against biblical teaching. Sometimes, we have to feel uncomfortable or even miserable before we're willing to make the necessary changes in our lives to be obedient to God. But when we make the right choice, we feel relief. The release that is so crucial in horse training is important in our lives as well.

> And I will give you a new heart—I will give you new and right desires—and put a new spirit within you. I will take out your stony hearts of sin and give you new hearts of love. And I will put my Spirit within you so that you will obey my laws and do whatever I command.
>
> *Ezekiel 36:26,27 TLB*

41

SPURS

When I first became a Christian, I used the NIV translation. One verse that jumped out at me was Hebrews 10:24. Here it is in a variety of Bible versions.

And let us consider how we may **spur** one another on toward love and good deeds, NIV

Let us think of ways to motivate one another to acts of love and good works. NLT

And let us consider how to stir up one another to love and good works, ESV

And let us consider one another to provoke unto love and to good works: KJV

and let's consider how to encourage one another in love and good deeds, NASB

and let us consider how to stimulate one another to love and good deeds, NASB 1995

And let us be concerned about one another in order to promote love and good works, HCSB

We must consider how to rouse one another to love and good works. NAB

You can probably see why the verse in the NIV stood out to me. That phrase "spur one another on" caught my attention. The Greek word is "paroxysmos," defined as a provocation which jabs or cuts someone so they must respond.

While the purpose of spurs is not to cut a horse, they are used to get a response from him.

When riding or training a horse, the rider communicates with him through the use of what are called aids. Natural aids are the rider's seat, legs, hands, and voice. Artificial aids include things that are not part of the rider's body, such as a whip and spurs.

Spurs have a bad reputation because they can be used cruelly. Anna Sewell describes this in the following excerpt from *Black Beauty*. In this scene, Ginger describes the cruel "breaking in" she received as a young horse by a man named Samson.

> I felt my whole spirit set against him, and I began to kick, and plunge, and rear as I had never done before, and we had a regular fight; for a long time he stuck to the saddle and punished me cruelly with his whip and spurs, but my blood was thoroughly up, and I cared for nothing he could do if only I could get him off. At last after a terrible struggle I threw him off backward. I heard him fall heavily on the turf, and without looking behind me, I galloped off to the other end of the field; there I turned round and saw my persecutor slowly rising from the ground and going into the stable. I stood under an oak tree and watched, but no one came to catch me. The time went on, and the sun was very hot; the flies swarmed round me and settled on my bleeding flanks where the spurs had dug in.

Note Sewell's name for this character—Samson. Sewell wove many scriptural themes into her story. Her Samson and the Samson in the Bible shared the characteristic of unusual strength. But force isn't a good way to train a horse.

A good horseman will not use spurs in a harsh manner. Properly used, spurs allow a rider to give a subtle and precise cue or signal. Think of the difference in pressure you feel when someone pokes your side with a finger versus pressing with the palm of a hand. The small tip of a spur allows the rider to apply it in a more precise location than is possible with the rider's leg or foot, to encourage movement, whether forward, backward, or sideways.

Spurs should be applied lightly. After all, a horse that can feel a fly land on him is capable of feeling extremely light pressure from a spur.

A horse has to learn what the application of the spur in different locations means. It's not something he'll automatically know. Spurs should only be used by competent riders who understand their proper use. A beginning rider may not be able to control his leg movement well enough to keep from jabbing the horse unintentionally.

Trainer Stacy Westfall calls spurs a motivator. "A motivator is something that encourages your horse to make a change in its behavior."

That sounds a lot like Hebrews 10:24.

> And let us consider how to spur one another on to love and good deeds.

The next verse in Hebrews reminds us not to be solitary Christians. It's important that we meet together periodically.

> Let us not neglect meeting together, as some have made a habit, but let us encourage one another, and all the more as you see the Day approaching.
>
> *Hebrews 10:25*

After all, if we don't meet with other believers, we can't apply our spiritual spurs. As Christians, we face enough opposition from the world. We need to support and encourage each other to live the kind of lives God has called us to—spurring, motivating, stirring up, provoking, encouraging, stimulating, promoting, and rousing each other to love and good works!

42

PHOBIAS

What is the most frequent command in the Bible? To love God? Love your neighbor? Don't lie? Actually, it's none of those. The most frequent command in the Bible is not to fear.

The phrases, "do not be afraid" and "fear not" occur over 200 times in the Berean Study Bible.

Why did God feel it was important to tell us that so often?

Fear is a lack of faith. If we fully trusted God, we wouldn't fear. Doubt and fear creep in when faith wavers.

Have you ever heard the word, "hydrophobia"? It's another name for the disease, rabies. Technically, the word means "an abnormal fear of water."

Our horses develop an abnormal fear when they reach a certain watery point on a metro park trail. But it's not the water they're afraid of—it's the bridge.

The bridge ramps up and down at each end. The flooring is constructed from thick wooden timbers that make loud, clip-clopping sounds as the horses walk on them. Metal framework on both sides extends up higher than their heads. It's the longest bridge we cross. And, to top it off, it's a dead-end trail. Not long after crossing the bridge, the trail ends. At that point, there's no other option than to turn around and return along the same path, to cross the bridge a second time.

I remember one ride when the horses acted as if not one of them had ever seen such a thing as a bridge before. That was hard to figure, since they'd crossed that bridge at least half a dozen times on previous rides. When we finally coaxed them to step onto the big, scary thing, my daughter's horse, Kody, startled at some object visible only to him and jumped sideways. His hooves came down hard on the timbers, making a louder than usual clomp that frightened them all even more. With lots of encouragement, we got the horses moving again and made it across. Soon, we hit the end of the trail, turned around, and found ourselves back at the bridge.

You'd think, since they'd just crossed that bridge fifteen minutes earlier, they wouldn't have been bothered by it. No. They still acted like silly bridgaphobics. Using my best horsey-reasoning voice, I tried to explain to the silly equines that it was safe and there was nothing to be afraid of. With great fear and trepidation, they finally made it across the terrifying bridge again.

How can you tell when a horse is afraid?

- They will hold their head up very high with their eyes open wide and ears back (check out my bridge photo for some scared horses!).
- They may snort or give a high-pitched whinny.
- If you're riding them, you can feel or sense an overall tightness in their muscles.
- They won't want to stand still, but will prance, try to take off, or whirl around.

When afraid, horses may run, kick, bite, or strike with their front feet. If you're riding them and trying to hold them back to keep them from running, they may rear or buck to get free.

Although my Foxtrotter mare, Ginger, was used extensively as a trail horse, she had an intense fear of a certain type of weed we encountered occasionally on rides. I'm not sure what the plant was. It grew low to the ground and had huge, wide leaves. Ginger would stop at a safe distance, stare, and snort at the evil weed. One of the girls would have to go around us and take the lead to get Ginger past the scary green monsters.

Sometimes, I marvel at the things horses find to be afraid of. Why don't they just trust us?

God must feel the same way as He watches me battle my own fears. He wants me to trust Him, but too often my fears get the best of me. The Bible tells us not to fear, because God is with us.

> Do not fear, for I am with you; do not be afraid, for I am your God. I will strengthen you; I will surely help you; I will uphold you with My right hand of righteousness.
>
> *Isaiah 41:10*

It may seem contradictory at first, but the one thing we are told to fear in the Bible is God. Some are quick to redefine the fear of God simply as reverence for Him. Reverence is included in the definition of the word, but so is "a terrifying fear." I believe the terror part is primarily intended for unbelievers. Dread or terror of God's wrath and judgment is designed to draw unbelievers to Him. That kind of fear is the beginning of wisdom—a first step toward God.

> The fear [yira] of the LORD is the beginning of wisdom, and knowledge of the Holy One is understanding.
>
> *Proverbs 9:10*

yira—terror, fear (of God), respect, reverence, piety

Too often, our fear of man, what other people think of us, is greater than our fear of God. Anything man can do to us is temporary. We need to keep an eternal perspective. God is the one who controls our eternal destiny.

> Do not be afraid [phobeo] of those who kill the body but cannot kill the soul. Instead, fear [phobeo] the One who can destroy both soul and body in hell.
>
> *Matthew 10:28*

phobeo—to put to flight by terrifying, to scare away, to be seized with alarm, to reverence

> Fear [phobeo] God and give Him glory, because the hour of His judgment has come. Worship the One who made the heavens and the earth and the sea and the springs of waters.
>
> *Revelation 14:7*

In this verse from Revelation, God gives people another chance to switch their fear and worship, from Satan and the Antichrist, to Himself.

As believers, we grow in our knowledge of God and our love for Him. We will always have a reverential fear of God but not a terrifying one. We will fear displeasing Him, not out of a dread of His wrath, but because we don't want to disappoint Him.

> There is no fear [phobos] in love, but perfect love drives out fear [phobos], because fear [phobos] involves punishment. The one who fears [phobeo] has not been perfected in love.
>
> *1 John 4:18*

Without the assurance of salvation, people live in fear of death and judgment. "Thanatophobia" is an intense fear of death or dying.

> Now since the children have flesh and blood, He too shared in their humanity, so that by His death He might destroy him who holds the power of death, that is, the devil, and free those who all their lives were held in slavery by their fear [phobos] of death.
>
> *Hebrews 2:14,15*

If we deliberately go on sinning after we have received the knowledge of the truth, no further sacrifice for sins remains, but only a fearful [phoberos] expectation of judgment [krisis] and of raging fire that will consume all adversaries.

Hebrews 10:26,27

phoberos—fear, dread, terror

krisis—divine judgment, sentence, accusation, verdict

The fear of unbelievers will be so great it will cause their hearts to fail, but as believers we don't have to fear judgment.

> Men will faint [apopsucho] from fear [phobos] and anxiety over what is coming upon the earth, for the powers of the heavens will be shaken.
>
> *Luke 21:26*

apopsucho—faint, breathe out life, die

paressia—freedom, openness, especially in speech; boldness, confidence

> In this way, love has been perfected among us, so that we may have confidence [paressia] on the day of judgment;
>
> *1 John 4:17*

When I look back over the years and remember how God has provided for and protected me, I realize most or all of my fears have been groundless. I've been just as safe as my horses were on that bridge.

I'm not sure whether the photo below is real. I don't know how someone could have gotten a photo at that precise moment. But that would be a legitimate phobia—for both horse and rider! Leapingdeeraphobia?

43

DIVING HORSES

Although he abandoned the practice of dentistry, William Frank Carver was known as Doc Carver for the rest of his life. Because of his remarkable shooting skills, he was invited to join Buffalo Bill Cody's Wild West Show. The two strong-willed men found it impossible to work together and parted ways. After leaving, Doc Carver started his own show. In 1894, he added an unusual attraction—diving horses.

According to Carver, a bridge had once collapsed under him, plunging horse and rider into the Platte River in Nebraska. This was the inspiration for Carver's diving horse act. The Great Carver Show was a family operation. Doc's son, Al, trained and cared for the horses. Al also supervised the construction of the tall ramp and diving platform. At the early shows, the horses jumped riderless, then Carver's daughter, Lorena, became the first to ride a horse off the diving platform. Performance dives averaged thirty to forty feet in height.

The human diver, almost always a young woman, climbed the tower first. Then she waited on the platform at the top for her horse to arrive. The horse traveled, unaccompanied, up the steep, wooden ramp, the height of a four-story building. As the horse reached the top, the rider vaulted onto his back and held on to leather straps on either side of his neck. The horse sometimes jumped immediately, so it was important to grab the straps as quickly as possible.

Carver determined the optimal depth for the pool was eleven feet. After the momentum of the dive was broken by the water, the horse needed to touch bottom quickly in order to maintain his balance and keep himself from flipping over. When his hooves touched, the horse gave a powerful push to return to the surface. The rider had to keep her head to the side of the horse's neck. If not, the sudden upward jerk of the horse's head and neck could break her nose, jaw, or cheekbones.

Diving horses were wildly popular with the crowds and soon became the only attraction at Carver's traveling show. When Lorena was injured during a performance, the eighty-four-year-old Carver advertised for a replacement diver. He hired Sonora Webster in 1924.

Sonora began training from a twelve-foot platform on Klatawah, a 1,250-pound sorrel gelding. He was the oldest but the liveliest of Carver's horses. After twenty-one practice dives from the low platform, Sonora expected to move up to practicing at the full height. But, to her surprise, Carver announced that Sonora's first dive from the top would be in front of an audience.

On the day of the performance, Sonora made her way through the crowds, climbed the tall tower, and waited for Klatawah. When Al Carver released the horse, his hooves clomped loudly on the wood surface of the steep ramp. Sonora could feel the tower vibrating. As soon as Klatawah reached the top, she vaulted onto his back and grabbed the harness handles.

But that day, Klatawah was in no hurry to jump. He stopped and stood still. Apparently basking in the attention focused on him, he surveyed the audience and pawed at the edge of the platform. Klatawah's hesitation gave Sonora a few moments to change her mind. She could have dismounted and not gone through with the dive. In the past, other young women had done just that. A sudden change of heart at this point would be understandable, but Sonora sat on the big horse's back and waited.

Finally, the big gelding leaped from the platform. Sonora felt as if she were flying. They entered the water smoothly, and when Klatawah surfaced, Sonora was still aboard. She was so excited that when she dismounted, Sonora forgot to bow as Carver had instructed her to do.

Sonora continued riding the diving horses and eventually married Al Carver. Doc Carver died in 1927, but the Carver Show continued with Al assuming his father's responsibilities. In 1929, the Carvers received their first season-long contract at the Atlantic City Steel Pier in New Jersey. Over the years, the diving horses who performed at Atlantic City included: Dimah, Duchess of Lightning, Emir, Gamal, Gordonel, John the Baptist, Judas, Junior, Klatawah, Lorga, Powderface, Pure as Snow, Red Lips, Shiloh, and Silver King.

During one of Sonora's dives on Red Lips in July 1931, the horse came off the platform in a nosedive. He sailed straight down rather than at an angle. Sonora feared that leaning forward as she usually did would flip the horse over—on top of her. She leaned back, trying to help the gelding regain his balance. Rather than hitting the water with the top of her head, Sonora landed face first with her eyes open. Other than her eyes stinging, she seemed alright. But later, Sonora's vision grew cloudy. She refused to go to the hospital and dove for two more days.

The diving injury had resulted in detached retinas, worsened by Sonora's decision to continue diving. Doctors operated, hoping to save her sight, but the surgery didn't help. At the age of twenty-seven, Sonora realized she would never see again. Alone in the darkness one night at the hospital, she felt a powerful presence of God surrounding her.

> Then one day as I struggled with my thoughts of a future that must be faced in darkness, a strange thing happened. As I lay there in the hospital, the silence around me seemed to deepen and become amplified. In the heart of this silence, seemingly at its very core, there was a feeling of presence. How else shall I describe it? There are no words. I can only say that I knew as emphatically as we know very few things in life that I was in the presence of God.

> The knowledge wasn't frightening. On the contrary, it was deeply reassuring. It contained peace and majesty and an infinity of comfort.

> Lost for a moment in its vastness, I thought and heard nothing. Then the quiet ebbed away as unobtrusively as it had come and I discovered that in some totally inexplicable manner I had received a blessing. It was as if God had laid His hand on my shoulder and said, "Don't be afraid. You will see."

> It took a while for me to absorb this experience, since it struck at the very bedrock of my existence, but when I attempted an interpretation I concluded that the promise had not meant the restoration of my physical sight. What God was promising was greater mental vision to compensate for the loss of eyesight. …

> With this understanding of God's promise to strengthen me, I prayed for the courage to hold firmly to my resolution, made so long ago, never to become a burden to those around me.

> *A Girl and Five Brave Horses*

Even before leaving the hospital, Sonora began to rely on her other senses, particularly hearing, to compensate for her loss of sight. While she recovered, her younger sister, Arnette, handled the diving performances so the Carver Show could finish out the season.

Over their winter break, Sonora grew restless. She was desperate to feel useful. By spring, she was contemplating diving again. Did it matter that she couldn't see? Sonora discussed the possibility with her husband. Knowing her as well as he did, Al wasn't surprised by her idea, but he insisted they talk to her doctor first.

The doctor didn't seem surprised either. He granted his permission—if Sonora wore a specially fitted helmet. As she waited for the helmet to be constructed, Sonora's biggest concern was whether she could mount the moving horse at the top of the platform before he leaped off.

As it turned out, Sonora never had a chance to practice. The woman who had been diving was called away suddenly. With just a few hours' notice, Sonora would make her first dive since losing her sight. She ascended the ramp as she'd done many times before, this time counting the wooden slats as she climbed.

At the top, she mounted the railing, and waited for the sound of Red Lips coming up after her.

> For a split second I thought I had lost my hearing, and panic seized me. Then I detected hoofs on the ramp and felt their vibration. Thank God! I could hear him, though not as clearly as I had expected. I realized that the foam rubber inside the helmet partially deadened sound. Still, I would be able to hear him better the closer he got, and I tensed on the railing, remembering how fast Red traveled. Then,

when pounding feet and vibration told me he was very close, I held out my hand and felt the tip of an ear flick by my fingers. Immediately I lowered my hand; I had reached too high. I found the side of his neck and felt the coarse hair of his body brush by. The next instant I closed my hand over the neck strap and threw my leg over Red's back. In one swift motion I mounted him and knew I had mounted him perfectly!

A Girl and Five Brave Horses

The gelding pranced a little, then jumped from the platform. Sonora clung to the straps and experienced the familiar sensation of flying, followed by a smooth splash at the bottom.

The audience seemed to be applauding as they had never applauded before. They could not have known and yet seemed to know that something special had happened. Al handed me Red Lips' sugar and I put it between my lips. For some time before I lost my sight we had been training him to take it from me in this fashion so that it appeared he was kissing me. Red leaned over and took it, and the audience clapped harder.

A Girl and Five Brave Horses

That was the first of eleven years' worth of dives Sonora performed after losing her sight. For half of those years, no one in the audience knew she was blind.

> Not all the dives went as smoothly as the first one; I had some close scrapes. Sometimes I became overanxious about mounting the horse and jumped on him the moment my hand touched his body instead of taking time to find the harness. When this happened I landed halfway between his head and withers—a very unhandy place—from which I had to move back quickly to get into proper position before he dived.
>
> *A Girl and Five Brave Horses*

Sonora Webster Carver didn't agree with people who called her brave for diving.

> Actually, true courage is what it takes to make yourself do something you're afraid to do. I was not afraid of riding the horses; on the contrary, I loved it and would not have given it up willingly.

Animal rights activists claimed the Carvers abused the horses in order to make them jump. There was never any evidence of neglect or abuse. In fact, Sonora's sister, Arnette Webster French, stated,

> What impressed me was how Dr. Carver cared for the horses. Wherever we went, the S.P.C.A. was always snooping around, trying to find if we were doing anything that was cruel to animals. They never found anything because those horses lived the life of Riley. In all the years of the act, there was never a horse that was injured.

I'll confess, I would be terrified to ride a diving horse. I'm not crazy about heights, and having almost drowned as a child, I'm not a fan of deep water, either. Fortunately, there are no diving horse acts anymore, so it's not even a possibility. But from the accounts of past divers, once the horses and riders overcame their nervousness about that first jump, many enjoyed it.

> But, the truth was, riding the horse was the most fun you could have and we just loved it so. We didn't want to give it up. Once you were on the horse, there really wasn't much to do but hold on. The horse was in charge.
>
> *Arnette Webster*

There is a fear or concern that involves common sense and self-preservation. That fear keeps us from doing foolish and dangerous things, such as running in front of a speeding car or touching a hot stove. I believe God is fine with that kind of fear and probably approves of it. The fear God doesn't want us to have is one that keeps us from doing what He calls us to do.

> Have I not commanded you to be strong and courageous? Do not be afraid; do not be discouraged, for the LORD your God is with you wherever you go.
>
> *Joshua 1:9*

I can do all things through Christ who gives me strength.

> *Philippians 4:13*

Here is 2 Timothy 1:7 in several translations, showing the type of fear God does not want us to have.

> For God has not given us a spirit of fear [deilia], but of power, love, and self-control.
>
> For God has not given us a spirit of cowardice, but of power, and of love, and of self-control. BLB
>
> For the Spirit God gave us does not make us timid, but gives us power, love and self-discipline. NIV

deilia—timidity, fearfulness, cowardice

It seems one of the most frightening things for Christians to do today is to witness about their faith to unbelievers. Although the New Testament is full of examples of Jesus and the disciples sharing the gospel, today many are reluctant to do so. It's as if the Good News isn't good, but rather bad news or nasty medicine.

Charles Spurgeon had some strong words about an unwillingness to share our faith.

> Have you no wish for others to be saved? Then you are not saved yourself, be sure of that.
>
> The saving of souls, if a man has once gained love to perishing sinners and his blessed Master, will be an all-absorbing passion to him. It will so carry him away, that he will almost forget himself in the saving of others. He will be like the brave fireman, who cares not for the scorch or the heat, so that he may rescue the poor creature on whom true humanity has set its heart. If sinners will be damned, at least let them leap to hell over our bodies. And if they will perish, let them perish with our arms about their knees, imploring them to stay. If hell must be filled, at least let it be filled in the teeth of our exertions, and let not one go there unwarned and unprayed for.

As believers, we should take the plunge and begin witnessing more. With the increasing darkness of this world, there is a greater need for our light to shine. The horses and divers took their first jump in spite of their fears. Every jump after that became easier.

> Do everything without complaining or arguing, so that you may be blameless and pure, children of God without fault in a crooked and perverse generation, in which you shine as lights in the world as you hold forth the word of life…
>
> *Philippians 2:14-16*

> I am not ashamed of the gospel, because it is the power of God for salvation to everyone who believes, first to the Jew, then to the Greek.
>
> *Romans 1:16*

> How then can they call on the One in whom they have not believed? And how can they believe in the One of whom they have not heard? And how can they hear without someone to preach [kēryssō]? And how can they preach unless they are sent [apostellō]? As it is written: "How beautiful [hōraios] are the feet of those who bring good news!"
>
> *Romans 10:14,15*

The preaching referred to in this verse is not that of our modern pastors before a congregation. We are all called to this type of "preaching"—a simple proclamation of the Good News.

kēryssō—to proclaim openly

apostellō—set apart, send out. This sending isn't specific to the Apostles. The word "apostellō" is used 133 times in the New Testament.

hōraios—blooming, beautiful, flourishing, belonging to the right hour or season

We proclaim Him, admonishing and teaching everyone with all wisdom, so that we may present everyone perfect in Christ.

Colossians 1:28

As God's witnesses, we'll face opposition from some, but that shouldn't stop us. The prophet Jeremiah was called to warn Judah that the Babylonians would soon conquer them. Unhappy with his messages, the Jews, among other things, dropped the prophet into a cistern to die (Jeremiah 38). Because of the persecution, Jeremiah resolved to stop speaking about God. It didn't take long before he realized he couldn't do that. God's word burned inside him like a fire, and it was impossible for him not to speak.

Then I said, "I will not make mention of Him, Nor speak anymore in His name." But His word was in my heart like a burning fire Shut up in my bones; I was weary of holding it back, And I could not.

Jeremiah 20:9 NKJV

44

UNTAMABLE

Cruiser was born in England in 1852. His sire was named Venison and his mother, Little Red Rover. Cruiser was considered vicious from the time he was a foal. He sometimes leaned against the wall in his stall and kicked and screamed for ten minutes at a time. It's said he once broke a one-inch-thick iron bar in half with his teeth.

Why would anyone keep such a horse?

From excellent racing bloodlines, Cruiser was valued at $15,000, a lot of money at that time—and he was fast. But because it was so difficult to control him, he'd only raced once, as a two-year-old, finishing second. After that, he never raced again, but Cruiser sired many colts and fillies. Their owners hoped the foals would grow up to become great racehorses—without their father's bad temper, of course.

The only grooms brave enough to enter Cruiser's stall or pasture did so carrying a thick, wooden club. The horse's owner had thought about blinding Cruiser in order to protect his caretakers.

Cruiser was considered untamable. Blinding him might sound cruel. However, many thought the horse should be put down before he killed someone.

Across the Atlantic, John Rarey, born in 1827, grew up on a small farm in Groveport, Ohio. When he was three years old, the boy rode bareback atop the large plow horse while his father used the horse to work the fields. By age four, John had graduated to his own pony, and at twelve, he trained his first horse.

John used gentle training methods that weren't common in his day. Most people "broke" horses with harsh, forceful techniques. As Rarey grew older, his fame as a trainer spread. He traveled around the United States and Canada taming horses and other animals. While in Texas, he trained a team of elk to pull a wagon, and he became one of the first men to tame a zebra.

He taught the cavalry his gentle training methods for use on their war horses. Rarey wrote a popular horse-training book and traveled around the world demonstrating and teaching his techniques.

Many people can train ordinary horses, but Rarey presented himself as an extraordinary trainer. Therefore, people were eager to present their most challenging horses for him to work with—animals everyone else had given up on. In 1857, Queen Victoria invited John Rarey to England.

The extraordinary trainer was about to encounter the untamable horse.

Rarey found the horse imprisoned in a brick stall with a solid oak door where he had been kept for three years. He wore an eight-pound, iron muzzle with a bar in front of his mouth to keep him from biting anyone. He ate by licking up feed with his tongue. The horse lunged twice at Rarey before the man could catch and tie him. For twenty minutes, the furious horse fought the restraint to the point of exhaustion.

Just three hours later, Rarey emerged from the stable on Cruiser's back. With horses as vicious as Cruiser, Rarey would tie up one leg and bring the horse down to lie on his side. This implanted in nearly all horses' minds the conviction that Rarey was stronger, resulting in the animals submitting to him.

Cruiser's owner was so impressed, he gave the horse to Rarey. (Maybe he was just relieved to be rid of him?) Cruiser traveled with Rarey on a worldwide training tour. In 1861, the two returned to Groveport where Rarey built a mansion that included a stable and paddock for Cruiser.

John Rarey became ill and died in 1866. He cared so much for his "untamable" horse, he'd provided for Cruiser in his will. After the death of the one man Cruiser trusted, the horse's vicious temper returned. Although no one was able to get close to him, they cared for Cruiser who lived another nine years. It's believed the horse was buried near the current site of the Groveport Middle School football field.

Cruiser lives on as the mascot for the Groveport schools' sports teams. The players' colors are red and black. Red represents Cruiser's fiery temperament and black stands for the horse's color. There is a statue of Rarey and Cruiser in front of the Groveport Community Recreation Center.

Scripture says there's something all of us have that's even harder to tame than Cruiser.

> We all stumble in many ways. If anyone is never at fault in what he says, he is a perfect man, able to control his whole body. When we put bits into the mouths of horses to make them obey us, we can guide the whole animal. Consider ships as well. Although they are so large and are driven by strong winds, they are steered by a very small rudder wherever the pilot is inclined.
>
> In the same way, the tongue is a small part of the body, but it boasts of great things. Consider how small a spark sets a great forest ablaze. The tongue also is a fire, a world of wickedness among the parts of the body. It pollutes the whole person, sets the course of his life on fire, and is itself set on fire by hell. All kinds of animals, birds, reptiles, and creatures of the sea are being tamed and have been tamed by man, but no man can tame the tongue. It is a restless evil, full of deadly poison.
>
> *James 3:2-8*

Maybe you've never considered your tongue to be more dangerous than a vicious horse. However, Cruiser was eventually tamed by a man. James says no man can tame the tongue. He compares our tongues to the bits attached to a horse's bridle. Tongues and bits are not similar in appearance or the material they're made from.

THE SUPPOSED INCURABLE HORSE "CRUISER" UNDER MR. RAREY'S TREATMENT.—DRAWN BY JOHN LEECH.

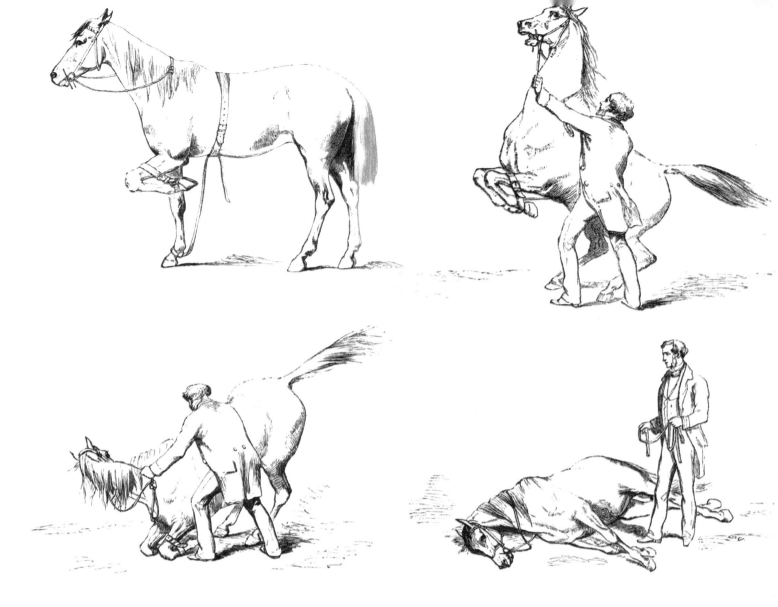

James is referring to their size and function. He wants us to understand how something so small can control something much larger.

Horses are large animals, weighing nine hundred or more pounds. Although bits vary in size, most bits weigh less than one pound. Yet, this little piece of metal, when placed in a horse's mouth, can force the animal to stop or change direction.

Although our tongues are small, they can determine our direction in life. The problem is that, rather than controlling our tongues, our tongues often control us.

> But the things that come out of the mouth come from the heart, and these things defile a man.

> *Matthew 15:18*

The words we speak reveal what is in our hearts. Imagine carrying a bucket full of water to your horse's stall. If someone bumped into you, what would splash out of the bucket?

Water, of course.

It wouldn't be possible for something else, like milk or juice, to spill out of a bucket of water. The bump reveals what is inside.

In life, annoying people or aggravating circumstances often "bump" us. When that happens, the words that spill out reveal what is inside us. If angry, hurtful words come out of our mouths, that indicates we have a heart problem. The angry words are only a symptom of our underlying disease.

We may apologize for hurtful words and excuse ourselves by explaining that we didn't mean what we said. But we can't totally undo the harm caused by thoughtless, unkind words.

> Speaking rashly is like a piercing sword, but the tongue of the wise brings healing.
>
> *Proverbs 12:18*

Picture a board with nails hammered into it. Each nail represents something unkind you've said to someone. Even if you pull the nails out with a hammer (apologizing), the holes remain. You could fill those holes with wood putty, but the board will never look the same as it did at first.

In the same way, you can't totally remove the harm inflicted on people you've pierced with unkind words. Others have used the comparison of a tube of toothpaste. Once the paste is squeezed out, it's impossible to put it back into the tube through the small opening.

When James says no man can tame the tongue, he means we can't do it on our own. But God is in the business of changing hearts and taming tongues. Just as it took a special man to tame Cruiser, God will help us bridle our tongues.

Here is a sampling of verses describing how we should use our tongues.

> May the words of my mouth and the meditation of my heart be pleasing in Your sight, O LORD, my Rock and my Redeemer.
>
> *Psalm 19:14*

> Keep your tongue from evil and your lips from deceitful speech.
>
> *Psalm 34:13*

> Set a guard, O LORD, over my mouth; keep watch at the door of my lips.
>
> *Psalm 141:3*

> A soothing tongue is a tree of life, but a perverse tongue crushes the spirit.
>
> *Proverbs 15:4*

> Life and death are in the power of the tongue, and those who love it will eat its fruit.
>
> *Proverbs 18:21*

> A word fitly spoken is like apples of gold in settings of silver.
>
> *Proverbs 25:11*

> Do you see a man who speaks in haste? There is more hope for a fool than for him.
>
> *Proverbs 29:20*

> Let no unwholesome talk come out of your mouths, but only what is helpful for building up the one in need and bringing grace to those who listen.
>
> *Ephesians 4:29*

> Let your speech always be gracious, seasoned with salt, so that you may know how to answer everyone.
>
> *Colossians 4:6*

Does that mean we should never say something that may hurt someone's feelings or offend them?

No. Sometimes a rebuke is necessary. But we must have the right motive and speak the truth in love for the benefit of the hearer. Typically, this would come from an older, wiser Christian to one who is younger or younger in the faith.

Truth and love go hand-in-hand. Because of our love, we must speak the truth. Love cannot remain silent. Part of loving those who don't know Christ is concern over where they will spend eternity. Unbelievers need to hear the truth of the gospel. They may not appreciate it, but seeds will be planted.

> Instead, speaking the truth in love [agape], we will in all things grow up into Christ Himself, who is the head.
>
> *Ephesians 4:15*

> All scripture is God-breathed and is useful for instruction, for conviction, for correction [epanorthosis], and for training [paideia] in righteousness, so that the man of God may be complete, fully equipped for every good work.
>
> *2 Timothy 3:16-17*

epanorthosis—restoration to a right state

paideia—instruction, discipline, training, education, chastisement, correction

45

BOOTS AND BIBLES

Many people picture cowboy boots as the tall, leather boots with pointed toes and high heels. That type of boot hurts my feet! I prefer the lace-up style that looks more like something you'd wear hiking rather than horseback riding.

One day, I made the mistake of wearing a new pair of riding boots to help run a horse show. For hours I had to stand in an arena full of soupy mud. Those boots were never the same after that extended mud bath. When the sides began to crack and leak, I picked up a new pair of Ariat boots.

I set the clean, new pair of boots alongside the old, cracked ones and stared at them. The difference in their appearance reminded me of a message I'd heard years before at a church service.

As a college student, the pastor was hired for a construction job, even though he'd never done that type of work. As he prepared to leave for his first day on the job, he looked down at his brand new boots and realized the spotless boots would be like a billboard to the other men, broadcasting his inexperience.

Not wanting his fellow workers to ridicule him, he walked outside, scooped up a handful of dirt, and rubbed it on the boots. Although now dusty, his boots were still obviously new.

I looked up as the pastor paused in the telling of his story. I was a new Christian and wasn't sure what the spiritual application of the message was. While I was pondering this, the pastor asked everyone to hold up their Bibles. (This was in the days before electronic devices.)

He asked what our Bibles looked like. "Does it have that brand new, right-off-the-bookstore-shelf look that announces to everyone you haven't been reading it? Or is it worn from months or years of soul-searching study? Perhaps even stained with tears?"

Ahh, now I saw his point.

> The law from Your mouth is more precious to me than thousands of pieces of gold and silver.
>
> *Psalm 119:72*

As Christians, we may acknowledge that worth in our mind, but do our lives show we really believe it? If we valued God's word more than silver or gold, wouldn't we spend more time reading it?

If so, our Bibles would resemble a well-worn pair of riding or work boots. There's only one way to make a pair of boots look used, and that is to use them! I doubt that the handful of dirt the pastor rubbed onto his boots fooled any of the men at the construction site.

Real scuffs, stains, creases, and perhaps a hoof print or two give riding boots an authentic, worn look that can't be faked. (check out the duct tape on the bull rider's boots)

Many people spend a lot of time each day on things that have little or no eternal value. For some, it may be texting, social media, music, TV, radio, shopping—or horses. Even good things can become bad if they pull us away from God.

We probably all have something we could give up or cut back on to make more time for reading our Bibles and learning from our heavenly Father.

46

THE MOCKER

Wine is a mocker, strong drink is raging: and whosoever is deceived thereby is not wise.

Proverbs 20:1 KJV

Many consider *Black Beauty* a children's book. However the author, Anna Sewell, did not write it for children. Her intended audience was the grooms, drivers, riders, and others who interacted daily with horses. The book was published in 1877, a time when horses provided most of the power to transport people and goods.

Sewell was concerned about the neglect and ill-treatment of horses. Her primary objection was to the use of the bearing or check rein, an additional strap used on harness horses to force an abnormally high head carriage which was considered fashionable.

While known primarily for its horse themes, Sewell was a strong Christian with a Quaker background. She wove many Christian principles into her book. One of those was her opposition to the use of alcohol.

Anna and her mother, Mary Sewell, were active in the temperance movement in England, attempting to eliminate, or at least reduce, the use of alcoholic beverages.

This topic comes up in several places in the book, but most notably in chapters twenty-five and twenty-six in the life of Reuben Smith, a groom at Earlshall where Black Beauty and the chestnut mare, Ginger, find themselves. Beauty describes Smith as follows.

> He was gentle and very clever in his management of horses, and could doctor them almost as well as a farrier, for he had lived two years with a veterinary surgeon. He was a first-rate driver; he could take a four-in-hand or a tandem as easily as a pair. … but he had one great fault and that was the love of drink. He was not like some men, always at it; he used to keep steady for weeks or months together, and then he would break out and have a "bout" of it, as York called it, and be a disgrace to himself, a terror to his wife, and a nuisance to all that had to do with him.

The Earl had fired Reuben Smith in the past when he had been so drunk he couldn't drive the ladies home from a ball, but he later rehired him when Smith promised he would never drink again.

One day, Smith drove Beauty in a carriage to the nearby village. He would leave the carriage there for repairs and ride Black Beauty home after running a few errands. But Smith gave in to the temptation of his old vice and drank all afternoon and into the evening. When he made it back to the livery stable, Smith mounted Black Beauty to return to Earlshall. He was so intoxicated, he didn't notice one of Beauty's shoes was loose. When Smith galloped him over rocky ground, Beauty lost the shoe and stumbled. The drunken Smith sailed over the horse's head and died from his injuries. Although Beauty recovered from the accident, his knees were permanently scarred.

Christians today disagree about the use of alcohol. When I'm asked about the topic, I tell people Carrie Nation is one of my heroes. Usually, that response produces a blank stare. That's a whole other story, but briefly, Carrie Nation was a radical member of the Woman's Christian Temperance Union in the early 1900s, becoming involved in the movement after her husband died of alcoholism.

She described herself as "a bulldog running along at the feet of Jesus, barking at what He doesn't like." But rather than barking, Carrie is best remembered for her "hatchetations." She often greeted bartenders of saloons and taverns with, "Good morning, destroyer of men's souls." Nation's hatchetations consisted of entering these establishments, singing hymns and praying while smashing bottles of alcohol with a small hatchet.

John MacArthur has an excellent message on the dangers of alcohol. He points out that the percentage of alcohol in drinks today is far higher than it was in biblical times.

> Thirty-eight million, the last count—this is a week ago—alcoholics in the U.S., and alcohol is produced at such mass volume that there is an unlimited supply, … A virtually unlimited supply, with a much higher alcohol content than the ancient counterparts.
>
> *2012 Sermon—Christians and Alcohol, John MacArthur*

Even people who believe some use of alcohol is acceptable should agree that drinking to the point of drunkenness is forbidden, since that is clearly stated in scripture.

> Do not get drunk on wine, which leads to reckless indiscretion. Instead, be filled with the Spirit.
>
> *Ephesians 5:18*

Rather than walking a line close to the edge of what is sinful, as Christians I believe we are called to steer far away from sin. We're also told to avoid practices that may cause others to stumble.

1 Corinthians 6:12 may seem confusing at first glance.

> "Everything is permissible for me," but not everything is beneficial. "Everything is permissible for me," but I will not be mastered by anything.

"Everything is permissible for me?" That cannot be true in a literal sense. Murder is lawful for me? No. We know it is not. When I find something in the Bible that doesn't make sense, I don't assume there is a mistake, only that I don't completely understand the passage. At that point, it's good to turn to a trusted pastor or commentator. In addition to MacArthur, Warren Wiersbe is one of my favorites. Here's what he has to say about that statement.

> "All things are lawful unto me." This was a popular phrase in Corinth, based on a false view of Christian freedom. We have not been set free so that we can enter into a new kind of bondage! As Christians, we must ask ourselves, "Will this enslave me? Is this activity really profitable for my spiritual life?"
>
> *Warren Wiersbe*

Our decisions should not be based solely on whether something is permissible, but on what is best, what will enhance our walk with Christ and our witness to others. We should avoid things that have the potential to enslave us. Alcohol falls into that category. Sewell addresses this in chapter 44 of *Black Beauty* when the cab driver, Jerry Barker, describes his own enslavement to alcohol.

> I found that I was not my own master, and that when the craving came on it was hard work to say 'no'. I saw that one of us must knock under, the drink devil or Jerry Barker, and I said that it should not be Jerry Barker, God helping me; but it was a struggle, and I wanted all the help I could get, for till I tried to break the habit I did not know how strong it was …
>
> Give up the drink or lose your soul! Give up the drink or break Polly's heart! But thanks be to God, and my dear wife, my chains were broken, and now for ten years I have not tasted a drop, and never wish for it.

Barker was able to break free of his addiction to alcohol, and encouraged his friend, Grant, to do the same. As Christians, we should be cautious about how our example affects others, especially those who are younger and more impressionable.

> So then, each of us will give an account of himself to God. Therefore let us stop judging one another. Instead, make up your mind not to put any stumbling block or obstacle in your brother's way. … It is better not to eat meat or drink wine or to do anything to cause your brother to stumble.
>
> *Romans 14:12,13,21*

I do not drink at all, however, if I drank alcohol, even in moderation, my example might encourage someone else to begin drinking. There's no guarantee the person I influenced would drink moderately. He or she might become an alcoholic. That's not something I want on my conscience. Unlike eating, drinking alcohol is optional. We can easily do without it.

I've never seen anything beneficial come from the use of alcohol—only harm—in my extended family and in our country. According to MADD (Mothers Against Drunk Driving), 10,142 people died in drunk driving accidents in 2019, twenty-eight people each day, or approximately one person every hour. Another 300,000 were injured in alcohol-related accidents.

In Ohio, we have a sizable Amish population. We're close to Pennsylvania which also has many Amish. Periodically, there will be news of an Amish person driving their buggy while intoxicated. Many find this amusing. I do not.

They put themselves, their horses, and anyone else on the road in danger. It's bad enough when motorized vehicles, traveling at high speeds, suddenly encounter a horse-drawn vehicle. It's even worse when an auto driver comes upon someone driving a buggy erratically because they are drunk. This usually occurs at night when poor visibility compounds the danger.

Here's an incident that happened in Kentucky. Fortunately, no one was seriously injured.

> An Amishman was arrested for DUI in Kentucky after sideswiping a car with his buggy last week. The 34-year-old man was traveling with his wife and seven children, ages 9 months to 12 years old. … The man first attempted to claim that one of his children was driving, but the children confirmed it was their father holding the reins.
>
> *AmishAmerica.com*

John MacArthur has two excellent sermons on whether Christians should drink alcohol. He asks and answers these questions.

- Is alcohol today the same as in biblical times? (the percentage of alcohol is far higher today)
- Is drinking alcoholic beverages necessary for health reasons?
- Is it the best choice to ensure no drunkenness?
- Is it habit forming? (1 Corinthians 6:12, could it master me?)
- Is it potentially destructive?
- Could my drinking cause someone else to stumble?
- Can drinking harm my testimony?
- Am I absolutely certain this is a behavior that is right? Will God be disappointed if I don't drink?

47

SORING HORSES

Anna Sewell, author of *Black Beauty*, fought to eliminate the use of the bearing or check rein on horses. If alive today, Sewell would be appalled by the soring of gaited horses, a cruel and senseless practice.

Like the bearing rein used to produce a high head carriage considered fashionable in the 1800s, horses are sored to create a fashionable, exaggerated gait that wins in the show ring.

Soring is practiced on "big lick" Tennessee Walking Horses, Racking Horses, and Spotted Saddle Horses. You can find photos and videos online of soring techniques and the unnatural gait it produces. I find the videos too painful to watch.

To sore a horse, chemicals or physical objects are used which cause pain when a horse's front feet hit the ground. To avoid the pain, the horse raises his front legs higher and faster, shifting his weight more onto his back end to keep his front feet off the ground as much as possible.

Some who don't go as far as soring may allow their horse's hooves to grow abnormally long and use weighted shoes with added pads (known as stacks). Those may be combined with weighted chains around the pasterns. Although not as bad as soring, these are at best questionable practices designed to create the same artificial, high-stepping gait.

Physical or pressure soring involves the use of objects to cause pain. They may insert nails in the stacked pads with the pointed tips pressing against the sole of the horse's hoof.

With chemical soring, a caustic (burning or blistering) chemical is applied to the pastern. The resulting pain increases when the horse wears chains that bang against his legs with every step. Outside the show ring, the treated leg is wrapped in plastic to increase the absorption rate. The plastic is then removed before entering their class. These chemicals often cause scarring, an obvious sign that a horse has been sored.

With the passage of the Horse Protection Act of 1970, soring was made illegal in the United States. However, the funds and manpower to monitor shows to enforce the act has been limited, so soring still occurs.

The Horse Protection Act specifies that soring has occurred when:

- an irritating or blistering agent has been applied, internally or externally, by a person to any limb of a horse

- any burn, cut, or laceration has been inflicted by a person on any limb of a horse

- any tack, nail, screw, or chemical agent has been injected by a person into or used by a person on any limb of a horse

- any other substance or device has been used by a person on any limb of a horse or a person has engaged in a practice involving a horse, and, as a result of such application, infliction, injection, use, or practice, such horse suffers, or can reasonably be expected to suffer, physical pain or distress, inflammation, or lameness when walking

Jackie McConnell received the Trainer of the Year award from the Walking Horse Trainers Association in 1986. But in a 2011 undercover investigation by the Humane Society of the United States, McConnell was recorded beating horses, using electric cattle prods, and soring their legs with chemicals. That footage aired in 2012 on the ABC show *Nightline*. You can find the video on YouTube if you dare to watch it.

In 2013, McConnell pled guilty to twenty-two counts of animal cruelty. He was sentenced to one year of house arrest, four years of supervised probation, and a $75,000 fine. McConnell was prohibited from owning or training horses for twenty years.

Although he was banned for life from attending the Tennessee Walking Horse National Celebration or any event on that show grounds, McConnell attended the national show in 2021. In fact, he was announced as the sponsor of a trophy for one of the classes.

There is no excuse for abusing horses or any other animals. God made us stewards over His creation. He calls us to care for the horses we've been entrusted with. That is the theme of my fourth book, *Tender Mercies*, taken from Proverbs 12:10.

> A righteous man regards the life of his animal, But the tender mercies of the wicked are only cruelty.

The practice of soring illustrates that people do their evil deeds in the "darkness." Attempting to hide their actions proves they know what they're doing is wrong.

> The Light has come into the world, but men loved the darkness rather than the Light because their deeds were evil. Everyone who does evil hates the Light, and does not come into the Light for fear that his deeds will be exposed. But whoever practices the truth comes into the Light, so that it may be seen clearly that what he has done has been accomplished in God.
>
> *John 3:19-21*

No one who practices soring does it in the open. They try to hide and cover it up. When the chemical agents cause scarring on a horse's legs, they use other chemicals to try to remove the scars or they apply dye to the legs so the scars aren't as visible.

Jackie McConnell is not the only trainer guilty of soring horses. Testing performed by the U.S. Department of Agriculture at the 2012 National Celebration in Shelbyville, Tennessee revealed seventy-six percent of the horses (145 of 190) tested positive for prohibited foreign substances. McConnell was just a prominent trainer who got caught.

I once attended a Saddlebred show to take photos of the horses. Saddlebreds perform a different gait that doesn't respond well to the soring techniques used with Walking Horses. Although they aren't sored, Saddlebred owners and trainers use similar weighted, stacked shoes, and other devices to produce an artificially enhanced gait. Also, most Saddlebred show horses have their tail bones broken or "set" to produce an unnatural tail carriage.

While walking through the barns, taking photos, several owners followed and questioned me in an unfriendly manner. I had the distinct feeling they didn't like me shining a light on what they were doing. I've attended many horse shows over the years and always take photos. This was the only time I was followed and interrogated.

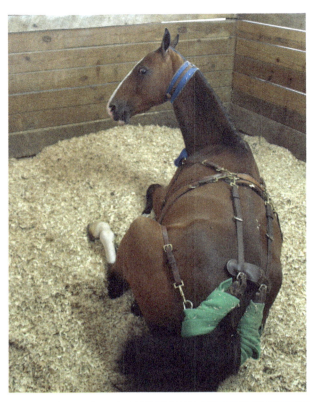

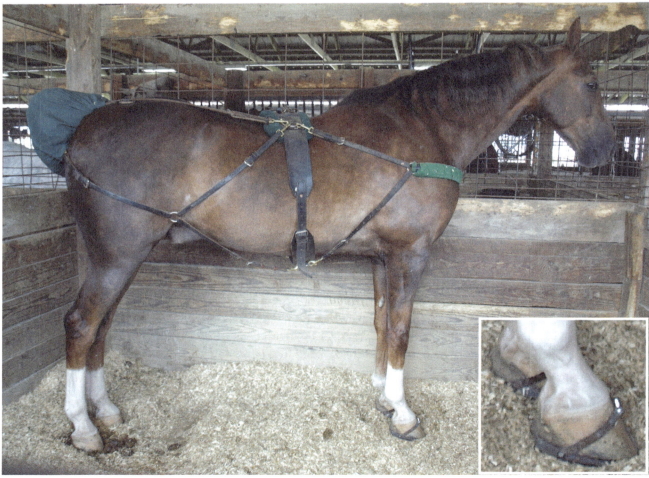

48

THE WAY

When trail riding, you often arrive at a fork where the trail branches off in two directions. Should you turn to the right or left? It's important to have a map or a trail marker that clearly shows the correct way to go.

My daughters and I covered a lot of miles trail riding together. I'll confess, I didn't always make the right turns, and sometimes we became lost. You'll find one of those stories in the next chapter. My mistakes were due to a combination of poorly marked trails, a bad or missing map, my limited sense of direction, and a tendency for my mind to wander and not pay attention to where we were going.

But even worse than being physically lost is to be lost spiritually. I had no spiritual sense of direction when I was younger. It wasn't until my late twenties that I realized I had taken several wrong turns in life and was going the wrong way. I needed to reverse course and find the right path before it was too late! I turned my life over to God and became a Christian at twenty-seven.

Followers of Christ today are nearly always referred to as Christians. That wasn't what believers were called at first, though.

The Greek word for "Christian" is "christianos," which means "a follower of Christ."

> Then Barnabas went to Tarsus to look for Saul, and when he found him, he brought him back to Antioch. So for a full year they met together with the church and taught large numbers of people. The disciples were first called Christians at Antioch.
>
> *Acts 11:25,26*

There are only two other uses of the word "christianos" in the New Testament.

> Then Agrippa said to Paul, "Can you persuade me in such a short time to become a Christian?"
>
> *Acts 26:28*

> But if you suffer as a Christian, do not be ashamed, but glorify God that you bear that name.
>
> *1 Peter 4:16*

At that time, the name Christian was likely used to insult the followers of Christ. In the New Testament, believers never refer to themselves or other believers as "Christians." The Jews wouldn't have called Jesus' followers Christians, because Christ meant Messiah, and most of them rejected Jesus as the Messiah.

Rather than "Christians," believers were known as followers of "The Way." The Book of Acts often uses "The Way" for the group of people who followed Christ. The main Greek word for "way" in the New Testament is "hodos," a traveled way, road, journey, or path.

It's important to know the way back to the campground on a horse trail. But it's even more important to follow The Way if we want to reach heaven. Although there may be several trails leading back to camp, according to the Bible, Jesus Christ is the only way to heaven.

> "You know the way to the place where I am going."
> "Lord," said Thomas, "we do not know where You are going, so how can we know the way?"
> Jesus answered, "I am the way and the truth and the life. No one comes to the Father except through Me."
>
> *John 14:6*

It's possible the early Christians adopted "The Way" as the name of their group because of Jesus' words in John 14:6. Despite the popular misconception that there are many roads leading to God and eternal life, Jesus insisted there was only one way—through Him.

> Enter by the narrow gate; for wide is the gate and broad is the way that leads to destruction, and there are many who go in by it. Because narrow is the gate and difficult is the way which leads to life, and there are few who find it.
>
> *Matthew 7:13,14 NKJV*

People contradict the Bible when they insist everyone goes to heaven, except a few horrible people like Adolph Hitler.

In Matthew 7, the way is described as narrow or difficult with few people finding and traveling it. The Christian life can be a struggle. Sometimes, it feels as if we're swimming upstream, against the flow, with nearly everyone else going the opposite direction.

Don't be discouraged. The Bible says it's supposed to be that way.

The following passages in Acts refer to Christianity as The Way.

> Meanwhile, Saul was still breathing out murderous threats against the disciples of the Lord. He approached the high priest and requested letters to the synagogues in Damascus, so that if he found any men or women belonging to the Way, he could bring them as prisoners to Jerusalem.
>
> *Acts 9:1,2*

> But when some of them stubbornly refused to believe and publicly maligned the Way, Paul took his disciples and left the synagogue to conduct daily discussions in the lecture hall of Tyrannus.
>
> *Acts 19:9*

> About that time there arose a great disturbance about the Way.
>
> *Acts 19:23*

> I [Paul] persecuted this Way even to the death, detaining both men and women and throwing them into prison, as the high priest and the whole Council can testify about me.
>
> *Acts 22:4,5*

> I [Paul] do confess to you, however, that I worship the God of our fathers according to the Way, which they call a sect.
>
> *Acts 24:14*

> Then Felix, who was well informed about the Way, adjourned the hearing and said, "When Lysias the commander comes, I will decide your case."
>
> *Acts 24:22*

49

FORK IN THE TRAIL

Years ago, one of my daughters and I were riding at a state park with a trail riding club. I hadn't realized the area was extremely rocky. Our horses weren't shod, and before long, they became uncomfortable on the rough trails. The other horses had shoes and could travel much faster.

Some of the riders were becoming impatient with our slow pace. Rather than holding everyone back, I insisted they go ahead without us. I'd never ridden at this park before. The trails were barely marked, and the park map wasn't much better. It wasn't long before we were lost.

I've heard of horses who have a built-in compass that guides them. But our two didn't have any better sense of direction than I did. They were clueless, relying on me for guidance. The later it got, the more tired and worried I became.

At the next fork in the trail, we stopped to rest. I stared at the two paths, wondering which would take us back to the campground. We hadn't seen any other riders since parting with our group. As we sat there, my inner GPS told me to take the left branch of the trail. I was about to start up again when I heard something behind us. I turned around and saw a man and woman riding two large mules. I've never been happier to see a mule in my life!

The couple was heading back to camp and invited us to follow them. When they turned to take the right fork, I breathed a prayer of thanks to God. If those mule riders hadn't arrived when they did, I would have started down the left fork, heading to who knows where.

There is a way that seems right to a man, but its end is the way of death.

Proverbs 16:25

Making the wrong turn and continuing to wander around the trails in the dark would have been scary, but not life-threatening. Just as we have choices about which path to follow on a horse trail, we also face

decisions about which way to go in life. The consequences for taking a wrong turn at critical forks in our life journey can be much worse than getting lost in the woods. Unfortunately, those kinds of bad choices may impact us for the rest of our lives.

God sometimes sends people to help us find and stay on the correct path. But it's up to each of us to listen to godly advice, learn about God and His way from scripture, and resolve to find and stick to the narrow path.

I could have insisted the mule riders were wrong and stubbornly gone my own way down the opposite trail. Instead, I accepted that they were more knowledgeable about the way than I was, and we followed them back to camp. In addition to godly people in our lives, God has given us written instructions. Unlike the terrible trail map I had that day, God reveals His will to us through His word, to help us stay on the narrow path.

> Thy word is a lamp unto my feet and a light unto my path.
>
> *Psalm 119:105 KJV*

If your heart is turned toward God, you'll have a desire to follow His ways and will be sensitive to His guidance. I love the following verse from Isaiah that illustrates what happens when we go a little off course.

> And whether you turn to the right or to the left, your ears will hear this command behind you: "This is the way. Walk in it."
>
> *Isaiah 30:21*

That guidance reminds me of what I do when driving my pony, Toby. Rather than traveling straight down the road, he likes to wander from side to side. When I sense him drifting, I give him a little nudge back in the opposite direction.

In my first book, *Rosie and Scamper*, I wrote about this experience of being lost on the trail. The grandmother in the book suggests the mule riders were angels sent to rescue them. Is that likely? Maybe not, but Hebrews indicates we may encounter angels without being aware of it.

> Be not forgetful to entertain strangers: for thereby some have entertained angels unawares.
>
> *Hebrews 13:2 KJV*

50

CIRCUIT RIDERS

Of all the things horses carried and delivered in the days before motorized vehicles, one of the most important was the Christian faith. More precisely, horses carried the men that preached God's word. These men, known as circuit riders, were generally Methodists, although a few Baptist pastors also rode preaching circuits.

A circuit rider sometimes traveled days before reaching a farm or village. Most Methodist circuits consisted of 200 to 500-mile routes. It took four to six weeks to complete an entire circuit.

When a minister in the East earned $400 a year, a Methodist circuit rider was paid $80. They relied on the hospitality of the families on their circuit for food and lodging. The traveling preachers usually served two years on a circuit, then switched to a new one. This allowed them to use the same sermons repeatedly.

The riders carried a variety of books with them. Besides the Bible, these might include a hymnal, prayer book, journal, the Constitution and Discipline of the Methodist Church, and Primitive Physic by John Wesley, which contained home remedies for illnesses. It was common for the preachers to read and study as they rode.

The circuit riders carried with them a simple message of repentance and faith in Jesus Christ.

> A Methodist preacher in those days, when he felt God calling him to preach, instead of hunting up a college or Biblical Institute, hunted up a hardy pony or a horse, and some traveling apparatus, and with his library always at hand, namely, Bible, Hymn Book, and Discipline, he started, and with a text that never wore out nor grew stale, he cried, "Behold the Lamb of God, that taketh away the sin of the world."
>
> In this way he went through storms of wind, hail, snow, and rain; climbed hills and mountains, traversed valleys, plunged through swamps, swam swollen streams, lay out all night, wet, weary, and hungry, held his horse by the bridle all night, or tied him to a limb, slept with his saddle blanket for a bed, his saddle or saddle-bags for his pillow, and his old big coat or blanket, if he had any, for a covering. …
>
> His text was always ready, "Behold the Lamb of God."
>
> *Autobiography of Peter Cartwright, the Backwoods Preacher*

An early circuit rider, Francis Asbury, averaged 6,000 miles a year on horseback, preaching at different stops nearly every day.

> I preached to any audience I could find, even when seriously ill or threatened by angry mobs. I preached hundreds of sermons with my throat so sore I could barely speak and fever burning so hot I could barely think. I was once so sick I had to be tied to my horse so I wouldn't fall off.
>
> *Francis Asbury*

In his journal, Asbury recorded the following incident with a new horse, Fox.

> On my way to Andrew Purdin's, (Delaware), I came on a race ground, where the sons of Belial had been practicing my horse; he ran away with me when he came to the end of the paths, but stopped, and I received no harm. I lifted my heart to God; and by the mercy of the Lord he stopped near a point of woods, which, had he entered, I might probably have lost my life: my heart was deeply humbled before the Lord, who preserved me from such imminent danger.

Whoever gave or sold him the horse neglected to inform Asbury that Fox had been used as a racehorse. When Fox recognized an area where he'd trained in the past, the horse took off, with Asbury clinging to the saddle for dear life.

Apparently, Asbury had no further problems with the horse as Fox remained one of his regular mounts. Additional excerpts from Asbury's journal give a glimpse of the arduous life of the circuit rider for both man and horse.

> After preaching on John vii. 17, we set out on our return. I was much fatigued, and it rained hard; my poor horse too, was so weak from the want of proper food, that he fell down with me twice; this hurt my feelings exceedingly—more than any circumstance I met with in all my journey beside.

> Since Thursday we have rode sixty miles along incredibly bad roads, and our fare was not excellent. O what pay would induce a man to go through wet and dry, and fatigue and suffering, as we do? Souls are our hire.

> We have had rain for eighteen days successively, and I have rode about two hundred miles in eight or nine days; a most trying time indeed. My horse lost a shoe on a bad road, and next day on the mountains dropped two more; so I rode my old baggage horse along a most dreary, grown-up path to brother C_'s

> We went on through devious roads and arrived at Guess's—here I set on a scheme to prevent my horse from falling lame, that had yesterday lost a shoe; it was to bind round his foot a piece of the neck of a bull's hide—my contrivance answered the purpose well.

> We hasted to O_'s in the Cove, where we met with a most kind and affectionate reception. But O the flies for the horses, and the gnats for the men! And no food, nor even good water to be had.

Asbury has been called the "George Washington of American Christianity." Later in his life, when Asbury could no longer ride because of rheumatism, he continued preaching but traveled by carriage.

Those old Methodist circuit riders have long been an inspiration. Robert E. Harris of Asheville, North Carolina used the circuit-riding technique well into the 1990s. He dressed in a plain white shirt, black frock coat, black pants, and a Stetson hat. Mounted on his horse, Sundance, Harris attracted attention and gained an audience in some unusual places.

The sixty-eight-year-old Harris showed up at craft shows, car races, amusement parks, and other places you wouldn't expect to find a preacher. But his favorite and most profitable location was a rest stop along the interstate. One day there, within fifteen minutes, he'd shared the gospel with people from Canada, New Zealand, and India.

The early circuit riders suffered hardships but not as many as the apostle Paul. However, the difficulties didn't stop any of them from continuing to spread the gospel.

> Are they servants of Christ? I am speaking like I am out of my mind, but I am so much more: in harder labor, in more imprisonments, in worse beatings, in frequent danger of death. Five times I received from the Jews the forty lashes minus one. Three times I was beaten with rods, once I was stoned, three times I was shipwrecked. I spent a night and a day in the open sea.
>
> In my frequent journeys, I have been in danger from rivers and from bandits, in danger from my countrymen and from the Gentiles, in danger in the city and in the country, in danger on the sea and among false brothers, in labor and toil and often without sleep, in hunger and thirst and often without food, in cold and exposure.
>
> Apart from these external trials, I face daily the pressure of my concern for all the churches.
>
> *2 Corinthians 11:23-28*

Few, or perhaps none of us, are called to be circuit riders today or to endure such hardships as Paul did. But we are all called to share the Good News, in some manner.

> But in your hearts sanctify Christ as Lord. Always be prepared to give a defense to everyone who asks you the reason for the hope that is in you. But respond with gentleness and respect,
>
> *1 Peter 3:15*

Paul asked for prayer that he might speak boldly and fearlessly.

> Pray also for me, that whenever I open my mouth, words may be given me so that I will boldly make known the mystery of the gospel, for which I am an ambassador in chains. Pray that I may proclaim it fearlessly, as I should.
>
> *Ephesians 6:19:20*

51

HORSE THIEVES

The eighth commandment, in Exodus 20:15, states, "You shall not steal." To steal is to take something without permission with no intention of returning it. The items most commonly stolen today are:

- money
- jewelry
- tools
- cars and trucks
- electronic equipment
- guns
- drugs
- identity or credit cards

What doesn't make the top of that list today is horses. But the theft of horses was a big problem in the 1800s when people's transportation and survival often depended upon horses, especially in the sparsely populated Midwest.

Stealing one or more horses was a serious offense that met with harsh consequences. In Pennsylvania, the "Act to Increase the Punishments of Horse Stealing," passed in 1780, was in force until its repeal in 1860. According to this act, the punishment for a first offense of horse thievery was standing in a pillory for one hour, thirty-nine lashes on the back, and the thief's ears cut off. A second offense received the same whipping and pillory; additionally, the thief would be branded on the forehead with the letters "HT" for horse thief.

Anti-Horse Thief Societies formed to help catch and administer justice to thieves. This justice was sometimes immediate, without a trial. Many considered hanging the best punishment for a horse thief.

Horse thieves sometimes worked alone. George White, one of those solitary thieves, was known to steal a horse, take it to the next town and sell it, then steal it again from the new owner of the horse. White might sell the horse a third time, then return it to the farm of the original owner before the horse was even missed.

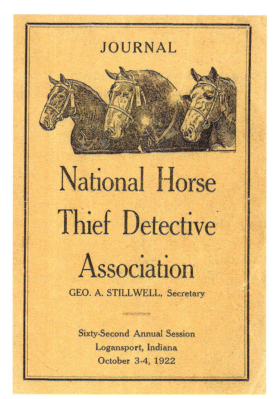

JOURNAL

National Horse Thief Detective Association

GEO. A. STILLWELL, Secretary

Sixty-Second Annual Session
Logansport, Indiana
October 3-4, 1922

Other thieves worked as part of a gang where each member had a specific role. A spotter visited a farm posing as a potential buyer. In reality, he was scouting out the place to see what horses were available, their location, and how best to access them. The gang allowed time to elapse after the spotter's visit so the theft wouldn't be connected to him. Then, other gang members would steal the targeted horse or horses.

It was important to get a stolen horse out of the immediate area where he might be recognized. They established relay stations where the gang's "runners" would ride a stolen horse to the next station, switching to the next rider for another leg of the journey. Relays allowed the horse to be quickly moved far away from its home.

When the horse couldn't be relayed, it was the job of other gang members to alter the horse's appearance by dying his hair, adding or covering up facial or leg markings, cutting his mane or tail, or altering brands. Sometimes horses were so unrecognizable they could even be sold in the same neighborhood where they'd been stolen.

The theft of horses, although much less frequent today, hasn't been eradicated. Stolen Horse International (SHI), also known as NetPosse, was formed in 1997 to help owners locate stolen or lost horses.

A sad, modern case of horse theft involved Wendi Cox, a home health care nurse, and her daughter, Jaci Rae Jackson. In 2011, the two, with the help of two men—Billy Hamilton and George Berrish, stole five horses and a horse trailer from the Southern Arkansas University stable. The horses and trailer belonged to members of SAU's rodeo team. Ironically, Jaci was a freshman at the college and also a member of the team, competing as a barrel racer.

The men took the horses and trailer to Cox's home in Oklahoma. It seems the motive was to resell the horses, so Cox could afford to buy a faster barrel racing horse for her daughter. Jaci's younger sister, Jade, recognized one of the horses, Credit Card, a fifteen-year-old sorrel roping horse gelding. She figured anyone on the rodeo circuit would also recognize Credit Card if they tried to sell him. Plus, the horse, owned by team member Shaun Smith, had multiple brands that would be impossible to cover up. Their plan started to unravel.

Not wanting to be discovered with the easily recognizable horse, either Jaci or her mother had Hamilton kill Credit Card.

When someone spotted the stolen trailer on Cox's property, things really began to go haywire. The thieves needed to get rid of the other horses, fast.

The remaining four horses were led to a remote area and tied to pine trees. Grey, a lighter-colored mare, was sprayed with camouflage paint to help conceal her. The horses were simply left there to die. The four went without food and water for two weeks before they were found, malnourished and dehydrated. They had survived by eating pine needles and bark from the trees. All four eventually recovered.

Wendi Cox, the mastermind of the plan, was tried, found guilty by a jury, and sentenced to sixty years in prison. Smiling for the television cameras after her sentencing, Wendy professed her innocence. She will serve at least ten years before being eligible for parole. Jaci Rae received a ten-year sentence, however, she was paroled after serving less than two years. Billy Hamilton was sentenced to twenty-five years and George Berrish to ten.

Coveting, prohibited in the tenth commandment, plays a role in theft. Wendi Cox wanted Jaci to be successful on the rodeo circuit. She coveted a top-level barrel horse for her daughter. Selling the stolen animals would have provided the money for Wendi to buy the horse she couldn't afford.

When asked what was the greatest commandment, Jesus replied,

> "This is the most important: 'Hear O Israel, the Lord our God, the Lord is One. Love the Lord your God with all your heart and with all your soul and with all your mind and with all your strength.' The second is this: 'Love your neighbor as yourself.' No other commandment is greater than these."
>
> *Mark 12:29-31*

While all sin is ultimately against God, theft has a big impact on other people. That goes against what Jesus called the second most important command—that we love our neighbor as we love ourselves.

The toll theft takes on others is apparent in the story of Wendy Cox and her daughter. The two were oblivious to the suffering inflicted on the stolen horses as well as the pain they caused the horses' owners.

In John 10:10, Satan or those under his control, are compared to a thief entering the sheepfold.

> The thief comes only to steal and kill and destroy.

52

BUYER BEWARE

In my book, *Outward Appearances*, Rosie and her grandmother went to look at a bay roan mare that was advertised for sale. When they arrived at the farm, they quickly realized the horse was nothing like she had been described in the advertisement.

Unfortunately, that happens too often in real life. That scene was based on an experience I had years ago when helping a friend find a suitable beginner's horse.

You'd think I would learn, but being a trusting person and one who loves most horses I see, I've been lied to and deceived several times when buying horses. Most recently, I was looking for a horse to use for light trail riding and as a companion for my driving pony, Toby.

I saw an ad for a large pony, 13.2 hands, a size capable of carrying a small adult rider. Plus, I figured if I fell off—something I dread at my age—it wouldn't be too far to the ground. The bay mare was also gaited, which is much easier on my back. She was listed as a Paso Fino, although not registered.

The seller's website had Christian messages all over it, which contributed to my lower level of caution. A Christian wouldn't lie about a horse, would she?

Because the woman claimed to be a Christian, I naively trusted her. (Whether she actually is one or not, I'll leave up to God.) I visited her stable for a trial ride on the horse. When I arrived, the mare stood calmly tied in the barn.

The horse's dead calmness impressed me. Could this be another Maggie? I commented on how well the horse stood tied, and the woman informed me, "Oh, she'll stand like that all day." (Later I realized why!)

I explained what I was looking for—a calm horse I could poke around easy trails on, almost always riding by myself. There were many horses at the stable, some in the barn and others out in pens. I rode around the stable yard, and the mare paid little attention to any of the horses. Her behavior convinced me she wasn't buddy sour—one of the problems I hate the most in a horse.

It's impossible to take a buddy sour horse out by herself. She will be obsessed with getting back to her friend. The reverse is true also. You can't do anything with her friend without the buddy sour horse having a nervous breakdown and potentially injuring herself. The woman assured me the horse was not buddy sour.

I felt safe riding the mare. She was a perfect size for me. That day, she was calm and obedient, with a very smooth gait—seemingly perfect for what I intended to use her for.

The horse was wearing new shoes. That nagged at me a bit. Most people selling a fairly low-end horse wouldn't put brand new shoes on right before they sold her. But her hooves looked healthy. I asked whether I could ride her on easy trails without shoes. The seller assured me that wouldn't be a problem. She claimed the mare had been extensively trail ridden.

Now, I see how ignorant I was, accepting everything she told me as true.

The horse was underweight, but I'm great at fattening animals. I figured it would just take some time to put weight on her. I agreed to buy the mare. I didn't have my trailer with me. My theory being that I'll be less likely to make an impulsive decision if I leave the trailer at home. But in this case, it didn't matter.

I returned a week later to pick up the mare. When I got home and unloaded her, I already sensed the horse was not behaving like the one I'd seen and ridden at the stable. She was anxious as soon as she came out of the trailer. I attributed it to the new, unfamiliar environment. However, horses that have been trail ridden "extensively" are used to being carted all over the place and aren't too bothered by a change in location.

After giving her a couple of days to settle in, I got the mare out to ride. I tied her to groom and saddle her. Unlike at her previous home, the horse would not stand still. It was a challenge, but I finally got her saddled and bridled, and I mounted for our first ride. We started down the driveway but only went a short distance before she began dancing and whirling around, calling for the pony. That ride consisted of going back and forth along Toby's pen to the extent the mare could endure without throwing a fit. Still rather naive, I figured I would gradually be able to extend the distance away from Toby with each ride.

She had an amazingly smooth, natural gait. But as I gaited her back and forth, I realized it didn't feel like the lateral gait of a Paso Fino. I studied the video the seller had made of her, slowing it down so I could see the footfall pattern. She wasn't doing a lateral gait at all, but a diagonal one—a foxtrot. On top of everything else the seller had gotten wrong, there was no way this horse was a Paso Fino. She had Foxtrotter blood somewhere in her past.

By now, I realized something was seriously wrong. The horse's personality could not have changed so abruptly in such a short time. I contacted the seller and asked if I could return or exchange her. The woman gave me a far-fetched story about not being with the stable any more and that any returns were out of her hands.

To top it off, the horse then came down with pneumonia, something she had obviously been incubating before I bought her. Now, I had vet bills and a couple rounds of antibiotics to nurse her back to health.

Finally, she was healthy and had gained a respectable amount of weight. My farrier removed her shoes, and I quickly learned her feet were sensitive to even the gravel in the driveway. This horse could never be ridden barefoot. During this entire time, I hadn't been able to do anything with my pony either, for fear the mare would injure herself in her panic over Toby leaving her.

To say, I was frustrated with the whole situation is an understatement. Part of that frustration was how gullible and easily deceived I had been. I wasn't able to return the mare, and I doubted I could find anyone interested in buying a horse with her issues. I decided I'd drop her price and try to sell her, being honest about her shortcomings.

Pointing out that the horse was buddy sour and had tender feet limited the number of prospective buyers. Fortunately, I finally sold her. She's now being used as a companion to a blind horse—a perfect role in life for her!

How had I been so deceived? Although the seller lied about nearly everything about the horse, I put most of the blame on myself. It's sad that it has to be this way, but you have to approach buying a horse with the assumption that the seller may be lying or hiding something about the animal.

Why was the mare so calm the day I went for my trial ride? I'm convinced the woman tranquilized her. Acepromazine is a tranquilizer used for horses, commonly known as Ace. When used at regular dosage levels

$ 6,800

Gentle Bay Paint Gelding for sale in Texas

TNT Ranch
Profile page

to calm a horse for veterinary procedures, the horse becomes almost zombie-like and will stand perfectly still or may stumble around if he walks. At lower dosages, Ace doesn't impact the horse's movement, it merely calms him. That calming effect lasts several hours. I had given the woman the time I would arrive, so she could have dosed the horse with Ace far enough ahead that it was in effect while I was there, but not so far ahead that it wore off before I left.

What did I do wrong?

I trusted the woman's answers to my questions. I tend to be too trusting anyway, but because she presented herself as a Christian, I was even more trusting (gullible?) than usual.

I didn't have a veterinarian examine the horse. It's good to get what is known as a pre-purchase exam. The vet might not have been able to detect the use of a tranquilizer, but she may have seen the early signs of pneumonia. The stable was two hours from me, so the cost of having my vet travel that far was a factor in my decision not to have the vet check done. But I ended up losing more money on this experience than the examination would have cost me.

A vet check would also have given me a firm idea of the horse's age. I was told she was fourteen. Later, I found a complaint online from another person with a bad experience from that stable. The horse they purchased was also said to be fourteen. A vet later informed them the animal was closer to thirty. I'm pretty sure I could tell the difference between a fourteen-year-old and a thirty-year-old horse, but I don't know for sure how old this mare was. It's likely the seller lied about that, too.

I should have insisted on a trial period with the horse (and gotten that in writing). I knew within days of bringing her home, the mare was not the horse I'd been led to believe she was. If I had a trial period agreement, I could have returned her and gotten my money back.

The number of things I did wrong is embarrassing. If I'd been more discerning, I never would have bought her.

The Bible warns us there are far more serious matters we need to have discernment about.

> But solid food is for the mature, who by constant use have trained their senses to distinguish [diakrisis] good from evil.
>
> *Hebrews 5:14*

diakrisis—to distinguish, separate out, investigate, examine, scrutinize, question, to hold a preliminary judicial examination

We need discernment in order to determine what is true about God, our relationship to Him, and how we are to live in this world. That type of discernment doesn't come from worldly knowledge or education. It's spiritual. Unbelievers cannot possess discernment about spiritual things. Spiritual discernment allows us to detect and avoid false teachers and their teachings that attempt to lead us astray.

> The natural man does not accept the things that come from the Spirit of God. For they are foolishness to him, and he cannot understand them, because they are spiritually discerned.
>
> *1 Corinthians 2:14*

> For many deceivers have gone out into the world, refusing to confess the coming of Jesus Christ in the flesh. Any such person is the deceiver and the antichrist.
>
> *2 John 1:7*

In Romans 12:9, we're instructed to, "Abhor what is evil. Cling to what is good." NKJV

How can we discern what is good and what is evil? The world calls good many things God considers evil. The world operates on a very different standard than that of God.

According to the world, just about everyone is a good person. We're encouraged to look out for ourselves (looking out for number one!). We need to be tolerant or even approving of sin—both in ourselves and others.

If you have spiritual discernment, you'll immediately recognize such worldly wisdom as contrary to scripture. It's more challenging to be discerning about false teachers and their teachings. False teachers often mix in enough truth so that their teachings or doctrines sound scriptural, but on closer examination they don't hold up.

> If you continue in My word, you are truly My disciples. Then you will know the truth, and the truth will set you free.
>
> *John 8:31,32*

Jesus warned us that discernment is even more important as we approach or enter the Last Days. We don't want to be deceived by a leader masquerading as Christ.

> At that time, if anyone says to you, 'Look, here is the Christ!' or 'There He is!' do not believe it. For false Christs and false prophets will appear and perform great signs and wonders that would deceive even the elect, if that were possible.
>
> *Matthew 24:23,24*

The pony "4 Sale" ad below is a joke, but it's not far from the reality of buying horses. The ones that are as obvious as this are easy to pass over. But as with false teachers, it's the ones that seem true, that are the most dangerous.

53

A SUCKER BORN EVERY MINUTE?

Phineas Taylor (P. T.) Barnum is credited with saying, "There's a sucker born every minute." He may never have said those words. Some argue that rather than being a fraud and a con man, Barnum simply wanted to provide cheap entertainment to make people laugh. He did this through publicizing and exhibiting a variety of oddities.

One of Barnum's exhibits was a woolly horse he claimed had been "captured at the risk of life and limb among the snow-capped impassable crags of the wildest mountains in America." He claimed Col. Fremont caught the animal after a three-day chase in California.

The true story of the animal's discovery was a bit more mundane. In 1848, Barnum came across the unusual horse while in Cincinnati, Ohio, where the animal was already being exhibited locally.

> My attention was arrested by handbills announcing the exhibition of a 'woolly horse.' Being always on the qui vive for everything curious with which to amuse or astonish the public, I visited the exhibition, and found the animal to be a veritable curiosity. It was a well-formed horse of rather small size, without any manner or the slightest portion of hair upon his tail. The entire body and limbs were covered with a thick fine hair or wool curling tight to his skin. He was foaled in Indiana, was a mere freak of nature, and withal a very curious looking animal. I purchased him and sent him to Bridgeport, Ct., where he was placed quietly away in a retired barn, until such times as I might have use for him.
>
> *The Life of P. T. Barnum, Written by Himself*

It wasn't long before Barnum took advantage of the opportunity the woolly animal presented. He promoted the exhibit as—

> COL. FREMONT'S NONDESCRIPT OR WOOLLY HORSE will be exhibited for a few days at the corner of Broadway and Reade street, previous to his departure for London. Nature seems to have exerted all her ingenuity in the production of this astounding animal. He is extremely complex—made up of the Elephant, Deer, Horse, Buffalo, Camel, and Sheep. It is the full size of a Horse, has the haunches of the Deer, the tail of the Elephant, a fine curled wool of camel's hair color, and easily bounds twelve or fifteen feet high. Naturalists and the oldest trappers assured Col. Fremont that it was never known previous to his discovery. It is undoubtedly "Nature's last," and the richest specimen received from California. To be seen every day this week. Admittance 25 cents; children half price.

In all reality, the animal was simply a woolly-coated horse, most likely related to today's Bashkir Curly Horse. But Barnum was delighted with the success of his fantasy tale about the animal.

> The community was absolutely famishing. They were ravenous. They could have swallowed anything, and like a good genius, I threw them, not a 'bone,' but a regular tit-bit, a bon-bon—and they swallowed it in a single gulp!

The ease with which P. T. Barnum was able to fool people with his exhibits serves to remind us of the Bible's warnings to have discernment and to "test the spirits."

COL. FREMONT'S NONDESCRIPT

FROM CALIFORNIA.

This Animal Captured by

COL. FREMONT and HIS PARTY,

Near the River Gila, New Mexico, after a Chase of Three Days, has arrived in this City on its way to Europe, and is

TO BE SEEN ALIVE,

At 290 Broadway, corner of Reade st.

FOR A FEW DAYS ONLY.

Beloved, do not believe every spirit, but test the spirits to see whether they are from God. For many false prophets have gone out into the world.

1 John 4:1

What does it mean to "test the spirits"? 1 John gives us the most important and obvious test.

By this you will know the Spirit of God: Every spirit that confesses that Jesus Christ has come in the flesh is from God, and every spirit that does not confess Jesus is not from God.

1 John 4:2,3

If a teacher, pastor, or anyone else, denies that Christ is God who took on human flesh as Jesus on Earth (fully God and fully Man), we shouldn't listen to them. This point is foundational to the Christian faith and makes it possible for Christ's death to pay for the sins of all mankind.

In general, you can be a discerning Christian, able to separate truth from lies, by continually studying scripture and growing in knowledge and wisdom. The better you know your Bible, the more obvious it will be when you're presented with falsehood.

False prophets or teachers are sneaky. They often present a good bit of truth with a few lies or distortions sprinkled in to get you thinking in the wrong direction. After you've studied the Bible for a while, you'll develop an internal radar that warns you when something is off. When you get warnings like that, search scripture, like the Bereans, to discover the truth.

> Now the Bereans were more noble-minded than the Thessalonians, for they received the message with great eagerness and examined the Scriptures every day to see if these teachings were true.

> *Acts 17:11*

Testing the spirits hinges on knowing the truth of God's word. The study of it is a lifelong practice. Be involved in a church, home group, or Bible study that believes in the authority and inerrancy of scripture, and takes the study of it seriously. Listen to teachers or read commentaries from people who have an established reputation of sticking to scripture.

54

PLAN B

I glanced at the blood dripping down my finger and realized I needed to come up with a Plan B. I had attempted to put one of our barn cats, Korrie, into a carrier for a trip to the vet for spaying surgery. She wasn't thrilled with the idea and expressed her disapproval by turning around and biting me. Korrie was normally a very sweet cat, so I hadn't expected such a violent reaction.

She was a beautiful calico, nearly full-grown, one of the many strays that adopted us. It seemed there was a big sign on our barn, printed in cat language, "Felines Welcome—Free Room and Board."

Ignoring the pain, I tried my best to hang onto Korrie. As scared and angry as she was, I figured if I let her go, I'd never catch her again, and we needed to leave soon in order to make it to the appointment. But Korrie wriggled out of my grasp and raced into the barn.

Plan B consisted of a couple of Band-Aids on my hand, a beach towel, and a large clothes hamper with a lid. Surprisingly, I was able to get close enough to the cat to drop the towel over her. I scooped her up, towel and all, and deposited her into the hamper. If you've lived on a farm, you understand that baling twine is as useful as duct tape. I tied the lid shut with some twine. The hamper had an open weave pattern, so Korrie had plenty of air. I received a few strange looks when I entered the vet's office with my unique cat carrier. Once we entered the examining room, Korrie came out of the hamper much more easily than she went in, and I left her there overnight for her surgery.

On the way home, I contemplated how the cat I had rescued, fed, and cared for had turned against me so violently. Korrie couldn't understand that what I was doing was for her own good. As humans, our thinking is at a much higher level than that of our pets. We know sometimes things are necessary, even though they may hurt or frighten us.

If I had the power to briefly become a cat, I could have explained to Korrie what was about to happen, and the reasons for it, in a way she would understand.

"For My thoughts are not your thoughts, neither are your ways My ways," declares the LORD. "For as the heavens are higher than the earth, so My ways are higher than your ways and My thoughts than your thoughts."

Isaiah 55:8,9

I can't become a cat or a horse to communicate better with my animals. But God did something similar when He became a man, Jesus Christ, in order to reveal Himself to us.

Although Korrie was a cat, the same principle applies to horses. Sometimes, it would be nice to communicate with our horses in a language they could fully understand, so we could explain things to them.

This would be one of my conversations, "You really don't need to be afraid of that. It's called a plastic bag. Although it seems to be able to fly, plastic bags never attack horses. Trust me on this."

The next time you find God placing you in a challenging or fearful situation, will you react like Korrie—biting and clawing to avoid what He has planned for you? Or will you cooperate with God and see what you can learn from the experience?

55

MIND READING

O LORD, You have searched me and known me. You know when I sit and when I rise; You understand my thoughts from afar. … Even before a word is on my tongue, You know all about it, O LORD.

Psalm 139:1,2,4

In this Psalm, we learn that God knows all our thoughts as well as what we are going to say, before it comes out of our mouths. In the New Testament, there are several examples of Jesus' ability to know our thoughts, also.

Knowing what they were thinking, Jesus replied, "Why are you thinking these things in your hearts?"

Luke 5:22

But Jesus knew what they were thinking and said, "Why do you harbor evil in your hearts?"

Matthew 9:4

Similar passages include Matthew 12:25, Luke 9:47, and 11:17.

It's possible for us to get an idea of what another person is thinking from external clues, such as their facial expressions and body language. But fortunately, people cannot read each others' thoughts.

Reading the mind of a horse is easier than reading a person's thoughts. You don't have to be a horse trainer to pick up on what a horse is thinking about doing. The more familiar you are with a particular horse, the better you'll be able to read his thoughts and predict the behaviors that will result from them.

Of all the equines we had over the years, one of my favorites was an 11.3 hand pony mare named Ebony. She was black with a couple of small, white patches. She was gaited, which is rare for a pony her size. I bought her from a woman who raised miniature horses. The first time we saw Ebony, she was in a corral with the minis. She looked like a draft horse in comparison.

It was the last time Ebony towered over anyone. After that, she was always the smallest at our place—physically smallest, that is. I don't think she ever realized she was short. Maybe she just never accepted it as a limitation. On trail rides, she not only kept up with the horses, she usually wanted to be ahead of them.

My middle and youngest daughters learned to ride on Ebony. That little pony was one of the most trustworthy equines we ever had. She had the same temperament day in and day out, which isn't always the case with mares.

But she wasn't perfect. As with many ponies, Ebony had her share of tricks and enjoyed pulling them on inexperienced riders. One of her favorites was taking a brief break by gaiting down to the corner of our riding arena. When she reached her destination, she would turn abruptly toward the gate and stop. If she stopped suddenly enough, the back of the saddle tipped up, flipping the rider onto Ebony's neck.

I could see this idea forming in her mind as soon as Ebony started down that long side of the arena. It wasn't hard to detect; she would have stopped at the gate on every lap if permitted. It took the girls some time before they could read the pony's mind and take precautionary measures to prevent this trick.

As with horses, our thoughts usually lead to actions—both good and bad.

For as he thinks in his heart, so is he.

Proverbs 23:7 NKJV

But each one is tempted when by his own evil desires he is lured away and enticed. Then after desire has conceived, it gives birth to sin; and sin, when it is full-grown, gives birth to death.

James 1:14,15

An experienced rider learns to read her mount's thoughts and can anticipate the horse's behavior, redirecting it to something more appropriate when necessary.

With our higher mental capacity, people should understand how our thoughts influence our behavior. Remember to use that Philippians 4:8 checklist as a filter for the inputs into your thought life—things that are true, noble, right, pure, lovely, admirable, excellent, or praiseworthy.

Scripture is the most beneficial thing we can put into our minds. Studying and memorizing scripture will transform us.

Do not be conformed to this world, but be transformed by the renewing of your mind. Then you will be able to test and approve what is the good, pleasing, and perfect will of God.

Romans 12:2

56

Donkeys

I found this statement on an internet resource site for pastors and Bible teachers. "First Kings 1:33 mentions Solomon riding a donkey on the day he was recognized as the new king of Israel." When I looked up the reference, I learned the statement on that website wasn't exactly true.

> "Take my servants with you," said the king [David]. "Set my son Solomon on my own mule and take him down to Gihon."
>
> *1 Kings 1:33*

Solomon rode a mule not a donkey. While some people may not be able to distinguish between the two or even realize there is a difference, donkeys and mules are not the same.

The genus Equus comprises horses, donkeys, and zebras. Since they belong to the same genus, any of these animals may be crossed with each other. Mules are the most common of these hybrids, a cross between horses and donkeys.

Donkeys are also known as burros. They are very social animals and bond strongly to other donkeys or humans. Most are smaller than horses, although some, known as Mammoths, can reach horse size. They are

sturdy, gentle, cautious animals. The donkey's powerful sense of self-preservation is often mistaken for stubbornness.

Because of their intelligence, they sometimes stop and think about things to ensure they aren't in danger before they obey a command. They may try to figure out, not only what they are supposed to do, but why they should do it.

In the past, donkeys were a common means of transportation and served as a low-maintenance beast of burden. In some parts of the world, they're still used in this manner.

Today, we may consider the donkey a comical animal, but he was not a subject of amusement in Bible times. The only animal in the Bible, besides the serpent, to be given the power of speech was the donkey. (Balaam's donkey, Numbers 22:21-35)

Some judges rode on white donkeys.

> You who ride white donkeys, who sit on saddle blankets, and you who travel the road, ponder the voices of the singers at the watering places.
>
> *Judges 5:10*

Donkeys were valuable and a sign of wealth. When Jacob left his father-in-law Laban to return to Canaan with his wives and children, he feared meeting his brother Esau, who in the past had threatened to kill him (Genesis 27:41). Jacob included twenty female donkeys and ten foals along with the other livestock he presented as a gift to appease Esau. (Genesis 32:5-15) Job's wealth, listed in Job 1:3, included five hundred female donkeys.

By far the most prominent use of a donkey in the New Testament was when Jesus rode one into Jerusalem on what we call Palm Sunday. It seems odd that someone as important as Jesus would ride a lowly donkey. But in Bible times, donkeys symbolized humility and service. A king riding a donkey meant he came in peace, while one on a horse meant war.

Zechariah prophesied the entrance of Jesus on a donkey more than five hundred years before it happened.

> Rejoice greatly, O Daughter of Zion! Shout in triumph, O Daughter of Jerusalem! See, your King comes to you, righteous and victorious, humble and riding on a donkey, on a colt, the foal of a donkey.
>
> *Zechariah 9:9*

All four Gospels mention Jesus' triumphal entry into Jerusalem.

Matthew 21:1-9 (mentions a donkey and her colt)

Mark 11:1-10 (just the colt, and the fact that he was never ridden)

Luke 19:29-38 (just the colt, never ridden)

John 12:12-15 (just the colt)

> As they approached Jerusalem and came to Bethphage on the Mount of Olives, Jesus sent out two disciples, saying to them, "Go into the village ahead of you, and at once you will find a donkey tied there, with her colt beside her. Untie them and bring them to Me. If anyone questions you, tell him that the Lord needs them, and he will send them right away."
>
> *Matthew 21:1-3*

All the Gospels, except John, state that two disciples were sent to get the donkeys. However, none of the accounts name those disciples. The account in Matthew includes two donkeys—a jenny and her colt. The person who owned the donkeys would release them when told, "The Lord has need of them." Perhaps Jesus had made prior arrangements with this owner.

In the New King James and other translations, Matthew 21:7 has some vague wording.

> They brought the donkey and the colt, laid their clothes on them, and set Him on them. NKJV

What does the last "them" in that verse refer to? Some interpret it to mean Jesus sat on both donkeys. That would be physically awkward. It seems probable that "them" refers to the clothes, and that Jesus sat only on the younger donkey with the mother perhaps being led alongside as a calming influence on her colt.

Other versions attempt to clarify this.

> and brought the donkey and the colt, and laid their cloaks on them; and He sat on the cloaks. NASB
>
> They brought the donkey and the colt and placed their cloaks on them for Jesus to sit on. NIV

Still others hypothesize that Jesus rode both donkeys, but not at the same time. He rode the jenny on the first, steeper part of the journey, then switched to the colt right before He entered the city. This is possible but seems unlikely to me.

Mark and Luke provide the additional detail that no one had ever ridden the donkey colt. Donkeys have a naturally calmer disposition than horses. Anyone jumping onto an unridden horse colt would most likely find themselves flying off again. A donkey wouldn't be as reactionary. And Jesus, who created the world and calmed storms, could instantly tame a colt if needed.

Because the colt was young and had never been ridden, it lends credence to the possibility of the mother walking alongside him. A common training technique for equines is to work them beside an older, more experienced partner. With his mother close, the colt would more readily accept the unusual happenings, like a rider on his back, stepping on the clothes spread on the ground, the waving palm branches, and the general noise and hubbub of the crowd. If you haven't had much experience with equines, you may find it surprising that a donkey might be afraid to step on clothing laid on the ground, but I've known horses who have shied away from markings painted on the road.

The colt, having never been ridden, may symbolize that the journey Jesus was about to make to Jerusalem, and shortly after to Calvary, was something no one had ever done before.

Before the donkey could do the work of carrying Jesus to Jerusalem, he had to be loosed or untied. Luke uses some variation of the words "loose" or "tied" five times in four verses.

> "Go into the village opposite you, where as you enter you will find a colt **tied**, on which no one has ever sat. **Loose** it and bring it here. And if anyone asks you, 'Why are you **loosing** it?' thus you shall say to him, 'Because the Lord has need of it.' "
>
> So those who were sent went their way and found it just as He had said to them. But as they were **loosing** the colt, the owners of it said to them, "Why are you **loosing** the colt?"
>
> *Luke 19:30-33 NKJV*

Why this emphasis on the detail that the donkey was tied and needed to be untied or loosed?

lyo—to untie, loose, break, destroy, unbind, release from bonds, set free

Just as the donkey couldn't carry Jesus anywhere while tied, in order for God to use us for the work He has planned for us, (Ephesians 2:10) we need to be set free from anything that holds us back. What is it in your life that prevents you from being free to worship and serve God wholeheartedly? Fears, worries, guilt, or the pursuit of money, power, or pleasure? Like the donkey, let yourself be loosed so you can freely serve God.

> Since we have such a huge crowd of men of faith watching us from the grandstands, let us strip off anything that slows us down or holds us back, and especially those sins that wrap themselves so tightly around our feet and trip us up; and let us run with patience the particular race that God has set before us.
>
> *Hebrews 12:1 TLB*

Almost all donkeys have a cross on their back. One dark line runs along their spine with a second crossing over the shoulders. Several legends offer explanations for the donkeys' cross. The following is my favorite.

A young donkey colt carried Jesus to Jerusalem on Palm Sunday. Several days later, when he heard the Romans would crucify Jesus, that same colt wanted to carry the heavy, wooden cross for Him. The soldiers laughed at the donkey and chased him away.

By the time the donkey found Jesus at Golgotha, He was already on the cross. The colt stood behind the cross, braying mournfully. It's said the shadow cast by the cross onto the donkey's back became a permanent marking passed on to every donkey from that day on.

57

MULES

You are to keep My statutes. You shall not crossbreed two different kinds [kil'ayim] of livestock; you shall not sow your fields with two kinds [kil'ayim] of seed; and you shall not wear clothing made of two kinds [kil'ayim] of material.

Leviticus 19:19

Today, we find it challenging to understand the reasoning behind such commands. The moral laws of the Old Testament still apply to us, but most agree the civil and ceremonial laws of the Old Testament were directed only to the nation of Israel.

Did this prohibition of crossing different kinds of livestock prevent the Israelites from breeding mules? I found some disagreement about that. It seems to hinge upon the definition of the word "kind."

kil'ayim—dual, two things of diverse kinds

The mule is a crossbred animal with a donkey father and a horse mother. Donkeys and horses are both from the Genus Equus. However, the species differ.

Horse—Genus: Equus, Species: Equus ferus caballus

Donkey—Genus: Equus, Species: Equus asinus

The word used for "kind" in Genesis 1 differs from the word used in Leviticus 19.

Let the earth bring forth living creatures according to their kinds. [min]

Genesis 1:24

min—kind, sometimes a species: livestock, land crawlers, and beasts of the earth according to their kinds.

Do not plow with an ox and a donkey yoked together.

Deuteronomy 22:10

In this verse, the two animals are very different. It's not possible to cross an ox with a donkey, and it would be difficult for the two to work together because of differences in their sizes, body structure, gait, and temperament.

If "kind" in Leviticus 19 means Genus, then the production of mules was permissible. If "kind" was more restrictive, meaning what we call species, then the Israelites would not have been permitted to raise mules. The consensus seems to be that the Israelites did not breed mules. However, they did use them—more about that later.

What was the purpose behind this prohibition of the mixture of animals, cloths, and seeds? God always has a reason for His commandments, whether we understand them now or whether the Israelites themselves knew the reason at the time of the Old Testament.

God may have had a natural, physical reason for prohibiting mixtures or hybrids both in plants and animals. Maintaining the purity of both would ensure their long-term viability. Mules are sterile; they cannot reproduce. If the Israelites had relied on mules as their work animals, the supply might have diminished, while donkeys could continue to produce natural offspring year after year.

There was most likely an additional spiritual or moral meaning behind the commandments. The Israelites, recently freed from slavery in Egypt, needed to be reminded that God had set them apart as His chosen people.

> for you are a people holy to the LORD your God. The LORD has chosen you to be a people for His prized possession out of all the peoples on the face of the earth.
>
> *Deuteronomy 14:2*

As God's chosen ones, the Israelites were not to intermarry with the nations around them or adopt their pagan practices. Many of the commandments God gave them were a reminder to maintain their purity and holiness. We aren't under the same civil and ceremonial laws, but they can serve as a reminder to us, as well.

As believers, we are not to blend in with the world. We cannot mingle false teachings with the truth of God's word. Marriage or close partnerships between believers and unbelievers are forbidden. We can't tolerate sinful behavior in our own lives or encourage such practices in others.

If the Israelites couldn't cross horses and donkeys to raise mules, why did some people in the Old Testament have them?

The animals were most likely imported from other nations. Was this importation merely sidestepping God's commandment on a technicality? Was God's intent for them not to have mules or not to raise them? It's interesting that the New Testament doesn't mention mules at all.

We first hear of mules in Israel during the time of King David. David's sons, Solomon and Absalom, both rode mules, one as he began his role as king, the other at the end of his life.

Absalom, rebelled and attempted to dethrone his father to become king of Israel. While fleeing from David's army on a mule, Absalom met an untimely death.

> Now Absalom was riding on his mule when he met the servants of David, and as the mule went under the thick branches of a large oak, Absalom's head was caught fast in the tree. The mule under him kept going, so that he was suspended in midair.
>
> *2 Samuel 18:9*

Later, when King David was near death, he arranged for his own mule to carry another of his sons, Solomon, to the place where he would be anointed as the new king.

"Take my servants with you," said the king. "Set my son Solomon on my own mule and take him down to Gihon."

1 Kings 1:33

David's choice to use a mule for this important journey is interesting. Horses were used in war rather than peace. But also, David was aware of God's commandment against kings accumulating horses.

But the king must not acquire many horses for himself or send the people back to Egypt to acquire more horses, for the LORD has said, "You are never to go back that way again."

Deuteronomy 17:16

Multiplying horses would encourage kings to rely on their own strength and power rather than relying on God. When Solomon became king, he disregarded this command.

Solomon had 4,000 [some say 40,000] stalls for his chariot horses and 12,000 horses [or horsemen].

1 Kings 4:26

Solomon's horses were imported from Egypt and Kue;

the royal merchants purchased them from Kue. A chariot could be imported from Egypt for six hundred shekels of silver, and a horse for a hundred and fifty.

1 Kings 10:28

Hundreds of years later, when some of the Israelites returned from captivity in Babylon, mules were one animal they brought to Jerusalem.

Their horses were seven hundred and thirty-six, their mules two hundred and forty-five, their camels four hundred and thirty-five, and their donkeys six thousand seven hundred and twenty.

Ezra 2:66,67

Note the large number of donkeys compared to the other animals.

Donkeys were apparently still the preferred beast of burden at that time.

58

MULE TRAINING?

Don't ask me why, but many years ago, I was certain I needed a mule. Strong feelings such as these are why I don't always trust myself when I think I'm hearing from God. I have an amazing ability to convince myself that my "wants" are things God also believes I should have.

Somehow or another, I did end up with a mule—Sassy. God must have agreed that I needed a mule—but for different reasons. Sassy taught me a few things about myself, and she became a favorite character in the Sonrise Stable series.

It quickly became obvious that Sassy was not the most obedient or respectful mule and that mules' brains work differently than horses'. Finding myself in need of help with correcting Sassy's wayward behavior, I searched the internet for mule-training advice. I came across a video I found disturbing. (They've since removed it.)

Although the men in the video claimed to be "training" mules, I felt sick to my stomach as I watched. Their practices were not training at all, but animal abuse.

One mule in a corral had a tire tied to his saddle and was forced to drag it around. While that was a questionable technique in itself, it didn't stop there. Whenever the mule stood still, one man threw a bucket or large plastic tub at him. If that didn't get him moving, another man struck him with a long whip. There was no logic to the men's actions. No matter what the poor mule did, he was punished.

Later in the video, they rode several mules on a trail. Two riders whipped the mule, who was "in training," several times for no apparent reason. Back at the corral, they rode the same mule with his left front leg tied up off the ground. The mule tried to kick the man behind him, which meant he had to balance on two legs. With his leg still tied, the mule reared and nearly fell over backwards.

Mules have a reputation for remembering abuse—and later, getting even. Not only was this cruel treatment of the animal, but it created a potential danger for anyone who would own him in the future. The mule might associate all humans with this type of abuse, and out of fear or anger, someday decide to get revenge.

The group PETA (People for the Ethical Treatment of Animals) holds some pretty extreme positions. When then president, Barack Obama, swatted a fly during a televised interview, PETA sent him a Katcha Bug humane bug catcher—a device that allows you to trap a housefly and release it outside.

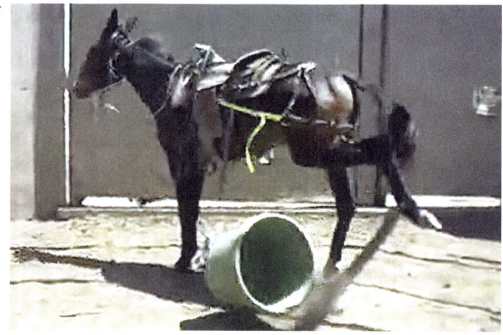

PETA president and co-founder, Ingrid Newkirk, described her group's overall goal as "total animal liberation." That included abolishing meat, milk, cheese, eggs, honey, zoos, aquariums, circuses, wool, leather, fur, silk, hunting, fishing—and even pet ownership.

Newkirk had one seeing-eye dog taken away from its blind owner. PETA opposes all medical research that uses animals. According to Newkirk, "Even if animal research resulted in a cure for AIDS, we would be against it."

There is an enormous gap between the two extremes of animal abusers and animal rights activists. As Christians, what should our position be on this issue?

In Genesis, after God created Adam and Eve, He gave humans dominion over all the earth. That included animals. Although we were created to be vegetarians (Genesis 1:29,30), after the flood, God granted permission to use animals for food. At the same time, He made the animals fear man. It seems He wanted to give them a chance to avoid being hunted and killed.

> "All wild animals and birds and fish will be afraid of you," God told him; "for I have placed them in your power, and they are yours to use for food, in addition to grain and vegetables."
>
> *Genesis 9:2,3 TLB*

I believe Proverbs 12:10 best sums up what God intended for our relationship with animals.

> A righteous man regardeth the life of his beast: but the tender mercies of the wicked are cruel. KJV

The Bible isn't a book on animal care, but it contains passages that describe kind and ethical treatment of animals. One image Jesus chose for Himself was a good Shepherd, who not only cared for His sheep, but was willing to lay down His life for them.

> I am the good shepherd. The good shepherd lays down His life for the sheep.
>
> *John 10:11*

You're probably familiar with the fourth commandment—to remember the Sabbath day and not work on it. Did you know it applied to animals as well as people? God wanted the animals to have a day of rest so they would not be overworked.

> Remember the Sabbath day by keeping it holy. Six days you shall labor and do all your work, but the seventh day is a Sabbath to the LORD your God, on which you must not do any work—neither you, nor your son or daughter, nor your manservant or maidservant or livestock, nor the foreigner within your gates.
>
> *Exodus 20:8-10*

Here are several other verses that illustrate God's concern for the animals He created.

> Do not muzzle an ox while it is treading out the grain.
>
> *Deuteronomy 25:4*

> He tends His flock like a shepherd; He gathers the lambs in His arms and carries them close to His heart. He gently leads the nursing ewes.
>
> *Isaiah 40:11*

> Be sure to know the state of your flocks, and pay close attention to your herds;
>
> *Proverbs 27:23*

> Look at the birds of the air: They do not sow or reap or gather into barns—and yet your heavenly Father feeds them. Are you not much more valuable than they?
>
> *Matthew 6:26*

Which of you, having a donkey or an ox that has fallen into a pit, will not immediately pull him out on the Sabbath day?

Luke 14:5 NKJV

What man among you, if he has a hundred sheep and loses one of them, does not leave the ninety-nine in the pasture and go after the one that is lost, until he finds it?

Luke 15:4

You don't have to be a PETA member to be opposed to cruel treatment of animals. The Bible is pretty clear that in giving us "dominion" over the animal kingdom, the expectation was that we would treat them humanely.

59

MY PATIENCE PROFESSOR

Before becoming a Christian, I had little patience with myself. Whether I felt good or bad about myself depended upon how well I performed or what I could achieve. I believed I had to do everything well, even things I'd never tried before. I was good at a lot of things—I received excellent grades in school, was reasonably artistic, and excelled at many sports.

I became the ultimate perfectionist. But there will always be someone who performs better than you—or something you can't do well no matter how hard you try. If you base your self-worth on those things, at times you'll have a low opinion of yourself. When I became a Christian in my late twenties, I realized my value came from being a child of God—not from my ability to perform.

As a new Christian, I remember praying for God to give me patience. I guess I expected it to arrive in a package with a bow on top. But I learned that isn't how God works. Patience isn't something God hands to you; it's something He develops in you. This happens over time as He takes you through challenging or frustrating situations.

God blessed me with three daughters and led me to homeschool them. Children aren't a "trial" in a negative sense, but they do require a lot of patience. After fifteen years of homeschooling, I believed I had become a very patient person, achieving what I considered the equivalent of a Bachelor's degree in patience.

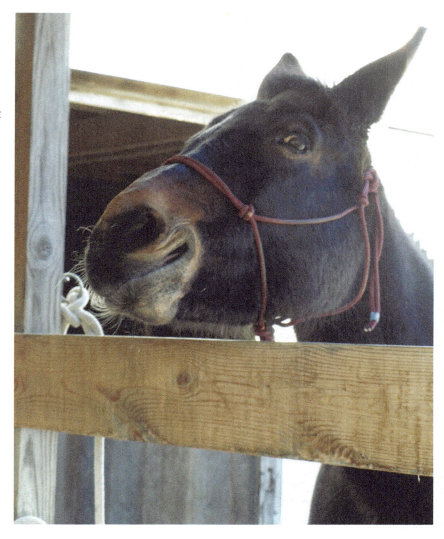

Maybe I was becoming smug about my level of patience. Somehow, I found myself buying a mule. Not just any mule—a thoroughly spoiled one that was used to getting her own way. I think it was all part of God's plan—allowing me to buy that cantankerous animal. Some of my interactions with Sassy must have made Him smile.

After a few days of working with Sassy, it was obvious I didn't possess as much patience as I had thought. Sassy was determined to take me on to a Master's degree in that area.

I studied mule-training videos, determined to outsmart—or outstubborn that mule!

Although Sassy taught me a lot about myself and about mules, I confess I didn't have the patience, or maybe the mule savvy, to stick it out long term with her. She ended up going to Texas, where her new owner used her in mounted shooting competitions.

James reminds us that trials help us develop patience or perseverance so we may become mature and complete. I hope you are growing in patience each day—with your horses or other animals, yourself, family members, friends, and acquaintances.

> Consider it pure joy, my brothers, when you encounter trials of many kinds, because you know that the testing of your faith develops perseverance [hypomonē]. Allow perseverance [hypomonē] to finish its work, so that you may be mature and complete, not lacking anything.
>
> *James 1:2-4*
>
> **hypomonē**—steadfastness, constancy, patient endurance

If you want a crash course in patience, I recommend buying a mule—especially one that isn't well-trained.

60

PERSEVERANCE

There are similarities between patience and perseverance. Different Bible versions use the words almost interchangeably. For example, in James, some versions translate "hypomonē" as patience, while others use perseverance.

> My brethren, count it all joy when you fall into various trials, knowing that the testing of your faith produces patience [hypomonē]. But let patience have its perfect work, that you may be perfect and complete, lacking nothing.
>
> *James 1:2-4 NKJV*

Webster's 1828 dictionary provides the following definitions.

> **patience**—the suffering of afflictions, pain, toil, calamity, provocation or other evil, with a calm, unruffled temper; endurance without murmuring or fretfulness

While patience seems passive—calmly waiting or enduring, perseverance is more active.

> **perseverance**—persistence in anything undertaken; continued pursuit or prosecution of any business or enterprise begun

The Bible has much to say about being patient and persevering. The parable of the persistent widow is an example of persevering.

> Then Jesus told them a parable about their need to pray at all times and not lose heart: [ekkakeō] "In a certain town there was a judge who neither feared God nor respected men. And there was a widow in that town who kept appealing to him, 'Give me justice against my adversary.'
>
> For a while he refused, but later he said to himself, 'Though I neither fear God nor respect men, yet because this widow keeps pestering me, I will give her justice. Then she will stop wearing me out [hypōpiazō] with her perpetual requests.'"
>
> And the Lord said, "Listen to the words of the unjust judge. Will not God bring about justice for His elect who cry out to Him day and night?"
>
> *Luke 18:1-7*

ekkakeō—to be weak, to fail (in heart), faint, be weary

hypōpiazō—many versions translate this as "weary me" or "wear me out," but its literal meaning is "to beat black and blue." Most translators have chosen its metaphorical meaning.

The parable is one of contrasts. The intent is not to portray God as One who only helps us when we nag Him as was the case with the corrupt judge. It shows how *unlike* that judge God is. He is a loving Father who delights in giving good gifts to His children.

The parable emphasizes the importance of persevering in prayer. Many of us have people or situations we've prayed about for years. It's easy to become discouraged and give up when we don't see anything changing.

Surely the arm of the LORD is not too short to save, nor His ear too dull to hear. But your iniquities have built barriers between you and your God, and your sins have hidden His face from you, so that He does not hear.

Isaiah 59:1,2

I believe God hears our prayers as long as we aren't willfully, continually sinning. We must have the right motives, and our requests must be in line with His will. If we don't see the answers we expect or hope for, it may simply be that God's timing is not the same as ours. Seemingly unanswered prayers for the salvation of a loved one are the most difficult to understand. How salvation works has been debated for years (predestination versus free will). But as humans, we cannot override another person's free will, and it appears that God chooses not to.

Pray without ceasing.

1 Thessalonians 5:17

Let us not grow weary in well-doing, for in due time we will reap a harvest if we do not give up.

Galatians 6:9

A bay Thoroughbred gelding, Zippy Chippy, foaled in 1991, may be the ultimate equine example of perseverance.

With a name like Zippy Chippy and a pedigree that includes some of the most famous race horses of all time, his owner, trainer, and jockey had high hopes for Zippy's racing career. The Thoroughbred colt was born into the equivalent of a royal family in the horse racing world with such ancestors as: Native Dancer, Bold Ruler, Northern Dancer, War Admiral, and Man o' War.

Zippy's first chance to show his stuff was as a three-year-old at Belmont Park on Sept. 13, 1994. Jockey Julio Pezua rode Zippy to an eighth-place finish out of ten horses. After five races, Zippy had finished no higher than third. When Belmont closed that fall, Zippy raced at the Aqueduct track in New York. In his first race there, Zippy finished ninth out of eleven horses. Two weeks later, he was dead last, eighth out of eight, and fifty-four lengths behind the winner.

They demoted Zippy from the big-name tracks to the minor leagues of horse racing. Although he was running against horses of lower quality, Zippy finished fourth in his first race at the Finger Lakes track. Zippy continued to rack up lackluster performances, but he never lost his enthusiasm. The Thoroughbred eagerly anticipated each race, and despite finishing third, fifth, or even last, he left the track prancing, tail held high, as if he'd won the Kentucky Derby.

After eighteen races, Zippy had finished second three times. But by then, his owner had given up on him. The horse had a reputation of being hard to handle and impossible to motivate. He was known for destroying stalls and water buckets. One of his favorite tricks was snatching items from the hands or head of an unsuspecting person walking past his stall. Zippy was sold several times. With each sale, his future grew bleaker.

A Puerto Rican trainer, Felix Monserrate, took a liking to Zippy. Wanting to keep the horse from ending up at a slaughterhouse, he traded his 1988 Ford pickup for him. Zippy had no way of understanding what had happened, and he wasn't particularly grateful to Felix for saving him. The first thing the temperamental horse did was bite his new owner on the back.

Felix was also Zippy's trainer. In their first seven races, Zippy had two third-place finishes. On September 23, 1995, Zippy came incredibly close to winning. In a heartbreaking finish, the big gelding lost by a nose, a mere one fortieth of a second behind the winner. Felix was pleased with Zippy's performance and, ever the optimist, believed their next race would be the one.

On his next outing, Zippy was in last place for most of the race. He came on strong at the end, finishing second and losing by a neck. After that, Zippy hit a bad streak, losing repeatedly. Felix switched jockeys, exercise boys, saddles; he even changed the horse's diet. Nothing made a difference.

Felix's devotion to the horse is difficult to understand. People who knew Zippy described him as mean to people and other horses. Grooms pushed his food into his stall from a safe distance, using a rake or pitchfork, so he couldn't bite them. It was difficult to find an exercise boy to ride Zippy, since he bucked most of them off. He was difficult to shoe and once kicked the farrier's truck with both hind legs.

One day, Zippy trapped Felix in the back of his stall for almost an hour. Each time the man tried to escape, Zippy threatened to strike or bite him. According to Felix, the horse never intended to hurt anyone. It was just Zippy's way of playing.

At six, Zippy extended his record to eighty losses. Felix attempted to retire him. But the horse was so miserable away from the track, the trainer brought him back.

Zippy became a favorite with the local

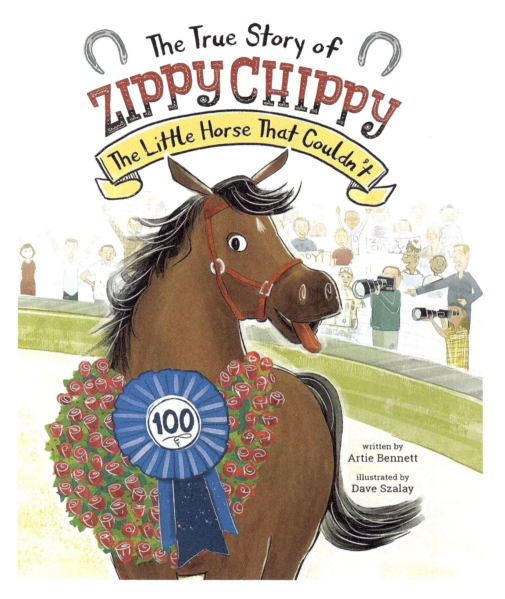

spectators. His fans flocked to races to cheer him on, rooting for the underdog to get his first win. The media was not so kind. Felix was bothered by newspaper headlines that referred to Zippy as ugly and stupid. He was determined to help Zippy win to prove the reporters wrong.

But Zippy had a trick he hadn't played yet. This would be a costly one. In many of his previous races, he'd started slowly, then made a valiant effort to come from behind. But on June 23, 1998, in a race at Finger Lakes, six horses flew out of the gates at the starting bell—while the seventh—did not.

Zippy didn't have much zip that day. His jockey finally got him going, but they finished last, his eighty-third loss. Not leaving the gate or leaving very slowly is called dwelling. It's highly frowned on in racing. But Zippy was so fond of it, he dwelt again a few weeks later.

Zippy was banned from the track for sixty days. During that time, Felix put the horse through remedial lessons with a focus on breaking quickly from the gate. In September, Zippy returned for his next race, but when he dwelt in the gate again, Zippy received a permanent ban. The horse was seven years old and had run eighty-five races. Most racehorses retire by age five, but Felix knew Zippy liked to run. And he wanted a win before retiring the horse. The only place Zippy wasn't banned was at the county fair level.

In 2004, fans crowded a Northampton, Massachusetts track to cheer Zippy on in his one-hundredth race. The atmosphere at the track was electric, the horse's fans decked out in Zippy hats and T-shirts. But, after a disappointing last place finish, Felix decided Zippy had run his last race.

Knowing how much his horse loved to be at the track, Felix thought working as a track pony would keep Zippy happy. His job was to ride alongside and lead a racehorse to and from the track to keep the other horse calm. Zippy didn't last long in that role. He tried to either race the other horse or bite him.

The perfect ending to this story would be that Zippy finally got the win Felix believed he had in him, but it wasn't to be. Zippy never won a race. He ended his career with eight second place and twelve third place finishes.

In 2010, Felix was seventy years old. It was time he and Zippy both retired. Zippy went to the Old Friends at Cabin Creek, a new Thoroughbred retirement farm in New York. For the grand opening ceremony, the owners had created a winner's circle from flowers and bales of straw with a sign that read: Cabin Creek Winner's Circle. The plan was for Felix to lead Zippy into the circle, a place he'd never entered by finishing first in a race. Then, everyone would take photos of the pair.

Zippy, apparently insulted by the idea, kicked the sign over.

Life at Cabin Creek was a big change for Zippy. But eventually, the cranky, old gelding made a friend, a chestnut named Red Down South. The two shared the same pasture and became inseparable. Tourists visited Cabin Creek each summer to see the famous retired Thoroughbreds, but one of the most popular was Zippy Chippy. The gift shop sold a mug with a photo of Zippy and the caption, "Winners don't always finish first."

Zippy even has his own picture book, *The True Story of Zippy Chippy: The Little Horse That Couldn't.*

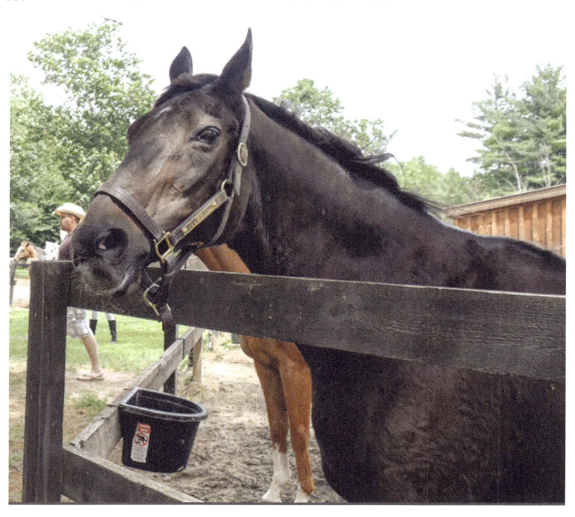

61

NOT LIKE THE HORSE OR MULE

Do not be like the horse or mule, which have no understanding; they must be controlled with bit and bridle to make them come to you.

Psalm 32:9

When my three daughters arrived in our living room, I began reading Psalm 32. We had six horses. Four were purchased several years earlier. The other two were foals we raised from our own mares. At first, several of the horses we bought were difficult to catch in the pasture.

If you've had the same experience, you know how frustrating that can be. You walk calmly up to the horse in the field. He stares serenely at you—until you get within an arm's length. Then he whirls and runs off a short distance and resumes grazing. This process often repeats until he—or you—tires of the game and gives up.

We had worked with the horses until we could catch each of them easily. In fact, there was usually a stampede as they all came charging to the gate at my whistle.

That morning, we had turned the horses out in the pasture in front of our house. That pasture didn't have any shelter or water, so after a few hours, we had to catch them and lead them back to the barn.

After we finished our Bible study and homeschool work, we went out to take care of the horses. I whistled as usual, and five horses stormed up to the gate. After we attached lead ropes to their halters, I looked up to see whether the remaining straggler had made it to the gate.

No. Ginger stood grazing in the middle of the five-acre field.

"Ginger," I yelled. "Come on, girl!" I gave my loudest whistle, but she paid no attention. I trudged through the tall grass to retrieve the rebellious one, but when she saw me coming, she turned and ran.

"You rascal!" She hadn't done that in a while. Knowing that pursuing her would be a game I didn't have time to win, I decided to outsmart her.

Ginger was the lead mare and hated to be without her herd. I figured once she saw the other horses leaving, she wouldn't be able to get to the gate fast enough. The girls and I started for the barn. Each of them led a horse. I had two, one on each side. I kept glancing back, confident that Ginger would gallop toward the gate as soon as she noticed the others leaving her.

But each time I looked back, Ginger was in the same spot—not the least disturbed about being left by herself.

When we had the other horses in the barnyard, I thought back to our Bible lesson. Was this evidence that God has a sense of humor? It seemed as if He was putting an exclamation point on the Psalm we had read earlier. "Do not be like the horse or mule, which have no understanding; they must be controlled with bit and bridle to make them come to you."

It worked. It's been years since that happened, but I still remember it well.

I had a plan for Ginger, which required her cooperation. It was a good plan—for her benefit. She needed water and shelter, but her unwillingness to come near me prevented me from providing it. At my approach, she ran away, so I left her there to come to her senses.

Remember Jonah? When God called him to preach to the Ninevites, he hopped on the next ship traveling in the opposite direction.

Jonah, however, got up to flee to Tarshish, away from the presence of the LORD. He went down to Joppa and found a ship bound for Tarshish. So he paid the fare and went aboard to sail for Tarshish, away from the presence of the LORD.

Jonah 1:4

The Psalm says that the horse has no "understanding." That doesn't mean horses are stupid, but their ability to reason and understand is not at the level of a human's. We can't use that "not under-standing" excuse when we run from God and attempt to avoid the work He's prepared for us.

Sometimes, the opportunities God has for us require immediate obedience. We may never have another chance to do some things. Erwin Raphael McManus calls this "seizing your divine moment" in his book with the same title.

For Ginger, there was a second chance. When I went back out later, she walked right up to me, apparently repentant for her previous misbehavior.

62

THE THRILL OF VICTORY

"The thrill of victory and the agony of defeat."

That phrase is from *The Wide World of Sports*, an old television show. Over the years, I saw it apply to the experience of 4-Hers competing at our county fair. For some, there is the excitement of winning or placing in a class. Others experience sadness, frustration, or anger when they do not do well.

I sometimes wonder how God views all the competition in our world. We are often pitted against each other to win or achieve something or to get ahead in a career.

> Do you not know that in a race all the runners run, but only one receives the prize? Run in such a way as to take the prize. Everyone who competes in the games trains with strict discipline. They do it for a crown that is perishable, but we do it for a crown that is imperishable. Therefore I do not run aimlessly; I do not fight like I am beating the air. No, I discipline my body and make it my slave, so that after I have preached to others, I myself will not be disqualified.
>
> *1 Corinthians 9:24-27*

The Isthmian Games in Corinth were second only to the Olympics in popularity. Paul used them as an example the Corinthians would be familiar with. He compared the effort required to win a race in those games to the diligence and devotion we need to put forth in our Christian life.

It's not a perfect comparison. In those races, and in horse show classes, there is only a single winner, but we can all be winners in the Christian life. The Corinthian runners disciplined themselves and trained vigorously for a prize that had little real value (a perishable crown).

In the Christian race, when we reach our goal, we'll receive an imperishable crown. As in the parable of the talents, we long to hear our Father greet us with, "Well done, good and faithful servant." Matthew 25:21

In the events of this life, I don't believe God cares so much whether we win or lose, as long as we compete honestly and give our best effort. Additionally, it's important how we handle both our victories and defeats. Can we win without being prideful and lose without becoming angry?

Romans 12:15 calls us to "Rejoice with those who rejoice; weep with those who weep."

Maybe it's just me, but I find it easier to sympathize with those who are weeping. It's the "rejoicing" part I find challenging. Take this scenario, for instance.

You've spent countless hours working with your horse, training and conditioning him yourself. Now, you're at the fair, the big 4-H event of the year. There are seven horses and riders in your class but only six ribbons. When the class ends, you feel good about how you and your horse performed. Maybe not your best, but nothing to be ashamed of, either.

The announcer begins calling out the winners.

The winning horse is an expensive animal, professionally trained, and ridden by a younger girl who isn't a very good rider. These are called push-button horses. The rider isn't required to know anything. The horse does it all; the rider is merely a passenger along for the ride. But you're okay with that. It's hard to compete against a horse of that caliber. You set your eyes on second place.

As the announcer goes through the remaining placings, your number is never called. You sit for a moment, alone, on your horse in the middle of the ring, tears burning in your eyes. Everyone in the audience seems to be staring at you—the only one in the class leaving without a ribbon. Slowly, you leave the ring frustrated and embarrassed.

At that moment, would you be able to rejoice with those who placed in the class? Even if you managed to speak words to congratulate the winner, would your heart be in it?

I'm not saying it's easy, but I think God is pleased when we are able to lose gracefully. Too often, I've heard the opposite at horse shows–whining, complaining, and envy. Comments like the following:

"Where did they get that judge, anyway? Is he/she blind?"

"How could they place that horse over me? She broke at least three times."

"If I had a horse that cost as much as hers, I'd win everything too. She doesn't even know how to ride."

"It's not fair!"

I was extremely competitive before becoming a Christian. I'm mostly recovered from that in terms of competitions I participate in. But when one of my daughters didn't place in a class in which she'd done really well, I'll confess I may have expressed a few thoughts along the lines of those previous comments.

Even worse than the whining and complaining—from the contestants and/or their parents—is when riders take their frustration out on their horses. I've seen kids viciously yank the reins, jerking their horse's mouth or kicking them for no reason other than being upset they didn't win.

Rather than seeing us win all the time, I think God is more interested in developing Christ-like character in us. And sometimes, the "agony of defeat" is one of His best tools to accomplish that.

While losing a horse show class seems a pretty minor thing at my age, it can be a big deal to a young person. It's disappointing and frustrating. I don't know that it qualifies as suffering as mentioned in the following verse from Romans, but the idea is the same—we can learn from our disappointing losses.

> Not only that, but we also rejoice in our sufferings, because we know that suffering produces perseverance; perseverance, character; and character, hope. And hope does not disappoint us, because God has poured out His love into our hearts through the Holy Spirit, whom He has given us.
>
> *Romans 5:3-5*

Winning a ribbon or trophy is fun, but even more important is that God is pleased with how we've lived our lives—what we've done with the skills and material possessions He's given us. This is explained in the parable of the talents in Matthew 25:14-28.

> Well done, good and faithful servant! You have been faithful with a few things; I will put you in charge of many things. Enter into the joy of your master!
>
> *Matthew 25:21*

We don't earn our salvation, that is by faith, but we will receive rewards based on our lives here on earth.

Blessed are you when people insult you, persecute you, and falsely say all kinds of evil against you because of Me. Rejoice and be glad, because great is your reward [misthos] in heaven; for in the same way they persecuted the prophets before you.

Matthew 5:11,12

Be careful not to perform your righteous acts before men to be seen by them. If you do, you will have no reward [misthos] from your Father in heaven.

Matthew 6:1

He who plants and he who waters are one in purpose, and each will be rewarded [misthos] according to his own labor.

1 Corinthians 3:8

Indeed, if anyone gives you even a cup of water because you bear the name of Christ, truly I tell you, he will never lose his reward. [misthos]

Mark 9:41

For we must all appear before the judgment seat [bema] of Christ, that each one may receive his due for the things done in the body, whether good or bad.

2 Corinthians 5:10

Behold, I am coming soon, and My reward [misthos] is with Me, to give to each one according to what he has done.

Revelation 22:12

misthos—of the rewards which God bestows, or will bestow, upon good deeds and endeavours; dues paid for work; hire, wages

bema—a step, pace, the space which a foot covers; a raised place mounted by steps; the official seat of a judge

63

TRANSFORMED

This is one of my favorite, real-life horse stories. If there weren't photos, books, and newspaper accounts to back it up, you'd think it was pure fiction.

One snowy day in February, 1956, Harry de Leyer was on his way to a horse auction in New Holland, Pennsylvania, deep in Amish country. He hoped to purchase a horse to use in his riding lesson program at a New York boarding school. When a tire blew out on his station wagon, de Leyer worried he wouldn't make it to the auction at all.

That annoying flat tire would change Harry's life forever.

Repairing the tire took so long that when Harry finally arrived at the auction, it was over. All that remained were horses no one had purchased. Those poor animals had been loaded into a large trailer that would soon be headed to a slaughterhouse—the fate of most unsold horses at these auctions.

After making the long trip, Harry didn't want to return home empty-handed. He walked over to examine the leftovers. Through the slats of the trailer, he saw that most of the horses had a dull, lifeless look—all but one. A tall gray returned Harry's gaze with what seemed like a hopeful look. De Leyer asked the truck driver to unload the horse, so he could have a better look at him.

Although not a draft, the 16-hand gelding had been used hard for farm work by someone. Harness marks were worn into his chest, and he had open sores on his legs. His hooves were overgrown and chipped with one shoe missing. The gelding's coat was caked with dirt and manure, his mane and tail ragged. He was so thin his hip bones stuck out. Someone had considered the gray used up at a relatively young age. Harry figured the horse to be about eight years old.

There was something about the gelding's kind eyes that appealed to de Leyer. The truck driver offered to sell him for $80 including delivery. Harry agreed, then returned to his station wagon and drove home through the snow to await the horse's arrival.

When he reached his farm, Hollandia, Harry's children couldn't wait to hear what kind of horse he had purchased. Joseph (Chef) was six, Harriet four, and Marty two. It was still snowing when the horse arrived that night and the gelding stumbled off the trailer.

Harry's wife, Johanna, stood quietly, not sure what to think about the mangy-looking horse. The children, however, didn't notice his faults. As they stood watching the new horse, the falling snow coated his back. Harriet laughed with delight, claiming he looked like a snowman. And that's how the big gray got his name.

Two-year-old Marty walked up and wrapped his arms around one of Snowman's legs. Johanna rushed over to rescue her youngest, but Snowman hadn't budged. He seemed to like the children as much as they liked him.

Over the next few days, as the family worked together, cleaning and caring for him, Snowman remained calm and gentle with the children. Under all the grime, they discovered he was a flea-bitten gray—gray with small dark flecks in his coat. After Snowman had gained weight, Harry began his training, line driving him at first. The horse didn't turn very well. Harry assumed he'd been used for plowing long, straight rows in the fields. Once Snowman became more flexible and adept at turning small circles, Harry was ready to saddle him. He was cautious, assuming the horse had never been ridden.

Uncertain about this new experience, Snowman was initially tense. What was this man doing on his back? But it didn't take long before Snowman relaxed and accepted his rider. Harry was relieved and now confident he hadn't made a mistake by taking a chance on the gelding. Snowman would make a great lesson horse at the Knox School.

Each morning, when Harry went to the barn, Snowman greeted him with three loud whinnies—always three. By March, he was ready to begin his new career as a lesson horse. Harry rode Snowman five miles to the Knox School. The stable at the school was shaped like a horse shoe. From their stalls, the horses could see each other across a central courtyard.

Knox was an all-girls boarding school with students from all over the United States and abroad. The girls loved their young riding instructor—once they could understand him. Harry and Johanna had immigrated from Holland just a few years earlier, and Harry spoke with a thick Dutch accent. If the students were surprised by the looks of the new lesson horse, they didn't let on to Harry. Snowman's first year as a lesson horse was an overwhelming success. The gentle giant was a favorite of the more timid riders at the school. His calm, gentle nature boosted their confidence.

When the school closed for the summer, Harry kept his lesson horses at Hollandia. Since he didn't have enough stalls for all of them or the money to feed that many horses all summer, he tried to find a buyer for Snowman. Riding the horse at the school had been one thing, but he wasn't flashy enough for the girls who participated in the summer show circuit. Snowman was broad and heavy-boned, not like the stylish Thoroughbreds the serious young horsewomen preferred.

Although none of the students were interested in buying Snowman, soon a doctor, who lived six miles down the road, appeared at Hollandia. Dr. Rugen was looking for a calm horse for himself and his twelve-year-old son. The doctor purchased Snowman for $160. Harry would miss the horse's friendly greeting each morning, but he had a family to provide for, and he'd doubled his money on Snowman. He reminded himself that horses were his business. He couldn't get sentimental about them.

Harry wasn't the only one that missed Snowman. His children were attached to him, too. The day after he left, even the other horses at Hollandia seemed unsettled with the big gray gone. His gentle nature had been a calming influence at the farm. Harry figured it would take a few days for everyone to adjust.

As a teen in his home country, Harry had been an almost certain choice for the Dutch Equestrian Olympic team, but World War II had changed all that. Now, although he was doing what he loved—working with horses—he struggled to make enough to provide for his growing family. And he dreamed of having the money and a horse talented enough to compete in the jumper competitions in New York. Harry's vision of owning a champion jumper wouldn't go away. If he continued to make a profit by training and reselling horses, like he had with Snowman, he could save enough to buy a horse of the caliber to compete at that level.

Harry was just beginning to adjust to Snowman's absence when he received a phone call from Dr. Rugen. The doctor reported that Snowman had gotten out of his pasture and trampled his neighbor's yard. He claimed Snowman had jumped the pasture fence. Harry assured him that was impossible. After he'd hung up the phone, Harry thought no more of it, assuming the inexperienced horseman had forgotten to latch the gate or Snowman had somehow figured out how to open it.

On his way to feed the horses a few days later, Harry heard something—a quick three whinnies.

He stopped for a moment, staring through the early morning fog. It sounded like Snowman, but his mind must be playing tricks on him.

Then suddenly, the gray gelding appeared out of the mist, walking toward Harry. Although de Leyer was delighted to see Snowman, and he regretted selling the horse, a deal was a deal. The horse no longer belonged to him. He led Snowman into a stall, fed him, and returned to the house to phone the doctor.

When Dr. Rugen came to retrieve his horse, he assured Harry he had checked all his fences. According to Rugen, Snowman was jumping over them. Harry found it hard to believe the large, awkward horse could jump at all, let alone over a pasture fence. He went to inspect the doctor's setup himself, but found nothing amiss.

For the next several days, this scenario was repeated. The doctor took Snowman home, only to have the horse reappear at Hollandia the following morning. Snowman was not only jumping out of the pasture at the doctor's farm, he had to jump a fence to get into the barnyard at the de Leyer's.

Seeing as how Snowman seemed determined to remain at Hollandia, Harry suggested the doctor board the horse there. Doctor Rugen agreed. As sometimes happens, the doctor and his son soon lost all interest in the horse. After a few months, Dr. Rugen gave Snowman back to Harry in exchange for unpaid boarding fees.

That concludes the middle chapter of Snowman's life. Such a strong bond between horse and human is rare. If not for Harry's flat tire that wintry day in 1956, Harry and Snowman would never have met, and the horse's life would have ended at a slaughterhouse.

As an adult, Harriet de Leyer said, "Snowman would do anything my dad asked of him, and I believe that's because Snowman understood my dad saved him."

It seems that in some sense, the horse did appreciate what Harry had done for him. Harry later returned to the auction to find out about Snowman's background. Where had the horse come from? What was his breeding? But de Leyer never learned anything about the horse's past. That first chapter of Snowman's life remains a mystery.

Snowman's final chapter is almost as amazing as the story of his rescue. With the dream of a champion jumper in the back of his mind, Harry began working with Snowman. If he could clear pasture fences, maybe there was a jumper hidden somewhere inside the big plow horse.

The early results were disappointing. Snowman repeatedly sent ground poles and low jumps scattering. The horse found it easier to go through rather than over them. Harry was persistent, but he grew discouraged by their lack of progress. One day, he sat on Snowman in the Knox School arena, staring absently at a five-foot jump left in the ring by a previous rider. Harry was deep in thought, debating whether he should give up on trying to turn the big gray into a jumper. Snowman was an excellent lesson horse, but he was just a lesson horse. The gelding apparently didn't have the coordination to jump while carrying a rider.

A stable boy passed by and teased Harry about taking the tall jump on Snowman. Feeling he had nothing to lose, Harry accepted the challenge and cantered his horse toward the jump. Snowman took a gigantic leap and sailed over it.

Harry was shocked. He'd just discovered the horse's secret. The ground poles and low jumps were too easy. Why put forth the effort when he could just clomp through them? But when faced with a challenge, Snowman literally rose to the occasion and cleared the highest of jumps.

For years, Harry had dreamed of a horse that could take him to the grand championship. And for the last year, Snowman had patiently been trying to tell him he was that horse. To make a long story short, Snowman won the U.S. Open Jumper competition in New York's Madison Square Gardens in 1958, just two years after working as a plow horse.

After that championship, a wealthy man offered Harry $35,000 for Snowman. At the time, Harry earned $4,000 a year teaching riding lessons at the school. The offer was tempting. But Snowman was more than a horse; he was part of the de Leyer family. Harry had already made the mistake of selling him once. He wouldn't sell Snowman again for any amount of money.

Snowman became known as the Cinderella horse—a grade plow horse destined for the slaughterhouse, but transformed into a champion jumper. Harry and Snowman won the jumper championship again in 1959.

I don't know whether Harry de Leyer was a Christian, but we can still learn from his amazing experience with Snowman. Their story reminds me of several things from scripture.

God is in the smallest details of our lives. He can work through things we view as frustrations or obstacles—things we think are keeping us from pursuing our agenda or achieving our goals. Harry's flat tire is a perfect example. Without the flat tire, Harry would have arrived at the auction on time. He would have purchased a more "respectable" horse—and poor Snowman would have died within days of the sale.

> A man's heart plans his course, but the LORD determines his steps.
>
> *Proverbs 16:9*

> And we know that God works all things together for the good of those who love Him, who are called according to His purpose.
>
> *Romans 8:28*

After creating man, God gave him dominion or the authority to rule over the animals.

> Let Us make man in Our image, after Our likeness, to rule over [rādâ] the fish of the sea and the birds of the air, over the livestock, and over all the earth itself and every creature that crawls upon it.
>
> *Genesis 1:26*

> **rādâ**—to have dominion over, to rule or reign over

This dominion by no means gave man permission to be cruel to animals. In fact, at that time, there was no death. All animals and people were vegetarians, and none of the animals feared people.

Whoever owned Snowman prior to the sale didn't take proper care of him. I'm not blaming the Amish. There are kind and cruel people in that community as well as in any other group of people. Snowman may not have even been owned by an Amish person; Harry never found out where the horse had come from. But Harry and his family showed proper dominion over their horses and nursed Snowman back to health.

One of my favorite verses is 1 Samuel 16:7.

> the LORD does not see as man does. For man sees the outward appearance, but the LORD sees the heart.

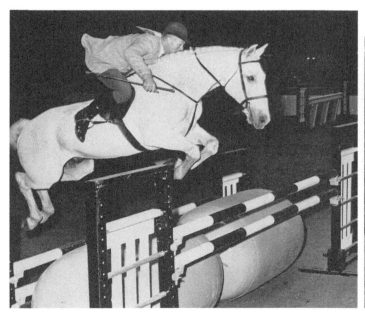

Harry looked past Snowman's scruffy outward appearance to see a spark of something inside. He saw what he hoped the horse would become, given the proper care. God sees us the same way. While the world focuses on youth and external beauty or handsomeness, God is more concerned with our heart and inner character.

Snowman and Harry were both looked down upon at the shows. The large, heavy-boned Snowman plodded around, often dozing outside the ring until it was his turn to jump. He was the opposite of the typical horses that dominated these events—high-strung, nervous Thoroughbreds who couldn't stand still. When the pair won or placed in a class, Harry often led Snowman into the ring to collect his award with several of his children on the horse's back.

Snowman's dramatic transformation reminds me of how God can change us. We don't have to remain stuck in our sinful past. When we're born again, we have a new life. I experienced this myself. Even as a young adult, I was extremely timid and insecure. After becoming a Christian, God began my transformation, still in process of course.

> Therefore if anyone is in Christ, he is a new creation. The old has passed away. Behold, the new has come!
>
> *2 Corinthians 5:17*

> Do not be conformed to this world, but be transformed by the renewing of your mind. Then you will be able to test and approve what is the good, pleasing, and perfect will of God.
>
> *Romans 12:2*

There are undoubtedly more lessons from Snowman's life, but I'll stop with this last thought. While it's unlikely Snowman fully understood that Harry had saved his life, there is no question the horse was devoted to him. Shouldn't we be devoted to Christ who saved us by taking the penalty for our sins and dying on the cross in our place?

> In Him we have redemption through His blood, the forgiveness of our trespasses, according to the riches of His grace that He lavished on us with all wisdom and understanding.
>
> *Ephesians 1:7,8*

> For you know that it was not with perishable things such as silver or gold that you were redeemed from the empty way of life you inherited from your forefathers, but with the precious blood of Christ, a lamb without blemish or spot.
>
> *1 Peter 1:18,19*

64

WHO'S SERVING WHOM?

Shortly after Jesus informed His disciples He would be killed, but would also be resurrected on the third day, James and John came to Him, requesting a favor.

> Grant that one of us may sit at Your right hand and the other at Your left in Your glory.
>
> *Mark 10:37*

Jesus must have been disappointed by this selfish request. The other disciples were definitely not pleased with the two brothers. Jesus used this opportunity to teach them what it meant to be a servant leader.

> You know that those regarded as rulers of the Gentiles lord it over them, and their superiors exercise authority over them. But it shall not be this way among you. Instead, whoever wants to become great among you must be your servant, and whoever wants to be first must be the slave of all. For even the Son of Man did not come to be served, but to serve, and to give His life as a ransom for many.
>
> *Mark 10:42-45*

The world's estimation of leaders is often proportional to how many people serve them. That leads to pride and grasping for even more fame and power. Many of the world's leaders today wouldn't be good leaders according to Jesus' standards. He defined greatness through humble service. The servant status of Christ is explained in Philippians 2:5-8

> Let this mind be in you which was also in Christ Jesus: Who, existing in the form of God, did not consider equality with God something to be grasped, but emptied Himself, taking the form of a servant, being made in human likeness. And being found in appearance as a man, He humbled Himself and became obedient to death—even death on a cross.

Jesus washed the dirty feet of His disciples as an example of how they should serve others.

> So He got up from the supper, laid aside His outer garments, and wrapped a towel around His waist. After that, He poured water into a basin and began to wash the disciples' feet and dry them with the towel that was around Him.
>
> *John 13:4,5*

Jesus' entire ministry was one of service to the people around Him—teaching, feeding, healing—but His most astonishing service was His sacrificial death on the cross. The sinless God-Man offering His own life to pay the penalty for our sins.

Over the years of owning horses, I've often contemplated who does the most work for whom. In my case, I've definitely served my horses more than they have served me. Taking care of a horse is a lot of work! Cleaning stalls, grooming and bathing them, cleaning and possibly trimming hooves, feeding and watering, stacking bales of hay, storing bedding material, and caring for them if they become sick.

None of that is glamorous work. In return, my pampered horses give me a brief horseback or pony cart ride a few times a week. When I get weary of all the work, I console myself with the thought that people pay for gym memberships to get the kind of workouts I have nearly every day—for nothing!

Part of Christ's definition of a servant leader was the humility with which one does their tasks. If I whined and complained all the time about the work I do for my horses, I wouldn't qualify as a servant leader. Or at the opposite extreme, if I bragged about how much work I do every day for them, that would disqualify me as well.

Jesus served people without complaining or boasting. Of course, it's not just with horses we're supposed to put the servant attitude into practice. We can serve in our families, churches, and communities. Our tasks may be small and perhaps go unnoticed, but we can still do them with the servant heart Jesus called us to have.

65

PECKING ORDER

I've been aware of the concept of a "pecking order" in horses for as long as I can remember, but I never gave much thought to the origin of the phrase. Upon even a cursory consideration, it's easy to see that it refers to birds.

Undoubtedly, anyone who raised chickens was aware of the birds pecking at each other. But it turns out that a young Norwegian, Thorleif Schjelderup-Ebbe, was the first to name the social hierarchy observed in chickens as the "pecking order." The official name came in 1913, when Thorleif was nineteen.

From the age of six, Thorleif had a fascination, bordering on obsession, with the chickens on a farm near Oslo, Norway, where his family spent their summers. He could tell all the chickens apart, named each one, and filled notebooks with diagrams and observations of their fowl behavior, paying particular attention to who was allowed to peck whom.

Thorlief called the chicken at the top of the order, the "despot." His childhood fascination with chickens never left him. When he earned his Ph. D., his dissertation was titled, "Gallus domesticus in Its Daily Life." I'm thankful God gave me an obsession with horses rather than with chickens!

Even though horses can't peck, they definitely have a similar hierarchical structure. A power ranking is established whenever there is more than one horse together. Rather than a "despot," the top horse in the equine version of the pecking order is usually a mare. This "boss" is called the lead mare.

The lead mare gets to eat and drink before any of the other horses. She has the best place in the barn or pasture and controls who may approach or stand near her. She will chase, kick, or bite any horse who dares to invade her space without her permission. Some horses enforce the pecking order with a good deal of ferocity.

Years ago, I bought a Rocky Mountain mare named Nikki. The online photos and video showed a beautiful, chocolate-colored mare with light mane and tail and a smooth gait. As it turned out, I ended up buying her because I felt sorry for her. She was a good example of the cruel nature of the horse's pecking order (and the negligence of the horse's caregiver).

The man who owned Nikki was working out of state. While he was gone, he left his teenage daughter in charge of feeding their six horses. She simply threw hay out in the pasture in one large pile—whether through ignorance or laziness, I'm not sure. Nikki was the lowest horse in that herd's pecking order. The other horses kept her away from the hay until they'd eaten their fill. Nikki got whatever was left, which was not much, as evidenced by her rundown condition. By the time I arrived, she was extremely thin, and her hooves were overgrown. If you're familiar with body condition scoring for horses, I put her at about a 2.5. The scores run from 1 (emaciated) to 9 (obese). Five is optimal. It was hard to believe no one in the family noticed Nikki's poor condition.

When feeding hay for several horses in a pasture, the best approach is to create at least one more pile than the number of horses, with the piles spaced a good distance apart. The first to choose a pile is the lead mare, of course. She'll walk around, sniffing the piles to determine which best suits her royal highness. Feeding them this way will quickly reveal the herd dynamics if you aren't aware of the horses' ranking already. They will shift around between the piles occasionally, with a higher-ranking horse able to take over the hay pile of any horse beneath him, forcing that horse to find another one.

Control structures similar to this exist outside the world of horses and chickens. Most groups, whether animal or human, function under some sort of hierarchical system. With people, we don't usually call it a pecking order—at least not out loud. As practiced in the human world, this ranking system violates many of the precepts for leadership and relationships given in the Bible.

Years ago, I heard an acronym for the word "joy." It's a simple reminder that to have joy and to bring joy to others, put Jesus first, others second, and yourself last.

In terms of your relationships, whether at school, work, or with family or friends, are you like the lead mare insisting, "Me first!" or do you put others ahead of yourself?

> Do nothing out of selfish ambition or empty pride, but in humility consider others more important than yourselves. Each of you should look not only to your own interests, but also to the interests of others.
>
> *Philippians 2:3,4*

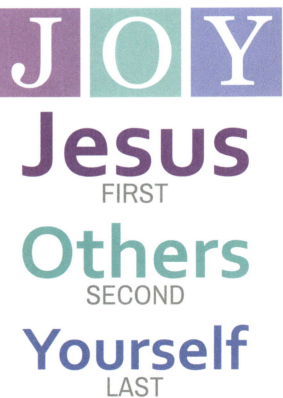

66

WAR HORSES

God commanded the kings of Israel not to accumulate horses, as that would encourage them to rely on their own strength rather than on God. Solomon ignored that command when he became king.

> But the king must not acquire many horses for himself or send the people back to Egypt to acquire more horses, for the LORD has said, "You are never to go back that way again."
>
> *Deuteronomy 17:16*

God repeatedly reminded His people that their trust should be in Him rather than in horses.

> Some trust in chariots and others in horses, but we trust in the name of the LORD our God.
>
> *Psalm 20:7*

> A horse is a vain hope for salvation; even its great strength cannot save.
>
> *Psalm 33:17*

> A horse is prepared for the day of battle, but victory is of the LORD.
>
> *Proverbs 21:31*

> Woe to those who go down to Egypt for help, who rely on horses, who trust in their abundance of chariots and in their multitude of horsemen. They do not look to the Holy One of Israel; they do not seek the LORD.
>
> *Isaiah 31:1,2*

In Bible times, horses, chariots, and horsemen were the equivalent of today's military, tanks, rockets, and nuclear weapons. Our rulers no longer rely on horses. However most of them certainly don't rely on God, either. Modern arsenals are no more capable of saving us, without God's protection, than the horses of old.

Horses have been instrumental in wars from ancient times until recently. The use of horses in wars peaked in World War I. But one of the best known modern war horses earned her fame in the Korean War.

Estimated Deaths of Equines in War (horses, mules, donkeys)

American Civil War (1861-1865) one to three million

World War I (1914-1918) eight million

World War II (1939-1945) two to five million

Korean War (1950-1953)

In Seoul, South Korea, a young man, Kim Huk Moon, was a successful jockey and trainer. He received a racehorse mare, Ah-Chim-Hai (Flame of the Morning) as payment for his work in a prisoner of war camp during World War II.

In June 1948, Ah-Chim-Hai gave birth to a filly. Kim called the chestnut filly with three white stockings, Flame. The filly grew to about 13 hands. She was of the Mongolian horse breed, although not as stocky.

Flame showed great promise as a racehorse, but when the Korean War began in 1950, all horse racing was suspended. Flame's racing career ended before it even began. Instead, Flame, hooked to a rickety cart, took Kim and his family two hundred miles to safety in the south. During their two years there, Kim used Flame to help unload supplies from American ships.

By 1952, Seoul was considered safe and Kim once again hooked Flame to a cart to return to the city. They had converted the racetrack where he formerly worked into a landing field for American troops. Kim lived in poverty, finding it difficult to earn enough money to feed his family and Flame. He used the mare to haul rice from the fields to a warehouse. The local children gathered grass for Flame to eat.

Chung Soon, Kim's sister, was injured by a land mine which exploded in a rice field. When Chung Soon's leg had to be amputated, Kim was determined to find a way to provide her with an artificial leg.

Kim knew Flame was fast. If she became a successful racehorse, he could earn money to help his sister. He began training and conditioning the horse, hoping she could soon begin her racing career. One fall day in 1952, Flame was resting in her stall after a workout when four American military officers appeared at the stable.

Kim knew what they were looking for, but he didn't have time to hide Flame. Lieutenant Eric Pedersen had a good eye for horses. He passed several up before reaching Flame's stall. Kim didn't want to part with the horse he loved, but Pedersen offered him $250—enough money to purchase an artificial leg for his sister. Kim tearfully agreed to sell his horse.

Flame was still young, just four years old. Her life was about to take a dramatic turn.

When Pedersen returned to base with her, two marines, Monroe Coleman and Joe Latham, were assigned to care for and train Flame. Her first meal at the camp was a loaf of bread and some uncooked oatmeal.

Pedersen planned to use the horse to haul their heavy guns and ammunition. The Marines gave the mare a new name—Reckless—after their weapons: recoilless "reckless" rifles. Each gun was almost seven feet long and weighed 115 pounds. It took two to four men to position a gun at the top of a hill. Each round of ammunition weighed twenty-five pounds.

The men built a special bunker for Reckless, although the mare didn't always use it. Horses are herd animals with a strong desire to live in a group. Since there were no other horses around, the men became Reckless' herd. She bonded to them and would do whatever they asked. The men loved Reckless as well, sharing their food and treats with her.

Once Reckless adjusted to her new life as a Marine, she was free to wander around the camp. Winters in Korea were cold with temperatures often dropping below zero degrees. On those bitterly cold nights, Reckless shared a tent with one of the men, warming herself at the Marine's stove.

But her favorite place was the cook's tent. When the cook was late getting up in the morning, Reckless would enter his tent and lick his face to remind him it was time for breakfast. Having spent most of her life being hungry, the little horse had an insatiable appetite and would eat almost anything—scrambled eggs, coffee, peanut butter sandwiches, fruit pies, hard candy, chocolate bars, cereal, graham crackers, and bread with jam. Reckless would even drink Coca-Cola or milk from a cup.

One Marine told the story of a time he bought a pack of cookies and hid them in his tent. When he returned, his tent was a disaster. Reckless' keen sense of smell directed her to his well-hidden treats. She'd not only eaten the cookies but the wrapper as well.

Joe Latham became Reckless' drill instructor, putting her through boot camp—or as he called it—hoof camp. Latham trained her to come when he whistled and to step carefully over barbed wire. She was sometimes transported in a small, open cart, standing at an angle in order to fit in the two-wheeled vehicle. Reckless learned to lie down when Latham tapped her front leg.

"Incoming, incoming" meant the enemy was about to fire on them. Reckless learned to run to her bunker or to the bunker of the closest Marine. When a pack saddle arrived from the United States, Reckless began

training to carry the large, heavy ammunition used by the reckless rifles. The horse could comfortably carry six rounds, but when needed, she took eight to ten at a time.

Reckless excelled in her training, but would she remain calm in an actual battle? In November 1952, the horse had her first test. After lugging six shells up a steep hill to the ridge, Reckless experienced the deafening blast of the recoilless rifle for the first time.

Latham could see the whites of the mare's eyes as all four of her hooves left the ground. Reckless began to sweat all over, a sign of her extreme fear. Latham did his best to calm her, and by the third round, she was less fearful. Reckless carried four more loads of ammunition to the ridge that day.

Reckless had passed the test. The mare proved herself repeatedly in battle. Not only was she a genuine help, but her quirky personality and fearless determination encouraged the men in her unit.

Reckless is best known for her heroic performance in the Battle of Outpost Vegas. She made fifty-one trips from the supply station to the battle site, most of those trips made entirely by herself. During that battle, she was wounded twice—once above the eye and a second time on her left flank. After being treated, Reckless went right back to work. The mare received two Purple Hearts for her role in that battle.

The Korean War ended with a cease-fire on July 27, 1953, four months after the Battle of Outpost Vegas. On April 10, 1954, Reckless, still in Korea, was officially promoted to sergeant. She received a red silk blanket with gold trim for the occasion—which she promptly tried to eat.

When a four-page article about Reckless appeared in the Saturday Evening Post, Americans began a campaign, Operation Bring Reckless Home, to bring the equine Marine to the United States.

Using a combination of military flight and transport ship, Reckless arrived in San Francisco, California on November 9, 1954. After a press conference, they lowered Reckless from the ship to the dock in a large wooden crate. Later that day, she was honored with a reception at the Marine's Memorial Club. She rode the freight elevator to the tenth-floor banquet hall. Before her handlers could stop her, Reckless dove into a two-foot-high cake. She finished that off by eating its floral centerpiece.

The Marines purchased Reckless for $1 in 1955 and moved her to the stable at Camp Pendleton. She was seven years old, still young for a horse. Without the constant contact of her fellow Marines, Reckless was lonely in her retirement. One spring, someone attached a sign to the fence around her pasture—"Mare-Ternity Ward." A colt, Fearless, was born to Reckless on April 5, 1957.

On March 2, 1959, Reckless gave birth to her second colt, Dauntless.

On December 6, 1964, she delivered a third colt. This foal didn't continue the tradition of having "less" at the end of his name. He was named Chesty after a Lieutenant General.

Reckless had her last foal in 1966, but the filly died when only a month old.

In her later years, Reckless suffered from arthritis and laminitis. She died at twenty in 1968. The engraving on her headstone reads, "In Memory of Reckless, Pride of the Marines."

> Reckless was a very special horse and undoubtedly bonded through a spiritual connection of love with her Marines. The noise and waves of concussion can't be described, but she endured it all. I believe an angel had to be riding Reckless, since she was alone and without a Marine to lead her. I have always cherished my horses. But after watching and learning more about that little mare of the Reckless Rifles, mine are even more special because I know they have the same Creator.
>
> *Sgt. Harold E. Wadley, USMC*

The use of horses in wars makes me sad. I'm reminded of Captain's words in Anna Sewell's, *Black Beauty*. Captain had been a cavalry horse in the Crimean War. In chapter thirty-four, the horse describes his master's death in a battle in which three out of every four horses were killed. Sewell uses Captain's confusion over the purpose of the war to express her own opposition to senseless wars.

> "I [Black Beauty] have heard people talk about war as if it was a very fine thing."
>
> "Ah!" said he [Captain], "I should think they never saw it. No doubt it is very fine when there is no enemy, when it is just exercise and parade, and sham-fight. Yes, it is very fine then; but when thousands of good brave men and horses are killed, or crippled for life, it has a very different look."
>
> "Do you know what they fought about?" said I.
>
> "No," he said, "that is more than a horse can understand, but the enemy must have been awfully wicked people, if it was right to go all that way over the sea on purpose to kill them."

In Matthew 24:3, the disciples asked Jesus, "What will be the sign of Your coming and of the end of the age?"

Jesus' response included the following:

> You will hear of wars and rumors of wars, but see to it that you are not alarmed. These things must happen, but the end is still to come. Nation will rise against nation, and kingdom against kingdom. There will be famines and earthquakes in various places. All these are the beginning of birth pains.
>
> *Matthew 24:6-8*

Wars have been fought throughout history, so war in itself is not a sign of the End Times. But wars will increase in frequency and intensity as the return of Jesus nears.

67

THE SAME FOREVER

Jesus Christ is the same yesterday and today and forever.

Hebrews 13:8

The older I get, the more I appreciate Hebrews 13:8. Years ago, I thought about this devotion for a long time, but couldn't write it, as if not writing would change the facts the photos clearly show.

The first photo is of my youngest daughter, Julie, age seven, and her pony, Ebony. The second photo shows Julie at nineteen with the same pony. Ebony was about twenty-six then.

Many things were changing in my life. Julie was about to move out to live with her oldest sister. I was selling my farm and downsizing. After seventeen years of homeschooling my three daughters and identifying as a homeschool mom, I was searching for a new identity.

I don't like change. My preference is to stay in a comfortable, predictable routine. My mother's death several years earlier brought many unwanted changes. Then, friends took their five-year-old daughter to the emergency room for a stomach ache and learned she had cancer. While some changes are good and exciting, many changes in this life are not.

When I look at these photos, I see Julie changing from a cute, mischievous little girl into a strong, talented, and capable young woman ready to tackle the world.

But I also see Ebony changing from a sassy, feisty little pony (who never knew she was little) into an old and increasingly feeble animal we couldn't keep weight on. She had Cushings, a disease that affects the pituitary gland. That's the reason for the long, shaggy coat. It's more common in ponies than horses. Not long after that photo was taken, Ebony became so weak we had to put her down. I have tears even now as I remember that sad day when we lost one of the best ponies we ever had.

In our constantly changing world, I hold on to the fact that God, and His love for us, will never change.

68

LEFT BEHIND

Years ago, I read the *Left Behind* series, a fictional account of what might happen in the End Times when Jesus returns to earth. The *Left Behind* authors wove fictional events into their stories, but much of it was based on scripture.

Many disagree about when, and in what order, the events in the book of Revelation will occur. One interpretation is that Christians will be taken to heaven (an event called the Rapture) before a seven-year period of turmoil on earth (the Tribulation). During the Tribulation, evil will increase, and God will send judgments, giving those left behind multiple opportunities to repent and turn to Him.

The main characters in the *Left Behind* series were unbelievers, not taken in the Rapture, despite having close friends or relatives who were Christians. When their loved ones disappeared, those characters became believers themselves and were filled with a sense of urgency to tell others about Christ while there was still time.

Whether you are pre-trib, mid-trib, post-trib or you don't have a clue what any of that means, one thing is certain—if you profess to be a Christian—you don't want to be left behind! When Christ returns for His people, you want to go with Him.

One day, I was at a horse show with my daughter Julie. We had taken her horse, Kody, and my mule, Sassy. My first classes were over, and one of Julie's was coming up. I tied Sassy to the trailer, then started back to watch Julie show. As I walked toward the arena, a large, dark animal flew past me, the sound of hoof beats pounding in my ears.

"Horse loose," people all around me yelled. Soon, that changed to, "Mule loose!"

Oh, no. That left no doubt as to who was loose. Sassy was the only mule on the show grounds. The mule raced down a narrow passageway between the announcer's booth and the arena fence, frantic to get back to her buddy, Kody.

It looked like the parting of the Red Sea as people scrambled to get out of Sassy's way. As soon as she reached Kody, Sassy stopped, content now that she had reached her goal.

I hurried to retrieve my wayward mule, relieved that she hadn't hurt anyone in her mad dash. I was too annoyed to immediately see any spiritual application to her behavior. Actually, I would have been willing to sell the mule right then and there, but no one appeared to be interested in buying her. With mules, people tend to either love or hate them.

After I got over my annoyance with the crazy beast, I considered Sassy's frantic fear of being "left behind" and her overwhelming desire to be close to Kody.

> Strive to enter through the narrow gate, for many, I say to you, will seek to enter and will not be able.
>
> *Luke 13:24 NKJV*

The New King James version uses the word "strive." Other translations say

> make every effort, work hard, keep on struggling, exert every effort, try hard, do all you can, do your best, contend

The Greek word is "agónizomai" which means a conflict or struggle. Our word "agonize" comes from it. That same Greek word appears in 1 Timothy 6:12 and is translated "fight." "Fight the good fight of the faith…"

Of course, we are saved through faith in Christ not by our own effort or works, but the Bible states in multiple places that the Christian life involves effort on our part.

Sassy was certainly striving, making every effort, even agonizing to return to Kody. She made it through a narrow gate—sort of. The passageway between the announcer's booth and the arena was a tight squeeze for that overweight mule!

Are you that intent on making sure you won't be left behind when Christ returns?

If you're already certain of your own salvation, what about your friends, family members, neighbors? Do you feel an urgency to make sure they won't be left behind, either?

Let Sassy's "agónizomai" remind you to strive to make it through that narrow gate and onto the narrow path that leads to life.

Love your neighbor?
Please, tell me Sassy
isn't my neighbor!

69

FOUR HORSES

Although in our day, "apocalypse" has taken on the meaning of catastrophic destruction, the Greek word "apokalypsis" actually means a revealing, disclosing, or unveiling. The book of Revelation is God revealing to us what will happen in the End Times. The events and judgments found in that book are His last attempt to persuade the unrepentant to abandon their sin and turn to Him.

In Revelation 5, John wept bitterly because no one in heaven was found worthy to open a scroll sealed with seven seals. Many believe the scroll represents the title deed to Earth, that Adam, through his sin, lost to Satan, and which was now about to be reclaimed by its rightful Owner.

Then one of the elders said to me, "Do not weep! Behold, the Lion of the tribe of Judah, the Root of David, has triumphed to open the scroll and its seven seals."

Revelation 5:5

A Lamb, looking as though it had been slain (5:6), took the scroll and opened the seals one by one, causing specific events to occur on Earth. The first four seals each released a horse. These are known as the Four Horses of the Apocalypse—or referring to the riders—the Four Horsemen of the Apocalypse.

1. The White Horse

Then I watched as the Lamb opened one of the seven seals, and I heard one of the four living creatures say in a thunderous voice, "Come!"
So I looked and saw a white [leukos] horse, and its rider held a bow. And he was given a crown, and he rode out to overcome and conquer.

Revelation 6:1,2

leukos—light, bright, brilliant, dazzling white (The same word is used in Revelation 19:11.)

The color white represents peace. Although some interpret this first rider to be Christ, most believe he is the Antichrist, riding a white horse in imitation of Christ. The Antichrist will reign during the seven years of the Tribulation. During the first half of those years, there will be relative peace. The Antichrist signs a peace treaty with Israel and unites the nations in a one-world government. After three and a half years, this leader, controlled by Satan, will break the treaty and demand that everyone worship him.

2. The Red Horse

And when the Lamb opened the second seal, I heard the second living creature say, "Come!"
Then another horse went forth. It was bright red [pyrros], and its rider was granted permission to take away peace from the earth and to make men slay one another. And he was given a great sword.

Revelation 6:3,4

pyrros—red, fire-like, flame-colored

The color red and the presence of a great sword mean this horse and its rider represent killing and bloodshed. During the last three and a half Tribulation years, nations, and individuals will rise up against each other and kill many.

3. The Black Horse

And when the Lamb opened the third seal, I heard the third living creature say, "Come!"
Then I looked and saw a black [melas] horse, and its rider held in his hand a pair of scales. And I heard what sounded like a voice from among the four living creatures, saying, "A quart of wheat for a denarius, and three quarts of barley for a denarius, and do not harm the oil and wine."

Revelation 6:5,6

melas—black, black ink

Black represents the famines that occur as a result of droughts and wars. A denarius was the average daily pay, meaning a man had to work all day to afford food for himself alone. Later in the Tribulation, people will be required to take the mark of the Beast and worship him in order to buy or sell.

4. The Green (Pale) Horse

> And when the Lamb opened the fourth seal, I heard the voice of the fourth living creature say, "Come!"
>
> Then I looked and saw a pale green [chloros] horse. Its rider's name was Death, and Hades followed close behind. And they were given authority over a fourth of the earth, to kill by sword, by famine, by plague, and by the beasts of the earth.
>
> *Revelation 6:7,8*

chloros—green. We get our word "chlorophyll" from this same Greek word. It's the same word used in Mark 6:39 where it is translated "green."

> Then Jesus directed them to have the people sit in groups on the **green** [chloros] grass.

While grass looks wonderful when it is bright green, horses (and people) don't. In fact, looking green is an expression used to describe someone who isn't feeling well. This fourth horse represents death caused by plagues, epidemics, famine, and wild animals.

The release of these first four seals results in the death of one fourth of the earth's population. And the four horsemen are just the beginning. Three additional seals follow the horses, then seven trumpets, and seven bowl judgments.

Why all the wrath and judgment in Revelation? Some people won't read this book because it doesn't fit their conception of a God they've invented who "loves" everybody and who will punish no one. This reveals a lack of scriptural knowledge and a poor understanding of God's character. Although He is a God of love, God's wrath is very real. It's not spoken of only in Revelation.

> The wrath of God is being revealed from heaven against all the godlessness and wickedness of men who suppress the truth by their wickedness. For what may be known about God is plain to them, because God has made it plain to them. For since the creation of the world God's invisible qualities, His eternal power and divine nature, have been clearly seen, being understood from His workmanship, so that men are without excuse.
>
> *Romans 1:18-20*

> But because of your hard and unrepentant heart, you are storing up wrath against yourself for the day of wrath, when God's righteous judgment will be revealed.
>
> *Romans 2:5*

> Whoever believes in the Son has eternal life. Whoever rejects the Son will not see life. Instead, the wrath of God remains on him.
>
> *John 3:36*

God's holy perfection requires that He be angry about sin and evil. But He has provided a way for us to escape that wrath. In fact, He wants everyone to come to repentance.

> The Lord is not slow in keeping His promise as some understand slowness, but is patient with you, not wanting anyone to perish but everyone to come to repentance.
>
> *2 Peter 3:9*

In Revelation, God offers many opportunities for people to repent and turn to Him. Rather than a book primarily of wrath, I see it as a book of amazing love—a last effort to reach those who have repeatedly rejected Him.

Surprisingly, throughout the book of Revelation, many cling to their sin and refuse to turn to God, regardless of the judgments they experience.

If the theory of the pre-Tribulation rapture is true, Christians will not be here when the four horses are released. According to that interpretation, all believers will be taken to heaven before the Tribulation begins.

Others believe the rapture occurs at the midpoint of the seven years. In that case, believers would experience the first half of the Tribulation but be spared the final, worst years.

Still others believe Christians will go through the entire seven years of the Tribulation.

Are the four horses real or symbolic?

It seems these horses are intended to be symbolic. Horses that very well could be real are the white ones Jesus and the saints ride when He returns to Earth, as described in Revelation 19.

70

WHITE HORSES

Then I saw heaven standing open, and there before me was a white horse. And its rider is called Faithful and True. With righteousness He judges and wages war. He has eyes like blazing fire, and many royal crowns on His head. He has a name written on Him that only He Himself knows. He is dressed in a robe dipped in blood, and His name is The Word of God. The armies of heaven, dressed in fine linen, white and pure, follow Him on white horses.

Revelation 19:11-14

The rider on the white horse in Revelation 6:2 seems to be the Antichrist. But there's no doubt the rider in Revelation 19 is Jesus, returning in power to judge the Earth. Satan often attempts to copy what God does. If Jesus rides a white horse, then it makes sense Satan would try to deceive people by doing the same.

In the days of the Old and New Testaments, horses were used for warfare. Rulers rode white horses into conquered cities to signify victory. Today, white horses are fairly rare. The skin of a true white horse is pink. They most often have brown eyes. Many horses that appear to be white are technically gray or cream. There are no albino horses.

If you're in doubt, check the horse's muzzle. That's the easiest place to see his skin. If the skin is dark, the horse is gray, no matter how light his coat is. A horse with a white facial marking will have pink skin under the white hair in that area, but other areas of his body will have dark skin.

A gray horse may be born any color. His coat fades with age until the horse can appear white. However his skin will remain dark. The Lipizzan breed is a good example. At birth, they are black, but when older, most appear to be white.

Horses with a cream gene, like cremellos and perlinos, can be harder to distinguish from a white horse. They vary from a light palomino color to a creamy almost-white. They also have pink skin, sometimes a more dusty pink, and usually have blue eyes.

The first white Thoroughbred was registered in the United States in 1963—a mare named White Beauty. White Beauty raced sixteen times with two wins in minor races. Out of 2.5 million Thoroughbreds registered with the Jockey Club, only about twenty have been white. Those white horses haven't been very successful on U.S. tracks. However Sodashi, a white filly, foaled in 2018, experienced some success racing in Japan. White horses aren't limited to Thoroughbreds. White Bliss, a registered white Standardbred pacer, was born in 2012 to two bay parents.

According to Zechariah 14:3-4, Jesus will return to Jerusalem. This appearance on a white horse is in contrast to His entrance to Jerusalem on Palm Sunday, riding a donkey. The donkey symbolized that Jesus came in peace and humility. His second coming, on a horse, shows Jesus is prepared for war.

On the cross, Jesus forgave those who crucified Him. Despite multiple opportunities for repentance during the Tribulation, some will continue to reject Christ. This time, they will not be forgiven; they will be judged.

Will Jesus literally return riding a white horse?

I don't see why not. Remember a man named Elijah?

> As they were walking along and talking together, suddenly a chariot of fire with horses of fire appeared and separated the two of them [Elijah and Elisha], and Elijah went up into heaven in a whirlwind.
>
> *2 Kings 2:11*

Later, when surrounded by the Syrian army, Elisha tells his servant not to fear "for those who are with us are more than those who are with them." 2 Kings 6:16

> And the LORD opened the eyes of the young man, and he saw that the hills were full of horses and chariots of fire all around Elisha.
>
> *2 Kings 6:17*

Some interpret much of the Bible symbolically, especially Revelation. I find it easier to interpret God's word literally unless it clearly indicates something is symbolic. For example, in Revelation 1:20, Jesus explains the symbolism of the stars and lampstands.

> This is the mystery of the seven stars you saw in My right hand and of the seven golden lampstands: The seven stars are the angels of the seven churches, and the seven lampstands are the seven churches.

It's possible to read all sorts of strange theories into the Bible if you see it all as symbolic. The possibilities are unlimited if we allow ourselves to begin imagining scenarios. At a bookseller event, my table was next to a woman who had written a book she described as "taking all the violence out of Revelation." I didn't understand how that was possible. When I questioned her about a few specifics in Revelation, she admitted she didn't understand the book. She simply chose to interpret it in a way that made her feel comfortable.

I don't see any reason why Jesus couldn't return on an actual white horse. Obviously, the horse had capabilities beyond those of earthly horses, since it could fly. But Jesus' resurrected body also had capabilities beyond our human bodies. In John 20:19, He appeared to the disciples in a closed room. It seems He passed through either the walls or the closed door.

It's not only Jesus who returns on a white horse.

> The armies of heaven, dressed in fine linen, white and pure, follow Him on white horses.
>
> *Revelation 19:14*

There's some debate over who makes up this army. It could be any, or all, of angels, Old Testament saints, the church, and Tribulation martyrs. Whomever it might include, this is an unusual army, even beyond the fact that they're all mounted on white horses.

In the history of battles here on Earth, I don't believe clean, white clothing has ever been an army's uniform. Those uniforms would be horribly stained in battle. In addition to their unusual attire, no mention is made of any weapons. How is this army supposed to fight?

The answer is—they don't! There's no need for them to engage in the battle, as Christ easily defeats His enemies.

The beast and the false prophet are thrown into the lake of fire. The rebels who joined them are killed, and Satan is thrown bound into the bottomless pit for a thousand years. I'll confess, I don't understand why Satan is released after those thousand years. But ultimately, he is defeated again and joins the beast and the false prophet in the lake of fire. (Revelation 20:7-10)

There are many ideas about how the end times will play out and what everything in Revelation means. Keep in mind that "apokalypsis" or "apocalypse" means a revealing or unveiling. The book of Revelation was given to reveal what will happen. It's not so mysterious that only the highly educated or enlightened can understand it. Even if we don't understand every part of it, it's not difficult to grasp the big picture. The book promises that those who read it will be blessed.

> Blessed is the one who reads aloud the words of this prophecy, and blessed are those who hear and obey what is written in it, because the time is near.
>
> *Revelation 1:3*

The more I read Revelation, the more I see God's love and patience displayed in it. God isn't willing that anyone should perish, but that all should have eternal life. (2 Peter 3:9)

In the book of Revelation, God gives people chance after chance to repent, but many refuse. Finally, the time for repentance runs out. C. S. Lewis expressed it well in *The Great Divorce*.

> There are only two kinds of people in the end: those who say to God, "Thy will be done," and those to whom God says, in the end, "Thy will be done." All that are in hell choose it.

> I call heaven and earth as witnesses against you today that I have set before you life and death, blessing and cursing. Therefore choose life, so that you and your descendants may live, and that you may love the LORD your God, obey Him, and hold fast to Him.
>
> *Deuteronomy 30:19,20*

At the time of Christ's return, look for me riding in His army on a magnificent white steed! I hope you'll be there riding along with me.

Bible Study Resources

Blue Letter Bible, blueletterbible.org

This is my favorite online Bible study resource. You can quickly look up any verse and see the transliterated Hebrew or Greek for each word, along with the defintions, commentaries, and much more.

Bible Hub, biblehub.com

This is a close second. When I want original definitions or commentaries, I use Blue Letter Bible. When I want to read a chapter or compare verses in various translations, I use Bible Hub.

Berean Study Bible, bereanbible.com

I've been reading this translation lately, and it's the version used for most of the verses in this devotional. The BSB version is the only one in print at this time, but several other translations are available on their website in various tranlation tiers—interlinear, literal, and emphasized.

Grace To You, gty.org

You can listen to any of John MacArthur's sermons on the GTY website. It's searchable by topic and Scripture. He also has a daily podcast.

Precepts Bible Studies, precept.org

I'm so thankful to Kay Arthur and her Precept Bible studies. When I begged the pastor of the church I attended as a new Christian to have a Bible study, he refused. Strange behavior for a pastor, I know. But God led me to another church that had a *Precept Upon Precept* study on the book of James. I didn't just learn about James, I learned how to study any book of the Bible. That's been decades ago. I don't know if the studies are still of the same quality. Back then, it wasn't a lightweight approach. The studies required a fair amount of time.

Warren Wiersbe Commentary Set

I devoured commentaries for about fifteen years as I had gotten a late start on my Christian walk. Recently, I bought this six-volume set by Wiersbe that covers the entire Bible. It's a handy reference without being overwhelming. Wiersbe provides a good balance of stories along with some deeper analysis. It's not overly academic by any means.

30 Days to Understanding the Bible, Max Anders

This title sounds presumptuous. No one can fully understand the Bible in just thirty days, but I loved this book as a new Christian. I didn't understand how the Bible fit together as a whole. This book cleared up a lot of that confusion.

Living Waters, Ray Comfort, livingwaters.com

If you want encouragement for witnessing or resources to use, this site has plenty to offer—videos, books, and tracts.

Big Picture Story Bible, bigpicturestorybible.com

In case you're looking for a children's story Bible, I like this one. A problem with many children's Bibles is that the stories seem disconnected. This one presents "the big picture," showing how everything in the Bible connects and leads to the coming of Jesus and His sacrifice for us.

Chapter Notes and Credits

Lisa, Kristy, and Julie are my daughters mentioned in the devotions and these credits. Julie's horse, Kody, is the horse Scamper in my Sonrise Stable series is patterned after.

Chapter 1

John Lyons no longer has a website. This is his son Josh's site—joshlyons.com.
Lew Sterrett—sermononthemount.org

Years later, I spoke with Lew Sterrett and asked him what had happened to Jessie. They discovered the horse had a back issue that caused pain when anyone tried to get on her. Thankfully, I've forgotten what he said happened to Jessie. It was probably not a happily-ever-after ending for the mare.
Photos (l to r): p. 4—Kody (Scamper), Kezzie, Sassy, Nikki; p. 5—Sassy, Nikki, Sassy, Kody

Chapter 2

Photos: Cricket and Dolly. Unfortunately, those are the only two photos I have of my first ponies. The second shows my show outfit from the Steffens family. Those were the days!

Chapter 3

The woman who dangled Julie's jacket in front of me was Sissy Burggraf, founder of Lost Acres Horse Rescue and Rehabilitation. She and I have been friends since that day.

Chapter 4

If you've never heard of the *5 Love Languages* or aren't sure what yours are, you can take a quiz on the author's website. 5lovelanguages.com/quizzes/love-language
Photo p. 11—Maggie. I wish I had gotten photos of the day I brought her home, but I didn't.
p.12-Maggie, years later with my daughter and some of our Christian Cowgirls.

Chapter 5

Illustrations from *Rosie and Scamper,* Jet and Rosie, Kezzie and Scamper, p. 16—Ebony with Christian Cowgirls

Chapter 6

Pit Ponies by John Bright, Batsford Books, 1986
Pit Pony Heroes by Eric Squires, David & Charles, 1974

Chapter 7

Outline of Biblical Usage, Larry Pierce, blueletter-bible.org/help/BLBStrongs.cfm
onlinebible.biz
Photo p. 23—Julie on Kody,
p. 27—love this stock photo! :)

Chapter 8

uscurrency.gov/sites/default/files/downloadable-materials/files/CEP_Dollars_In_Detail_Brochure_0.pdf
Illustration from *Black Beauty*

Chapter 9

Animal counts will vary based on translations. These numbers were taken from: thebibleanswer.org/animal-mentioned-most-often-bible
Illustration is the cover for book 3 *Clothed With Thunder,* eohippus illustration is a t-shirt Rosie came up with in the book.

Chapter 10

Photo p. 37—not really Apache, but similar coloring, p. 38—Ginger, she loved to retrieve that orange cone, p.39—Toby greeting Gemma, the day I brought her home. She's supposed to be a Haflinger/Fjord cross, that may explain her gray mane color. Technically crossing a Fjord with another breed isn't permitted by the Fjord registry, but it happens.

Chapter 11

The story of Satin and Kezzie is included in book 2, *Carrie and Bandit*. It becomes one of the seeds planted in the foster girl, Carrie, which leads to her becoming a Christian. I doubt the tranquilizer was good for the foal, but Satin's behavior was so unexpected, I couldn't come up with a better alternative at the time.
Illustration p.40 is of Satin and Kezzie. I have photos of the newborn Kezzie, but they are too small for

print. The Standardbred mare and foal photos are from my neighbor.

Chapter 12

Multiple Births in Horses
skydogranch.org/elsa-then-now
ruralheritage.com/horse_paddock/horse_twinsmule.htm
thelickingnews.com/2021/09/08/rare-horse-twins-thrive
horseyhooves.com/mare-has-two-sets-of-twin-foals
www.deepdyve.com/lp/wiley/birth-of-live-triplets-in-a-mare-XqVh2d61vA

Chapter 13

The saddle pic is one I took at Equine Affaire. Some of these saddles are thousands of dollars! My main concern at my age is a saddle's weight! I don't like hoisting those thirty or forty pound saddles onto a horse's back. Photo p.46—my middle daughter helping one of the girls during our Christian Cowgirl Club. The horse is my Foxtrotter mare, Ginger. She was hard to fit to a saddle. I finally tried an Aussie saddle and it worked well on her.

Chapter 15

americasbestracing.net/the-sport/2022-meadow-stables-true-hero-riva-ridge

Chapter 17

Photo—Beka Setzer and her blind horse, Stormy, at Equine Affaire in Columbus, Ohio. Illustration from *Outward Appearances*

Chapter 19

Photo—Patch in his retirement at Old Friends Equine Retirement farm in Kentucky, Photo p. 66—from Sissy Burggraf of two horses at LAHRR.

Chapter 20

This was taken in 2004. Looking back, I'm amazed at what good horses those four were. The last few years I've searched for a safe, calm trail horse. When I was younger, Maggie seemed a bit too tame, but I'd love to have a Maggie horse now. Gemma is fairly calm, but nothing like Maggie was. Technically, Maggie was a pony, an inch or two short of being a horse.

Chapter 21

These ponies look like they're at Chincoteague or Assateague Island. We visited there in 2004, but I didn't get any beach photos of the ponies. Photo p. 73—this shows the mare sleeping standing up with one hind leg cocked. They'll usually doze with their head hanging over the foal to protect them.
This video has a great description of the stay apparatus components and their function—what a great example of intelligent design!
youtube.com/watch?v=eFWhIyOyKFU

Chapter 22

Photo p. 76—Sassy's first winter in Ohio. She came from South Carolina. I'm sure she wondered what all the white stuff was.

Chapter 23

Photo—a foal at Last Chance Corral giving Julie a good sniff. :)
Terry Nowacki author of *The Air Scenting Horse*
airscentinghorse.com
mainemountedsar.org/equine-air-scent-training
youtube.com/watch?v=9NZIq8EEYPI

Chapter 24

Toby in his favorite rolling spot!

Chapter 26

Equine Resources International is currently not operational equineresources.com
historic-uk.com/CultureUK/Old-Billy-The-Barge-Horse

Chapter 27

Julie at about five, riding Ginger. Kristy hadn't passed Ebony down to her yet.

Chapter 28

wesley.nnu.edu/john-wesley/the-sermons-of-john-wesley-1872-edition/sermon-60-the-general-deliverance/

Chapter 30

Charmayne James website: charmaynejames.com

This is the video of the amazing run when the bridle comes off her horse. youtu.be/ARYlauTj2lE

The barrel racing photo on p. 101 is not Charmayne James, just a stock photo.

Chapter 32

The amazing painting of Secretariat is used by permission, artwork by Nadina Ironia, ironia-art .com

Some consider the X-Factor to be an unproven theory and not the cause of the larger hearts found in some horses.
laminitis—inflammation of the tissues that hold the hoof wall to the underlying bone

Website of the great racehorse, secretariat.com

Penny Chenery, "The First Lady of Racing," passed away September 16, 2017, at the age of 95. January 27, 1922—September 16, 2017

Chapter 33

Sports Illustrated article about Rich Strike's win. si.com/horse-racing/2022/05/08/in-result-no-one-saw-coming-rich-strikes-kentucky-derby-win-helps-redeem-racing

Chapter 34

The illustration shows me on the left. The other girl is supposed to be Candy, but in reality the artist used a photo of a cousin and me for that illustration. Fun times. Old Frosty was a great pony!

Chapter 35

Carmel was a Foxtrotter gelding we briefly owned. He was too young and inexperienced to be safe around my girls. I'm sure he turned into a fine horse with further training, though. Photo p. 117—I took a lot of bull riding photos for my ninth book, *With All You Are*. That little cowboy was so adorable out there with his dad. The horse seems to be staring at the men praying, like he's trying to figure out what they're doing.

Chapter 36

Photo p. 120—Julie on Kody and a friend on Kezzie.

Chapter 37

A photo I took at a horse and pony pull. Those animals were monstrous, the equivalent of extreme human body builders.

Chapter 38

While it's true that every time you ride a horse, you're training him, to train a horse from start to finish, I recommend a professional trainer, unless you're very experienced or are working alongside a trainer. Depending on the horse, it can be dangerous. The illustration is of a young Scamper, adapted from a photo of the filly, Kezzie.

Chapter 40

A few horse people object to the use of pressure and release techniques, believing it causes fear in the horse. Some even consider it abuse. I'm not sure what they use instead.
The illustration is of Carrie helping train foals at Last Chance Corral, from book 4. The lead rope around the hindquarters helps the foal get the idea of leading. The photo p. 129 of the brown and white pony makes me cringe. I took it at our county fair. The poor thing is obviously in pain from the girl's tight pressure on the reins.

Chapter 41

Trainer Stacy Westfall article on the use of spurs. stacywestfall.com/when-and-why-to-use-or-not-to-use-spurs

Chapter 42

I love this photo! Our crazy bridgaphobics. Left to right: Kezzie, Sassy, Kody (Scamper).

Chapter 43

Charles Spurgeon sermon 349 hearspurgeon.com/349-2
A Girl and Five Brave Horses, Sonora Webster, 1961

Photo p. 142—you'll see these cross banners in several photos. A friend made them for me to use in parades, a simple way to show my faith. This was a musical fantasia performance at our county fair. That is Nikki a few months after I'd gotten her. She was still very thin in the neck area. Kezzie is there, mostly obscured by Nikki and me. It felt good to be on the horses with "Be in the Light" by DC Talk blaring over the loudspeakers. :)

Chapter 45

My two pairs of boots. The pair on the right don't look that bad in the photo, but the sides were cracked enough to leak!

The young bull rider has applied some duct tape to his well-worn boots. :)

Chapter 46

gty.org/library/sermons-library/80-380/Christians-and-Alcohol
gty.org/library/sermons-library/80-381/interrogating-alcohol
Madd.org; amishamerica.com/amishman-arrested-for-driving-buggy-while-intoxicated

Chapter 47

Although soring most often occurs with Tennessee Walking Horses, not all Walkers are sored by any means. It's typically limited to some of the top show horses. In their natural state, the Walking Horse is a wonderful breed. In addition to their beauty, the horses are smooth-gaited, intelligent, and make excellent trail horses.
fundforhorses.org/fact-sheets/horse-soring-fact-sheet
humanesociety.org/resources/what-soring
billygoboy.com

I don't see how horses can even walk with those extremely tall, stacked shoes. P. 156, these are two of the photos I took at the Saddlebred show. It makes me sad to see the horses in these ridiculous contraptions. They have to continually wear that harness to keep the tail set in place. You can find photos online of these tail operations gone awry, giving the tail a permanent sideways twist or curl. The inset shows the hoof pads, not as extreme as the TN Walkers, but still totally unnecessary. I've seen Saddlebred owners on horse forums vehemently defend these practices. Usually the rationale is that they're not as bad as the TN Walker people.

Chapter 48

"The Way" mentioned in my devotion and the Bible should not be confused with "The Way" or "The Way International," a cult founded in 1942 by Victor Wierwille. That cult denies the deity of Christ and maintains that we can get to heaven by good works. Photo p. 159—Gemma and I on a metro park trail. I considered using this photo for the book's cover. It depicts the concept of the narrow way mentioned in Matthew 7 extremely well. I probably took a

hundred photos from this view, on several rides, before finally getting one I liked.

Chapter 49

Photo—this is a people hiking trail at Highbanks Park in Delaware, Ohio. Every time I'm there, I think about how much fun it would be to ride my horse on those trails! The driving team is a stock photo.

Chapter 51

Lost or stolen horse site: netposse.com
Articles on the horses stolen by Wendi Cox and her daughter.
ksla.com/story/16205191/motive-behind-sau-horse-theft-investigated

Chapter 52

Those photos are not of the horse I bought, just a random selection from a typical horse sale website.

Chapter 53

Phineas Taylor (P. T.) Barnum (July 5, 1810—April 7, 1891) Quotes are from his autobiography, *The Life of P. T. Barnum, Written by Himself*, 1855

Chapter 54

This devotion is the only one that isn't mainly about horses. The photo is Korrie. At one time, I think we had fourteen cats in that barn, all of whom just showed up. It seemed every morning I'd see another one lurking around the food bowls, demanding their breakfast. P. 174—a couple of the other Sonrise Stable felines.

Chapter 55

Julie and Ebony. I loved that spunky little pony (the little girl also!)

Chapter 56

Confusion over donkey and mule was from:
preachitteachit.org/ask-roger/detail/triumphal-entry-what-you-never-knew-about-jesus-and-the-donkey
This same page states Mary rode a donkey to Bethlehem, which may or may not be true. It never says that in the Bible.

Photo p. 178—My middle daughter encouraging Digory, our miniature donkey, to pull that big, heavy cart. :) I should have included Digory in the Sonrise Stable books, but I had way too many animals to keep track of. He was a real character.

Chapter 57

A hinny is similar to a mule but is the offspring of a female donkey and a male horse.
Photos (l to r): Sassy and I at a horse show, Sassy illustration, Sassy and I as part of a drill team. P. 183— Sassy Sparkles getting ready to ride in a parade.

Chapter 58

Photo p.186—a filly at the Last Chance Corral. She really liked me. It's a wonder I didn't come home with her. :)

Chapter 59

That look captures Sassy's personality perfectly. :)
Photo p. 188—Sassy looking very calm on a trail ride—only because her beloved Kody was nearby.

Chapter 60

webstersdictionary1828.com

Zippy Chippy finished 2nd eight times and 3rd twelve times, earning $30,834 during his eleven-year racing career. The horse died in April 2022.
Old Friends at Cabin Creek Thoroughbred Retirement Farm, oldfriendsatcabincreek.com. View photos of Zippy Chippy on the In Memoriam page.
The True Story of Zippy Chippy: The Little Horse That Couldn't by Artie Bennett, available on Amazon

Chapter 61

A Sonrise Stable illustration. Hard to catch horses are so annoying!

Chapter 62

Photo p. 197—Julie showing Ginger.

Chapter 64

Digory helping clean his pen. The illustration is of Scamper (Kody) standing in a wheelbarrow/cart. He actually did that. The Rubbermaid wheelbarrow survived. I'm still using it almost twenty years later. I wish I'd gotten a photo, Rubbermaid might have

paid me to use it in an advertisement. P. 204 some Christian Cowgirls helping with barn chores.

Chapter 65

Gallus domesticus—Genus and Species for domestic chickens;
Chart showing horse body condition scoring: extension.iastate.edu/equine/body-condition-score

Chapter 66

All about Reckless, "America's Greatest War Horse" sgtreckless.com

Chapter 67

I think I said it all in the devotion text. :(

Chapter 68

The *Left Behind* series got me interested in studying Revelation and gave me an urgency to witness to people. tyndale.com/sites/leftbehind
Illustration shows Sassy chasing after Kody/Scamper, much as she did at the horse show. In the photo, note Kody's ear position. He's not thrilled to be that close to the mule. I had the cartoon on p. 214 drawn by Janet Griffin-Scott. It captures Sassy's love for Kody that he never returned.

Chapter 69 & 70

Four Horsemen artwork by Pat Marvenko Smith ©1982/1992 revelationillustrated.com, Image used by permission.
Christ on a white horse artwork by Pat Marvenko Smith ©1982/1992 revelationillustrated.com, Image used by permission.

Pat Smith's book, *Revelation Illustrated: An Artist's View of the Bible's Last Book*, contains 42 color illustrations, including these two.

I'll give Pat Smith a break, as an artist and not a horsewoman. If you read chapter 70, you'll know how to identify a white horse. The artist's horse is actually a gray—note the dark skin around the muzzle. It's an impressive illustration, nonetheless.

ker.com/equinews/white-thoroughbreds-come
paulickreport.com/news/thoroughbred-racing/pure-bliss-rare-white-standardbred-to-race-at-the-meadowlands

SONRISE STABLE

Wholesome and horsey with strong Christian themes, the Sonrise Stable series is unique among modern children's literature.

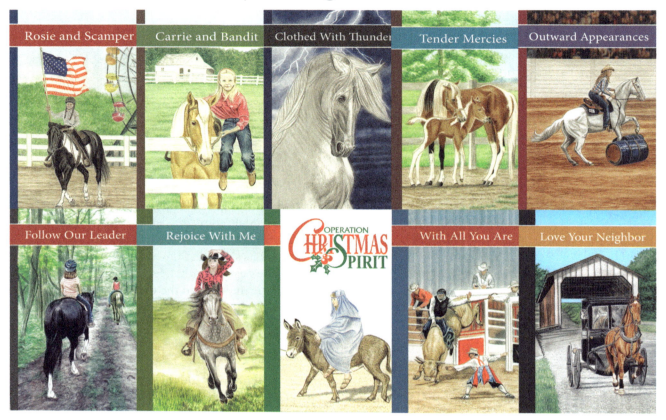

Read the books alone or use the Companion Guides for additional activities to supplement the series.

sonrisestable.com

HISTORY ON HORSEBACK

Through their bond with humans,
horses shaped history in ways no machine ever could.
Their contribution was absent from history textbooks—until
History on Horseback!

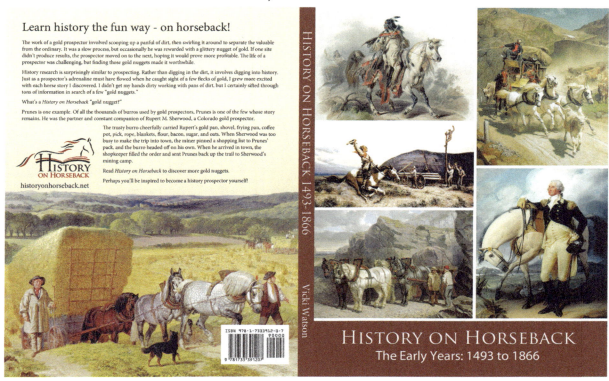

Learn history the fun way - on horseback!

The work of a gold prospector involved scooping up a panful of dirt, then swirling it around to separate the valuable from the ordinary. It was a slow process, but occasionally he was rewarded with a glittery nugget of gold. If one site didn't produce results, the prospector moved on to the next, hoping it would prove more profitable. The life of a prospector was challenging, but finding those gold nuggets made it worthwhile.

History research is surprisingly similar to prospecting. Rather than digging in the dirt, it involves digging into history. Just as a prospector's adrenaline must have flowed when he caught sight of a few flecks of gold, I grew more excited with each horse story I discovered. I didn't get my hands dirty working with pans of dirt, but I certainly sifted through tons of information in search of a few "gold nuggets."

What's a *History on Horseback* "gold nugget?"

Prunes is one example. Of all the thousands of burros used by gold prospectors, Prunes is one of the few whose story remains. He was the partner and constant companion of Rupert M. Sherwood, a Colorado gold prospector.

The trusty burro cheerfully carried Rupert's gold pan, shovel, frying pan, coffee pot, pick, rope, blankets, flour, bacon, sugar, and oats. When Sherwood was too busy to make the trip into town, the miner pinned a shopping list to Prunes' pack, and the burro headed off on his own. When he arrived in town, the shopkeeper filled the order and sent Prunes back up the trail to Sherwood's mining camp.

Read *History on Horseback* to discover more gold nuggets.

Perhaps you'll be inspired to become a history prospector yourself!

historyonhorseback.net

HISTORY ON HORSEBACK 1493-1866

Vicki Watson

ISBN 978-1-7333912-0-7
90000
9 781733 391207

HISTORY ON HORSEBACK
The Early Years: 1493 to 1866

Use it as a homeschool textbook or just read it for pleasure. *The Early Years* is the first in the HOH three-volume set.

History
ON HORSEBACK
sonrisestable.com

24
Pit Ponies at Work

A pit pony driver's day began early. He would rise before sunup, eat a quick breakfast, then set off for the mine in order to have his pony ready when the miners arrived. Former driver, Tony Bunks, recalled one of his ponies.

I used to have a pony called Tod. He was a great pony to drive. I used to give him a nice brush down before we left the stable before I fitted his collar and mobs. Then the next job

was his nose bag for snap [lunch] time. He would get a mint or spangle [a boiled candy] just before we set off on our way. I used to whistle on my way up to his stall and he knew it was me. It was a sad time when I had to give him up when I went coal face training.

After grooming his pony, the driver would harness him, in some places called "gearing up." The mining harness was similar to a regular horse har-

72

Made in the USA
Las Vegas, NV
12 May 2025

21990405R00131